M000189522

Forging Rights in a New Democracy

PENNSYLVANIA STUDIES
IN HUMAN RIGHTS

Bert B. Lockwood, Jr., Series Editor

A complete list of books in the series
is available from the publisher.

Forging Rights in a New Democracy

Ukrainian Students Between Freedom and Justice

Anna Fournier

PENN

UNIVERSITY OF PENNSYLVANIA PRESS

PHILADELPHIA

Copyright © 2012 University of Pennsylvania Press

All rights reserved. Except for brief quotations used
for purposes of review or scholarly citation, none of this
book may be reproduced in any form by any means
without written permission from the publisher.

Published by
University of Pennsylvania Press
Philadelphia, Pennsylvania 19104-4112
www.upenn.edu/pennpress

Printed in the United States of America
on acid-free paper
10   9   8   7   6   5   4   3   2   1

Library of Congress Cataloging-in-Publication Data
Fournier, Anna.
    Forging rights in a new democracy : Ukrainian students
between freedom and justice / Anna Fournier.
        p. cm. (Pennsylvania studies in human rights)
    Includes bibliographical references and index.
    ISBN: 978-0-8122-4426-7 (hardcover : alk. paper)
    1. Youth—Civil rights—Ukraine—History—21st
century.   2. Youth—Political activity—Ukraine—
History—21st century.   3. Social change—Ukraine—
History—21st century.   4. Ukraine—History—Orange
Revolution, 2004.   5. Ukraine—Politics and
government—1991–.   6. Ukraine—Social
conditions—1991–.   I. Title.   II. Series.
HQ799.U38 F68 2012
323.1477   2012004084

In memory of my grandparents, May and Jean Fournier

Contents

Note on Transliteration and Translation

Ukrainian and Russian terms have been transliterated into English according to the Library of Congress system. I have followed Ukrainian geographical names (e.g., the transliterations "Kyiv" and "Chornobyl'").

Most conversations in the school context as well as during the Orange Revolution were held in Ukrainian. Those words transliterated from Russian appear with the mention "Rus." before the transliteration, and those that reflect a mixture of Ukrainian and Russian are preceded by "Ukr./Rus."

All my informants have been given pseudonyms. When my informants' real names were used daily by themselves and others in their Russian versions, I chose the Russian spelling of their pseudonyms (e.g., Svetlana instead of the Ukrainian version Svitlana; Pavel rather than Pavlo).

All translations are my own.

Figure 1. Eastern Europe. Map by R. Dohan, 2011, based on Bjorn Sandvik, World Borders www.thematicmapping.org [shapefile], 1st ed., 2011, using ESRI. *ArcGIS* [GIS software], 10th ed. (Redlands, Calif.: Environmental Systems Research Institute, 1992–2011).

Chapter 1

Young Citizens and the Meanings of Rights in a Globalizing World

On my first day of fieldwork in Ukrainian schools, I was leafing through a ninth-grade history textbook in the teachers' lounge when I realized that the pictures in the section on the French Revolution had been radically altered. With the help of ink and liquid corrector, someone had transformed all the great figures of the French Revolution into pirates with scars and eye patches. Marat had become Captain Barbarossa! I was thrilled with the students' superimposition of "outlaws," and spontaneously shared my discovery with a biology teacher sitting in the lounge. We marveled at students' creativity, as, holding the book up to the light, he attempted to uncover the identities of the revolutionaries who had been so artfully defaced. Both revolutionaries and pirates bore a particular relationship to the law (that is, they existed "outside" of it), and valued a certain kind of freedom. Yet the students had preferred to depict those unconstrained by an ideology of justice.

How do young people come to participate in larger contests about the nature of freedom and justice under conditions of social change? More specifically, how does the concept of "rights" emerge in the tension between different articulations of freedom and justice, and how does it come to figure in the everyday discourses and practices of youth? How do young people in post-Soviet countries negotiate the relation of citizenship amidst conflicting Western-democratic, market-capitalism, and (reconfigured) Soviet-era discourses? Since 1991, the post-Soviet region has seen momentous changes in forms of governance. The reduction and partial privatization of the state associated with the processes of democratization and marketization have meant the redefinition of citizens' rights and entitlements (see, e.g., Petryna

2002, Phillips 2008, Caldwell 2004). This had been accompanied by a proliferation of pedagogies that aim at instilling in citizens the kinds of dispositions necessary to survival in a market economy (e.g., individualism,
risk-taking, and self-regulation) (see, e.g., Dunn 2004, Phillips 2008, Matza
2009, Hemment 2007). These post-Soviet developments have reconfigured
the meaning of civic rights and responsibilities. My goal is to investigate the
making of the first generation of post-Soviet youth (children born after 1991)
into rights-bearing citizens, and to explore how young people's exposure
to both the ideals of democratization and the realities of increasing social
inequality shapes their articulations of civic and human rights. This study
seeks to contribute to a growing body of anthropological work that explores
young people's experiences of citizenship, including their own interpretations and appropriations of rights (see, e.g., Cheney 2007, Hall 2002, Hurtig
2008, Bloch 2003).

Schools are major sites for the negotiation of civic values, and extensive
fieldwork in Ukrainian schools allowed me to access pedagogies around
rights, as well as to explore young people's everyday struggles to define themselves as rights bearers. To get a more complete picture of the dynamics of
students' quest for rights, however, it was necessary to go beyond official state
pedagogies and explore the impact of *informal* pedagogies on the making of
citizens. The streets emerged as a key site of informal pedagogies at the time
of my fieldwork. In fact, in the era of engagement with Western/global concepts, new actors (be they post-Soviet "violent entrepreneurs," or the leaders
of nonviolent "democratic" protests) operated in the public sphere in ways
that profoundly influenced young people's understandings of citizenship.
Their exposure to the new disciplines of the streets impelled students to
rethink the meanings of justice and freedom. My study investigates how
high-school students (ages fifteen to seventeen) attempt to translate the tension between justice and freedom into a new political vision for the future.

Fieldwork in Ukrainian Schools

It seemed fitting to conduct research in the capital city of Ukraine, Kyiv,
since the symbols and pedagogies of citizenship tend to be more salient in
cities that host the seat of parliament and other major symbols of the state.
In addition, Kyiv is located in central Ukraine, and by concentrating on this

region, I hoped to find a kind of middle ground between Western Ukraine's predominantly European orientation (historically, it had been under Polish and Austrian rule, had experienced a relatively short period of Soviet rule, and now shared a border with the European Union), and Eastern Ukraine's predominantly Russian orientation (it had been part of the Russian Empire and one of the first regions to be incorporated into the Soviet Union).

I found Svetlana, my contact person in Ukrainian schools, through a female friend I met at a conference in Kyiv in 1998. This friend had a cousin who had just graduated from the private school where Svetlana[1] taught. This was the beginning of my involvement in a network of contacts (one marked by the exchange of favors) referred to as *blat*. Svetlana taught Ukrainian in that private school and was also involved in the reform of the Humanities curriculum. We met in 2003 when I conducted preliminary fieldwork, and she agreed to rent me a room in her apartment, which she shared with her daughter, her son-in-law, and two grandchildren. This arrangement allowed me to get a sense of a teacher's home life. Svetlana introduced me to other schoolteachers who were part of her *blat* network. After visiting a few schools, I settled for extended work in a public school (*zahal'na shkola*) which I felt would provide a contrast with Svetlana's private school. I applied directly to the Ministry of Education and Science of Ukraine and received written permission to conduct research in the schools I had proposed. Official letters from the ministry to the school principals would inform them of the theme and purpose of my research. I dealt mainly with the vice principals, assuring them that the schools would never be mentioned by name. They transmitted the letters to the principals, who agreed (somewhat reluctantly at first) to my presence. Overall, I felt welcome in both schools, where many teachers would graciously invite me to attend their classes, especially when they knew the topic of the day to be of interest to me. During the fourteen-month fieldwork that I conducted in 2004–2005, I focused on students from grades 9 to 11 (ages fifteen through seventeen). This age range was ideal for the purposes of my study because students in that age group tended to be vocal about power and politics and were very aware of the fact that they would soon (at eighteen) be granted a major citizenship right, the right to vote. In each school, I concentrated on three classes (one per grade, for grades 9–11). I followed these groups in their courses in Ukrainian literature, folklore, geography, and history (i.e., dealing with elements of national culture), as well as civics and military preparedness (the latter two courses dealing with principles of statehood and the law). I engaged in participant observation, administered surveys and questionnaires, and conducted interviews with students, teachers, and administrators. Overall, my research included 182 students and 43 teachers and administrators.

Students ranging in age from fifteen to seventeen might be thought of, in the North American context, as "adolescents." While working with high school students in Ukraine, I hardly ever heard the term for adolescent (*pidlitok* in Ukrainian), as school administrators and teachers invariably chose the word "children" (*dity*) to refer to students.[2] Ukrainian schools typically house grades 1–11 under the same roof, and this perhaps made the sweeping label "children" more convenient, but the use of the term also revealed something about local definitions of childhood under conditions of social change. Students, legally minors until the age of eighteen, typically referred to themselves as "children," and the next meaningful age category, eighteen to about twenty-five, was subsumed under the label "youth" (*molodist'*). This study is in part about the negotiation of the boundary between childhood and adulthood in students' day-to-day engagement with citizenship, and the generic term "young people" is used in my narrative to avoid the bias of either "children" (a local category with its own politics), or "adolescents/teenagers" (a North American category only marginally relevant to the Ukrainian context). In local usage, those who attend school are referred to as "pupils" (*uchni*) rather than "students," but because my focus is on the high school population, I use the term students (as in "high school students").

The private school's aim was to prepare students for higher education. There were tuition fees (unlike in the public school), but these fees could be waived for gifted students who could not afford tuition. Some students in the public school continued on to university studies, but many would also enter technical colleges, and some with no inclination for higher education would be drafted for the compulsory military service. Students from both schools routinely participated in European competitions, often bringing back awards, especially in the hard sciences. This enhanced feelings of pride and belonging among students, especially in the private school. The private school served about 800 students, while the public school had around 500 students. Both schools taught grades 1 to 11, and class composition remained basically the same throughout these eleven years, unless students were transferred to or from another school. Therefore, students knew each other well, and graduation was a particularly emotional ceremony.

Both the schools in which I worked had been Russian-language schools in Soviet Ukraine. This meant that all subjects had previously been taught in Russian except for elective Ukrainian language classes. The situation was now reversed, with only a few Russian-language schools left in Kyiv. In order to attend those schools, one had to prove that at least one parent was Russian-speaking. In the schools where I worked, Ukrainian was usually the language of pedagogy, and all the textbooks used were written in Ukrainian. The two schools, both located within a reasonable distance of downtown Kyiv, looked much the same from the outside, old buildings with several floors. Both schools were guarded by uniformed men sitting in the foyer. The inside of the two schools differed, however. The private school had undergone some renovations right before I arrived for long-term fieldwork, and included a new computer center. The public school was less well equipped, and many classrooms were in disrepair. The blackboards were so old in some classrooms that students could barely make out the teacher's notes. Every homeroom teacher had his or her own classroom and often requested contributions from parents for new curtains or a fresh coat of paint. Students in the older grades sat in pairs sharing one elongated seat and desk (*lavka* and *parta*). I marveled (and sometimes cringed) at the inscriptions that students had carved onto the wooden desks. Only the younger children (grades 1–5) had individual laminate covered desks, and this was a new phenomenon.

The students attending the public school were usually part of the rising middle class. Parents were doctors or lawyers, many worked for the government, and some had blue-collar jobs in construction or factories. Both parents usually worked. In contrast, the parents of children in the private school were often part of the new business elite (the so-called New Rich), or otherwise held important government positions. Many of the students' mothers were homemakers. This new designation (which did not exist as a permanent category in the Soviet Union) held a certain prestige since it signified that the husband was wealthy enough to support the whole family. Because the students' parents were mostly part of the business world, a sphere of activity where Russian was spoken (business links with Russia were also prevalent), practically all families spoke Russian at home. The students also spoke Russian to one another during breaks or when gossiping during class. Private-school teachers also tended to communicate to one another in Russian outside the class setting, though a few of the younger teachers communicated in Ukrainian. Teachers not fluent in Ukrainian had received language training following independence in 1991, but with mixed results, especially in the hard sciences. Russian-language teachers had had to be retrained in other subjects because Russian was no longer taught in most schools. Many of those teachers became "world literature" teachers, and the world literature course became, for some, a way to smuggle Russian classics back in, in addition to other world classics often available only in Russian translation.

I sometimes witnessed code-switching in the classroom, as the teacher would lecture in Ukrainian, only to joke informally with students in Russian. The situation was slightly different in the public school, where more students, although still a minority, spoke Ukrainian at home. Some students who had moved to Kyiv from nearby villages spoke fluent Ukrainian. More teachers also interacted in Ukrainian outside the classroom setting. In the school context, I spoke Ukrainian with students. Ukrainian was the "official" language of the school and principals went to great lengths to enforce this. Therefore, I complied by addressing students in Ukrainian, and they mostly replied in Ukrainian. Outside the school, we spoke what they spoke among themselves: "Russian" pronounced the Ukrainian way, strewn with some Ukrainian and English words. I spoke Ukrainian with Svetlana, the teacher with whom I lived, in school and at home. This language came more naturally to her since she had taught it all her life. Svetlana's daughter spoke Ukrainian with her mother and with me, but not with her husband, who was Ukrainian but Russian-speaking like almost all young people in Kyiv. The daughter and her husband spoke Russian to their two children.

The broader language situation in Kyiv was also complex. In the public realm, almost everyone interacted in Russian. The market was a notable exception: since most sellers had come from nearby Ukrainian-speaking villages, they often addressed customers in Ukrainian. Figures of authority such as police officers or subway attendants always hailed citizens in Russian ("Zhenshchina!" [Hey, woman!], or "Devushka, idi siuda!" [Young lady, come here!]). Street signs were in Ukrainian (except the Soviet ones that had not been changed yet), and all public information (for example, recorded directives in the subway) and advertisements were in Ukrainian. Media broadcasts over Ukraine were mostly in Russian, except for the government channel (Pershyi Kanal, or First Channel) that broadcasted exclusively in Ukrainian. The other privately owned channels (ICTV, 1+1, Novyi Kanal) had broadcasts in both languages, but Russian dominated. The channel Ukraina, reportedly owned by Eastern Ukrainian oligarchs, broadcasted only in Russian. The "Fifth Channel" (Piatyi Kanal) broadcasted in both languages, but mostly in Ukrainian.

On the Eve of "Democratic Revolution"

At the beginning of my fieldwork in 2004, several media sources outside of Ukraine started reporting that the country was becoming "authoritarian." On the ground, this was more elusive. Channel 5 (Pyatyi Kanal) had become the only television station that did not give in to the pressures exerted on all television channels under the government of President Leonid Kuchma (1994–2004). This pressure took the form of *temnyky*, or secret government directives faxed to television stations telling them what they should or should not report on the news. An oligarch who sided with the opposition rather than the government in power owned Channel 5, and the latter became *the* forum for opposition views. Not everyone in Ukraine (or even in Kyiv) received this channel. I was told that the Kuchma government had threatened to take them off the air for having an expired license, and that some investigative journalists had been detained. Nevertheless, the channel continued its broadcasts through Ukraine's so-called Orange Revolution of November–December 2004. This "revolution" (a nationwide protest against electoral fraud) led to the sudden democratization of the media, as news anchors from all the main television channels appeared on air to state that they would no longer comply with the *temnyky* or "lie to the public."

Svetlana often remarked to me that "Now [in post-Soviet Ukraine], we are free [*vil'ni*]," or "Now, we can say whatever we want." Yet some of her reactions betrayed a different sentiment. One particular incident made this clear. After shopping with Svetlana, I stopped at the post office. She waited for me outside while I mailed some letters. When I stepped out, I saw that across the street, a woman was standing in front of a government building and yelling something angrily in a megaphone. I could not make out what she was saying and asked Svetlana what this was about. "Oh, she's just crazy," said Svetlana dismissively.

"How can you tell?"

"If she weren't, they [the police] would've taken her away a long time ago!" The idea that one would have to be in an abnormal state to protest against the government circulated widely. Even during the Orange Revolution, both sides of the political divide accused one another. The supporters of Viktor Yushchenko, the leader of the opposition and self-proclaimed "pro-democracy" candidate, claimed that those supporting Viktor Yanukovych (the prime minister under Leonid Kuchma's presidency and thus the candidate associated with the government in power) were there "because they had been paid to attend." Yanukovych supporters in turn argued that pro-Yushchenko protesters had been "zombified [*zombovani*]," brainwashed, or drugged.

"It's a little scary [*troshky strashno*]," a friend of mine had said upon hearing that the Ukrainian Security Services (SBU) was raiding the dorms of university students who had participated in pro-opposition rallies. Needless to say, the presence of an anthropologist during a period of political turmoil was inconvenient at best. In the summer of 2004, Russian President Vladimir Putin had declared that Ukraine would see an influx of Western spies on its territory before the presidential elections. And indeed, especially in the private school (where a lot of the students had influential parents on both sides of the political divide) some teachers were suspicious, asking Svetlana, "Who's this 'journalist' [*korespondent*] in your class?" Some of the students whom I knew less joked around about me being a spy. An eleventh grader in the private school simply asked me one day, after we had been talking about different things: "And you are a spy?" He was half-joking, but I had to answer (this felt rather silly): "I'm not a spy, I'm an ethnologist [*etnoloh*]" (in Ukraine, the category "anthropologist" refers to a physical anthropologist or archaeologist). I doubt this answer could have reassured him, as Soviet ethnologists were by nature politically involved. I tried to make my presence more inconspicuous than it had been at the beginning of my fieldwork. Interviews or questionnaires no longer seemed appropriate. Because I did not want to lose my access to the schools, or to add in any way to the vulnerability of my informants, I kept a low profile, concentrated on observing as well as engaging in informal conversations, and refrained from taking notes in class while teachers expressed their political views. The atmosphere became even heavier in late September 2004, when rumors started circulating about Yushchenko being poisoned by the government. While the political climate was somewhat constraining methodologically, it did compel me to rely more heavily on the observation and description of concrete practices. Anthropologists are enjoined to record, about their informants, both "what they say they do" and "what they do." The latter half seemed especially important under conditions of political struggle.

Theoretical Orientations

Youth, Citizenship, and Rights

Children have long been seen as "transitioning" toward adulthood—as human becomings rather than human beings (Montgomery 2009: 9). The perception of young people as "incomplete or incompetent adults" (Montgomery 2009: 9) has often meant an emphasis on their status as *potential* or *future* citizens rather than their recognition as agents and political actors in the present (Taylor and Smith 2009: 17). If we view citizenship as "a status bestowed on those who are *full* members of a community" (Marshall 1950: 14; emphasis added), then we must ask ourselves in what sense children, who do not yet possess certain rights (such as the right to vote), may be considered citizens. Anthropologists have noted that while in theory, citizens in liberal democracies are equal in rights, certain populations may be excluded from, or differently incorporated into, citizenship (Paley 2002, see also Ong 1999, Holston and Caldeira 1998, Gal and Kligman 2000, Povinelli 2002). Lazar (2010) defines "citizenship regimes" as the ways in which societies "organize and challenge political participation and exclusion (historically, of workers, women, illiterates, *and children*)" (2010: 182; emphasis added).

The arguments put forth to limit children's citizenship rights draw, for example, on the idea that children are not experienced enough to understand, use, or claim rights properly (e.g., Grisso 1981), so that they may, especially in early childhood, have "egocentric" rather than "universal" conceptions of rights (Melton and Limber 1992). Brocklehurst (2006) argues that traditionally, the concept of the "child" and the concept of "rights" are incommensurable because children, and especially young children, "have been seen as people without responsibility, for whom obligations, that is the obverse of rights, are not applicable" (10). Paradoxically, adults often seek to protect children from the responsibilities that would enable them to participate more fully in the web of entitlements and obligations that is citizenship. The rationale at work here is that citizenship duties could overburden children, potentially robbing them of their "childhood" (Morrow 1999: 150). This leads us to the question of whether children need to be "saved" (along with their childhood), or whether they need, rather, to be liberated from the prison that is childhood (see, e.g., Holt 1974). Scholars of human rights have pointed to a similar tension between what the United Nations Convention on the Rights of Children (UNCRC) poses as children's *participation rights*, and their *protection rights* (Woodhead and Montgomery 2002, Harris 1996, Marshall 1997). On the one hand, the convention portrays children as "autonomous individuals" with rights to freedom of expression and freedom of conscience; on the other hand, it constructs children as "objects of protection." My study investigates how this tension between two discourses of childhood comes to be played out in the pedagogies connected with citizenship education. More importantly, it asks how children's ambiguous location vis-à-vis rights impacts their *own* perspectives on and performances of rights. It is the everyday struggles of young people to be recognized as rights bearers that is the subject of this book.

In the last two decades, anthropologists have begun putting children and youth at the center of their analyses (Scheper-Hughes and Sargent 1998, Lancy 2008, Montgomery 2009), recognizing young people as constructors of meaning and culture-makers. Rejecting the view of children as mere "reproducers" of culture, anthropologists of childhood have examined how children use dominant cultural representations as a basis for "making sense of the world and organizing action in it" (Hirschfeld 2002: 615). Not only can children manipulate these representations and harness them for their own purposes (Harris 1998), but their particular interpretations ultimately contribute to adult culture (Hirschfeld 2002; see also Hardman 1973). Children have also increasingly been recognized as agents of social and political transformation (Reynolds 1995). Ethnographers have sought to deconstruct the discourse of the "innocent child" that can be traced back to Jean-Jacques Rousseau, and have increasingly looked at young people as actors whose relation to and negotiation of particular social orders must be investigated. Cheney points out that while adults presumably have some degree of influence over children's political beliefs, young people "engage politics in distinct ways *based on their own positions in the social hierarchy*" (2007: 136; emphasis added). Young people are indeed in a unique position to contest particular political projects. Durham (2000) argues that youth "enter politics as saboteurs; their potential for political sabotage comes from their incomplete subjugation to contexts and co-opters, and from their own power for action, response, and subversion in contexts of political definition" (13). Veloso (2008) shows how young people's creative and playful appropriation of rights may cast them as "'arrogant' negotiators of . . . citizenship" (52).

The types of engagement with politics and citizenship specific to youth can include seemingly exuberant discourses and performances around rights. Young people associate the concept of rights not only with justice and law, but also with the freedom grounded in whim and desire. Consequently, they at times challenge the traditional definition of rights as "*justified* claims to the protection of persons' important interests" (*Oxford Companion to Philosophy* 1995: 776; emphasis added). From an adult perspective, these kinds of claims may appear excessive or irrational. Traditionally, children, but especially adolescents, have been regarded as prone to acting on their desires. According to what Jenks calls the "Dionysian" discourse of childhood, "the child is Dionysian inasmuch as it loves pleasure, it celebrates self-gratification and it is wholly demanding in relation to any object, or indeed subject, that prevents its satiation" (2005: 63). Another strand of the Dionysian discourse views children as "unruly" and "anarchistic" (see the work of Thomas Hobbes in particular) and thus presumably unable to exercise the self-control and rationality required for the exercise of politics. In view of the constructed nature of these discourses, it seems necessary to move away from explanatory models that revolve around the "natural rebelliousness of youth"[3] and toward a better understanding of the connection between young people's performances as rights bearers and their ambiguous location, as children, minors, and so-called "citizens-in-the-making," vis-à-vis rights and the law.

This study examines how the adult/child relation is negotiated in everyday life in schools and beyond, and how this relation might come to bear on children's negotiation of the concept of rights. The latter cannot, however, be suitably addressed without also taking into account formulations of rights circulating in the wider social context. Young people engage with competing discourses and practices of rights, whether these be Western/global notions of rights (deployed in school textbooks, or apparent in new local statutes guaranteeing the dignity of children), or popular and media articulations of rights embedded in Soviet understandings of reciprocity and redistribution. We must also pay particular attention to new formulations of rights arising out of the local encounter with capitalism. In particular, the increasing polarization of wealth seems to have given rise to new "kinds" of citizens (e.g., the so-called New Rich) whose orientations toward citizenship rights and obligations may differ from traditional (Western or Soviet) understandings, and who may claim and use rights in new ways. Young people's exposure to different models of citizenship allows them to "play" with the notion of rights, and thus to expand or reformulate the latter according to context. In addition, as Sarat and Kearns (1997) have noted, rights can be understood as vehicles through which social actors come to experiment with different subjectivities and relate to the world in novel ways (8). Rights can also be thought of as a "resource" for political struggles (Wilson 1997), and thus allow youth not only to try on different social roles but also to explore new positionings vis-à-vis power and authority.

This experiential approach to rights is in line with anthropological definitions of citizenship as a "process" involving people's engagement with various state discourses, representations, and everyday routines (Sharma and Gupta 2006). Recent ethnographies have explored citizenship by focusing on the *meanings* associated with political membership and participation (Levinson 2005: 336). Those scholars who view citizenship as *social practice* (see, e.g., Ong 1996, Holston 2008, Lazar 2010) emphasize "the experiences of citizens with the elements—such as property, illegality, courts, associations, and ideologies—that constitute the discursive and contextual construction of relations called citizenship and that indicate not only particular attributes of belonging in society but also the political imagination that both produces and disrupts that citizenship" (Holston 2008: 13). Young people's everyday experiences of belonging and participation, as well as the "political imagination" that shapes and reflects these experiences, are key to my study.

Locating the "Pedagogical State" in the Era of Globalization

Corrigan and Sayer (1985) have pointed to the role of the state in constructing the range of identities (or subject positions) available to people, that is, in defining "the kinds of people there are and the kinds there ought to be" (Nagengast 1994: 109). Citizenship education is often looked upon as a state project that instills social and cultural norms in such a way that they come to seem "natural" and commonsensical (Durkheim 1956; Gellner 1983). Thus, ethnographies of formal schooling have traditionally focused on the process of "inculcat[ing] the skills, subjectivities, and disciplines that undergird the modern nation-state" (Levinson and Holland 1996: 1).

Influenced by the work of Radcliffe-Brown (1940) and Abrams (1977), anthropologists have come to acknowledge the fluidity and paradoxes inherent in what we conceive of as "the state." Sharma and Gupta (2006) define the state not as a unitary and autonomous actor that exercises power (or, we might add, wields pedagogies) over a particular population, but rather as "a multilayered, contradictory, translocal ensemble of institutions, practices, and people" (6). Drawing on these insights, ethnographies of education have begun to deconstruct the image of a coherent state "behind" the official curriculum, and to explore how pedagogies around citizenship may be the result of struggle and negotiation among various elements of society, whether political elites, intellectuals, or bureaucrats. In his ethnography of education in Turkey, *The Pedagogical State*, Kaplan (2006) explores how different sections of society with at times conflicting interests (in this case the military, religious nationalists, and neoliberal industrialists) come to be involved in defining the content of citizenship education. He shows how the struggles that constitute the "state" are instrumental in shaping schoolchildren's subjectivities. Similarly, Wanner (1998) argues that educational reform in Ukraine issues from a "compromise reached among divergent ideological groups wielding zones of influence in the government" (80), resulting in various contradictions, such as school textbooks in which the new nationalist historiography is conveyed through Soviet concepts and "language" (94).

The process of globalization has expanded the range of actors who may be involved in the making of governable citizens. Trouillot (2001) speaks of "tensions in the location of state power," tensions found in "many practices through which citizens encounter not only government but also a myriad of other statelike institutions and processes that interpellate them as individuals and as members of various communities" (133). He adds that what we might think of as "state effects" (e.g., atomized individuals who feel a sense of belonging to larger national collectivities) may be produced by such institutions as transnational corporations, nongovernmental organizations (NGOs), or community associations, with the result that citizens experience in their everyday lives a form of power that is "at once internal and external to the state" (Foucault 1991: 103). Taking a Foucauldian approach, Ong defines citizenship as a process of "self-making and being made within webs of power linked to the nation-state and civil society," emphasizing the role of "civil institutions and social groups as disciplinary forces" (1996: 738).

Recent anthropological writings on post-Soviet states have focused on "state power" as it is deployed by supranational organizations such as the

European Union (see, e.g., Dunn 2005), as well as informal networks such as mafias (Humphrey 2002, Volkov 2002, Ries 2002). This study explores how post-Soviet "violent entrepreneurs," or "bandits" in local parlance, come to influence young people's conceptions of citizenship. The violent pedagogies deployed by bandits on city streets also expand the range of meanings that young people associate with rights (see next section), and are thus central to my analysis. Also key to my analysis are the pedagogies associated with the leaders of democratic NGOs and civic groups (what we might call "democratic entrepreneurs"?), that is, the pedagogies of "peaceful and democratic" street protests. "Democratic revolution" as a form is gaining momentum in other parts of the world, including Africa and the Middle East, and it is thus crucial to investigate its effects on young people's articulations of citizenship.

The relationship of both violent entrepreneurs and leaders of civic groups to government authorities is complex. It is difficult to establish the boundaries of the "state" when a civic organization working for democracy actively supports/is supported by a political faction such as the opposition.[4] Similarly, the popular expression "bandit state [*bandyts'ka vlada*]" attests to the perceived entanglement between government and violent entrepreneurs at the time of my fieldwork. While the notion of "bandit state" should not be taken necessarily as *evidence* of what Bayart, Ellis, and Hibou (1999) have called the "criminalization of the state," it is nonetheless an important *representation* of power in the era of privatization of the state, and as Gupta and Sharma (2006) have argued, such representations are key to apprehending the state ethnographically. Gupta (2006) claims that the popular discourse of "state corruption" in India produces the "state" as bounded and separate from "society," simultaneously constructing citizens as innocent victims of state dishonesty. While the expression "bandit state" in Ukraine similarly reinforces the symbolic divide between the people and the authorities, it simultaneously *blurs* the boundary between the "state" and the violent entrepreneurs traditionally viewed as part of "civil society,"[5] thus yielding a complex representation of power and its boundaries that is significant to my analysis.

While my study does not cover the whole range of informal pedagogies at work in the post-Soviet context, it does examine in detail two sets that citizens came to associate with divergent engagements with capitalism (one, "bandit-like," and the other, "democratic and just") and divergent models of citizenship. In the period of political turmoil coinciding with my fieldwork, young people were heavily involved in the negotiation of these models, at time violently rejecting one or the other, and at times subtly reconciling the two. It is indeed through contact with different (though not necessarily incompatible) instantiations/extensions of the state that what Luykx (1999) calls "governable subject-citizens" (125) come to be produced. The emergence of new actors and their involvement in state power reframe the relation of citizenship in important ways. How do the "changing technologies of governance" associated with these actors "target and redefine youth through schools and other educational initiatives"? (Durham 2000: 114). This question suggests that we move away from the idea that schools are "monolithic purveyors of dominant ideologies" (Levinson and Holland 1996: 9), and toward new sites of learning. For example, Mazawi (1998) poses "the street" as a major agent and context of political socialization for Palestinian children and adolescents, and explores how their witnessing of and participation in violent confrontations influence their perception and experience of citizenship (90). The "streets" come to be the stage of various pedagogies and disciplines that feed into the educational process and come to shape young people's understanding of citizenship and rights.

Informal pedagogies do not necessarily undermine or subvert the formal pedagogies of the school. In her ethnography of schooling in rural France, Reed-Danahay (1996) points to the centrality of the home in negotiating and reconfiguring the dominant French culture disseminated in schools. She investigates both schoolchildren's attempts at accommodation and their efforts to keep the state "at bay" in some ways. The picture that emerges from my analysis of informal pedagogies in the post-Soviet context points to the challenges of keeping the state "at bay." Pedagogies of the streets and of the state may mesh in unpredictable ways so that the "location" of the state becomes complex. In fact, young people negotiate these pedagogies so that the latter come to overlap and diverge in new, unexpected ways. Anthropologists have increasingly recognized children as agents capable of both absorbing *and contesting* the ideologies meant to shape them (e.g., Foley 1990, Reed-Danahay 1996, Shaw 1996), including ideologies around citizenship (Lazar 2010, Luykx 1999, Golden 2001, Rival 1996, Rodgers 2008). Herzfeld's concept of social poetics as "the creative presentation of the individual self" (2005: x) achieved by "using, reformulating, and recasting official idioms" (2005: 2) allows me to move away from the resistance/compliance model that has sometimes been used in ethnographies of schooling. The model of "cultural engagement" (Herzfeld 2005) acknowledges the kinds of conversations that may be had between competing imaginaries of citizenship and rights.

In the Margins of the Law: Citizenship in the "Zone"

There has been a move in social theory from viewing the state as a bulwark against uncontrolled violence and therefore a protector of the people (social contract theory) to viewing the state as itself grounded in violence. The new anthropology of violence claims that "order" and "stability" are dependent upon various forms of "disorder," and that this is true of all systems, including liberal democracies. Recent ethnographic work has attempted to account for forms of sociality in which structure and chaos coexist. For example, based on Benjamin's (1969) view of the state of emergency as the rule rather than the exception, Taussig develops the concepts of "terror as usual," and the "nervous system." Other formulations of this tension have included the notions of "unruly order" (see Poole's 1994 work on Peru), and "sovereign exception," in which bare life emerges as an effect of power (Agamben 1998). In his study of post-Soviet Kazakhstan, Nazpary (2002) suggests that chaos is not the opposite of order, and that we should think of a "chaotic order" instead. He argues that in fact, what people in Almaty perceive as chaos is not "meaningless anarchy" but has "pockets of order" (for example, the order produced by racketeers protecting private property). In addition, the chaos experienced is not a *return* to savagery or barbarism, but the *effect* of certain forces, including "the speculative logic of accumulation of capital in the post-Soviet historical conjuncture" (Nazpary 2002: 38), or what his informants refer to as "wild capitalism."

Increasingly, citizenries have had to reckon with actors who pose themselves as "guarantors of the law" while also operating at the margins or outside the law. While the concept of a "criminal state" might seem paradoxical, it has been argued that criminals can perform many of the functions traditionally associated with the state, for example, protection/security, taxation, and the redistribution of resources (see Blok 1974, Tilly 1985, Roitman 2005). In fact, criminals do not necessarily operate in a manner that fundamentally challenges the rule of law. In their volume *Law and Disorder*

in the Postcolony (2006), Jean and John Comaroff claim that criminal violence "does not so much repudiate the rule of law or the licit operation of
the market as appropriate their forms" (5), and that this might account
for the "simulacra of social order" (ibid.) produced by power arrangements
in which "bandits" rule. Scholars of the post-Soviet region (e.g.,Varese 2001,
Volkov 2002) have examined how the power vacuum left by the collapse of
the Soviet state came to be filled by actors who operated in the margins
of the law, and yet could also produce a certain kind of order. Ries notes of
the Russian context that citizens have come to view the mafia as both as "the
destroyer of any hopes for . . . social order and also the most likely potential
source of . . . order" (2002: 278). Thus, ethnographic evidence belies the assumption that bandits are inherently "chaotic" and the state is by nature "orderly," and instead suggests that both state and bandits possess elements of
chaos and order that may easily mesh.

The concept of "bandit state" I encountered in the field is tied to the notion of structured or intentional chaos referred to above. *Merriam-Webster*
defines chaos in terms of unpredictability, as "a state of things in which
chance is supreme" (1993: 191; emphasis added). Chance itself is usually
understood as a realm removed from human intention. Yet, as Berdahl suggests in her work on socialist East Germany, randomness, or the arbitrary
and "inconsistent use of state power" (1999: 65), could be used as a form of
social control, producing in citizens political subjectivities useful to the
regime (Verdery 1996). In post-Soviet Ukraine, citizens often interpret
chaos (rightfully or not) as something "staged" by those in power. In fact,
life in the so-called "bandit state" comes to mean the experience of the
melding of the *randomness* of street criminals and the *intentionality* of
state officials. The inscrutability, "illegibility" (e.g., Sanford 2004), or duplicity of the state in the age of globalization (Derrida [1990] speaks of the
state's "spectral double," in which violence is always a possibility) produce
among citizens not only anxiety, but also a desire to uncover the state's "true
face," (see, e.g., Taussig 1999, Nelson 2004). In Ukraine, this desire can
manifest itself in the youth practice of "defacing" representations of political leaders.[6]

As populations are faced in everyday life with actors that are "representative[s] of *both* the state and the principal forms of private, extrajudicial,
and even criminal power" (Poole 2004: 43; emphasis added), it becomes
virtually impossible to apprehend the "boundaries" of the law. The conditions

under which the law may be suspended, thus leaving certain categories of people without legal protection or status, are the object of several recent anthropological analyses, many of which draw on the work of political philosopher Giorgio Agamben. Influenced by the work of Walter Benjamin and Carl Schmitt, Agamben (1998) theorizes the "state of exception" as one in which a particular population is included in the law *as an exception to the law*, and thus reduced to "bare life." In Western philosophical thought, political power is traditionally defined against the "state of nature," but Agamben points to a space of violence and vulnerability located at the margins of the political order yet also *produced by* power. The "zone of irreducible indistinction" (Agamben 1998: 9) between *bios* (political life) and *zoe* (natural life) is occupied by the *homo sacer,* a being divested of rights and who may be killed with impunity. For Agamben (2000), the inhabitant of a concentration camp most adequately personifies the figure of the *homo sacer.* Yet several anthropological studies have drawn on Agamben's conceptualization to analyze other kinds of spaces of "exception," including the checkpoint, the state border, and the refugee camp, among others (see, e.g., Das and Poole 2004, Alonso 2005). Anthropologists have also theorized the spaces of insecurity produced by power systems in terms of "free zones" (see, e.g., Gregory and Timerman 1986 for a description of the improvised spaces of impunity in which abductions took place in Argentina under the military dictatorship), or "wild zones" (see, e.g., Buck-Morss 2002 on spaces of banishment from modernity in the Cold War era). At the time of my fieldwork, it is the popular image of Ukraine as a potential Gulag or prison camp (or what people refer to simply as the "zone [*zona*]") that comes to stand for citizens' growing sense of political and legal vulnerability. This image in turn has a profound effect on people's representations of citizenship, so that adults and young people come to imagine themselves as "slaves," that is, as "politically irrelevant being[s]" (Arendt 1963: 107) with obligations (e.g., obedience) but no rights.

It is difficult to predict the effects on youth of everyday insecurity, and therefore it is critical to examine these in detail. On the one hand, the randomness and ever-present threat of violence by state/nonstate actors can produce in youth a sense of vulnerability (one that compounds their already ambiguous position, as "potential" citizens, vis-à-vis the law[7]). On the other hand (and this is key), young people are able to *model* some of the aggressive performances associated with the exercise of power under "wild capitalism," and to deploy them in their own power struggles, including, somewhat paradoxically, their struggle for more rights in the school context.

Human Rights and Democracy at the Intersection
of Two Modernities

It has become common to refer to a "global culture of human rights" (Cowan, Dembour, and Wilson 2001), and Merry (2001) claims that the language of human rights itself has become the "preeminent global language of social justice" (13). Critiques of human rights have underlined the fact that human rights are neither transcendent nor truly "universal," but rather firmly rooted in Western philosophical thought (e.g., Sarat and Kearns 1997). Consequently, rights, understood as "rights talk, rights-thinking, rights practices—entail certain constructions of self and sociality, and specific modes of agency" (Cowan, Dembour, and Wilson 2001: 12). Anthropologists have explored human rights as a *normative* framework" (Goodale and Merry 2007: 31) not only because human rights are thought to apply to all (to the extent that everyone is human), but also because human rights are "informed by particular values among a range of alternatives, and . . . embedded in . . . particular alignments of power" (Goodale 2007: 140). The human rights discourse tends to be prescriptive and is often transmitted in practice as a set of pedagogies that support the Western concept of the autonomous, rational, and individualized self.

While human rights are of the realm of norms or standards, we should perhaps be wary of treating them as what Latour (1987) has called "immutable mobiles," or "objects transferred from one community of practice to another, which have profoundly transformative effects without being transformed themselves" (Dunn 2005: 176). Norms and standards may be "immutable" in their written incarnation, but when transferred to different social and cultural contexts, they are unwittingly engaged in conversation. What is more, "normality" itself may be appropriated and inscribed with new meanings. As Speed suggests with respect to rights, social actors "bring to bear their own particular understandings and goals in ways that reshape the meanings and functions of the [human rights] discourse in interesting and at times contestatory ways" (2007: 165). In fact, the global discourse of human rights is often subjected to "creative reinterpretation" or what Merry

(2007) calls "vernacularization," a process that may result in something along the "replication/hybridity" continuum (Merry 2005). In his study of children and rights in Lebanon (2005), Joseph points out that the engagement with rights can be complex and that "the practices deployed by families in teaching children rights and responsibilities in Lebanon entail paradoxical incorporations of notions which both support and undermine both international conventions and locally upheld ideals" (1007).

In examining post-Soviet citizens' current engagement with the liberal model of rights, we must pay particular attention to the continuing influence of Soviet theories and practices around human rights. Cold War–era writings on the concept and practice of rights in the West and in the Soviet Union often posed the two positions as antagonistic or even incommensurable. For example, Donnelly (1982) claims that in the Western context, "human rights are rights that one has simply because one is a human being (person)" (304), whereas in the Soviet Union, rights are dependent on an individual's performance of duties. Other scholars writing at the time argued that within the socialist system, a citizen's dignity and rights depend on the "social significance of a person . . . the criterion of value of a person lies in his/her relation to work, in the socially useful work of the individual" (Petrosjan 1958, in Hawkesworth 1980: 72). In addition, much was made of the Western legal system's focus on political and civic rights, and the Soviet legal system's emphasis instead on social and economic rights (e.g., the right to food, work, rest, and education) (Donnelly 1982: 309).

How do these different orientations come to figure in post-Soviet imaginaries and practices of citizenship? In her analysis of the aftermath of the 1986 Chornobyl' disaster in Ukraine, Petryna (2002) argues that some citizens had to convert themselves into biological citizens ("sufferers" entitled to certain forms of care) to avoid abandonment in the era of state collapse. In this context, "collective efforts are not so much aimed at securing political rights as they are at guaranteeing a probability of economic survival through an injured biology" (Petryna 2005: 172). Citizens' focus on economic rights challenges the classical model of citizenship by underlining the fact that the latter's "principles cannot guarantee the basic biological existence of populations that precedes political life" (Petryna 2005: 173). When new regimes disrespect former entitlements (Hann 2002: 11), citizens may not perceive their humanity as guaranteed, and thus, in the Ukrainian context, they are likely to articulate human rights in terms of the "right to be human," or the right to the material conditions that guarantee their humanity. Thus, post–

Cold War discourses that "equate political freedom to liberated market forces" (Paley 2002: 486) may be contested. Paley (2002), drawing on Ong (1999), points out that in some contexts, democracy itself may be associated with "state provision for collective well-being" rather than with elections or individual freedoms (2002: 475). This suggests that we should expand the understanding of human rights simply as "a set of universal claims to safeguard human dignity from illegitimate coercion, typically enacted by state agents" (Brysk 2002: 3). While it would appear that "limits on existing political powers" (Speed 2007: 170) is what enables democratization and political freedoms (Ferguson and Gupta 2005: 118), the withdrawal of the state in the neoliberal era may produce a longing for state care that comes to be articulated in the language of human rights. The result, as described by Goodale (2007) in his work on social resistance in Bolivia, is a situation in which communities appropriate the discourse of human rights so as to critique and resist the (capitalist) system that gave rise to the concept of human rights in the first place.

While we might expect the new generation of post-Soviet youth to be drawn to the image of the individualized autonomous self that permeates liberal democratic models, we must also ask how they reconcile the latter with the realities of increasing social inequality, and whether (or to what extent) they reproduce the language of interconnectedness, collectivity, and moral obligation that has gained currency in a society facing "wild capitalism."

Rethinking Social Change

Following the collapse of the Soviet Bloc, there was a shift from imagining Eastern Europe and the Soviet Union in terms of an "area," to imagining them in temporal terms, that is, as undergoing a "transition." While the shift from a spatial to a temporal model signified the possibility for change and process, it seemed to merely reconfigure the Cold War–era boundary between East and West. The Transition model, rooted in the notion of progress, reproduces a boundary in time. This boundary is reinforced, for example, in popular comparisons of contemporary Ukraine's or Russia's "wild capitalism" with the economic practices of the American frontier. While these kinds of comparisons may be revealing in some respects, they seem to come uncomfortably close to the nineteenth-century model of unilineal cultural evolution according to which contemporary "savages" represented a stage in the past of "civilized" nations. In addition, the term transition suggests that countries positioned between socialism and capitalism are in some sense in a state of "liminality" (Buchowski 2001). Because these countries are thought to be in a state of in-betweenness, the assumption is that the social forms that emerge during transition are *impermanent*, and as such, lack legitimacy. Anthropologists have taken issue with the teleological and evolutionary underpinnings of transition. Some have argued that "transformation" might be a more accurate description for the process (Verdery 1996) because it allows for multiple directions of change, while also accounting for its complexity and indeterminacy (Burawoy and Verdery 1999).

Part of the effort to move away from transition has focused on transcending the hierarchy implied in the model. Some scholars (e.g., Buck-Morss 2002, Verdery 2002) have proposed that we think back to Cold War "opponents" as each seeking to produce a particular kind of modernity. Susan Buck-Morss (2002) suggests, for example, that both parties to the Cold War were engaged in a quest for utopia, and that while they wished to be looked upon as regimes ruled by the masses, they also constructed "wild zones" or spaces in which citizens came to be excluded from the "dreamworlds" of modernity. Drawing on Verdery (2002), Brandtstadter writes that scholars might explore postsocialism "as a cultural process shaped by the ideological opposition between socialism and capitalism, *and* their similarities as modernist projects" (2007: 134; emphasis added). This perspective may be usefully applied to the study of rights discourses in the post-Soviet space. In a 1980 article on Soviet and Western conceptions of human rights, Hawkesworth claims that "Because of [the] radical divergence in understanding the concept of human rights, one could predict that any dialog on the subject by proponents of these two world views would be at cross-purposes" (1980: 73). In the *post*–Cold War period, however, a dialogue between articulations of rights previously seen as incommensurable is in fact possible. What emerges from my study is that post-Soviet rights discourses tend to contain elements of (imagined) Western modernity *and* selected, reconfigured elements of Soviet modernity. Young people play a key role in reconciling these elements into new forms of claims making.

Scholars using the "Transition" model have often defined change as the evolution from Soviet values (collectivism, planned economy) to Western values (democracy, capitalism). We may wish to view change in the region not as the gradual replacement of Soviet by Western modernity, but rather as a constant engagement between Western and Soviet modernities. The notion of "becoming" developed by Deleuze (1987) is useful in thinking through change-in-process. He notes that

> Becomings are not phenomena of imitation or assimilation, but of a double capture, of non-parallel evolution, of nuptials between two reigns. Nuptials are always against nature. Nuptials are the opposite of a couple. There are no longer binary machines: question-answer, masculine-feminine, man-animal, etc. This could be what a conversation is—simply the outline of a becoming. The wasp and the orchid provide the example. The orchid seems to form a wasp image, but in fact there is a wasp-becoming of the orchid, an orchid-becoming of the wasp, a double capture since 'what' each becomes changes no less than "that which" becomes. . . . It is like Mozart's birds: in this music there is a bird-becoming, but caught in a music-becoming of the bird, the two forming a single becoming. (Deleuze and Parnet 1987: 2–3)

Similarly, we could argue that on the ground in post-Soviet countries, there is not only a "Western" becoming of former Soviet practices (i.e., the region is being Westernized), but also a "Soviet" becoming of Western practices (i.e., local populations appropriate and thus transform the concepts, practices, and standards around "democracy," the "free market," "private property," etc). In contrast to the transition model, premised on the eventual replacement of Soviet by Western modernity, "it is not one term which becomes the other, but each encounters the other, a single becoming" (Deleuze and Parnet 1987: 6–7). There is no direction to this encounter, no notion of "progress": elements may come together in unexpected and unintended ways. Newness thus emerges as something "between" and "outside" (7).

This is not to suggest that we think of this engagement in terms of "hybridity." The latter concept does not seem adequate because Western and Soviet modernities are not clearly bounded things to begin with (e.g., they have each emerged as a result of struggles between various actors and as products of various influences, including different national influences). In fact, as Buck-Morss (2002) suggests, the two modernities developed to a large extent *in relation to one another* during the Cold War. Moreover, labeling the engagement "hybridity" might lead us back to the stereotype of the region's "in-betweenness" and thus risk imposing upon people a category that is potentially demeaning (Friedman 1990). To think about change instead in terms of a conversation that leads to new forms allows us to undermine what

Deleuze calls "binary machines as apparatuses of power [that] break up becomings" (Deleuze and Parnet 1987: 33). This approach contributes not only
to an anthropological critique of Transition (e.g., Burawoy and Verdery
1999), but also to long-standing anthropological debates on the nature
of social change (e.g., Sahlins 1981, Ortner 1989), including change brought
about by globalization (e.g., Inda and Rosaldo 2008). While much valuable
work has come out of exploring the interpenetration of local and global, the
engagement between Western and Soviet modernities cannot be adequately
theorized with reference to Robertson's (1992) model of "glocalization." As
Caldwell points out in her analysis of the domestication of McDonald's
in Russia, there is a need to "depart from local/global paradigms that juxta-
pose 'the global' with an authentic and unquestionably indigenous 'local'"
(2008: 238). To speak of the interpenetration of the local and the global, or
the "universal" and the "particular," fails to acknowledge that Western and
Soviet modernities were both "global" to a certain extent. Indeed, the fact
that they both vied for universalism may help explain why *post*socialist
struggles may be conceived of as "struggles over the meaning and owner-
ship of modernity" (Brandtstadter 2007: 135).

Chapter 2

Order, Excess, and the Construction of the Patriot

In his 2004 Motherland Defenders' Day Speech, former president of Ukraine Leonid Kuchma stated: "The real patriotism of our time lies in safeguarding the public order (*poriadok*) established by our independence and by the historical wisdom of Ukrainians. That is what it really means to be a modern patriot [*suchasnyi patriot*]" (UT-1, February 23, 2004). Why would order and its maintenance become the central element of real Ukrainian patriotism? On the one hand, order was tied to the present (the patriotism "of our time," the "modern" patriot.) On the other hand, the president also pointed to the "historical wisdom" of the Ukrainian people (*narod*) as a guarantee of the maintenance of order. The term historical wisdom was reminiscent of another term, people's wisdom (*narodna mudrist'*), which refers to a set of dispositions, beliefs, and values attributed to the Ukrainian people and internalized (to some extent) by the latter. The authorities often portrayed the Ukrainian people as naturally "patient [*terpliachyi*]," or willing to endure a lot. In addition, state discourse, from official speeches to school textbooks, typically characterized Ukrainians as a "peace-loving" nation. Yet Leonid Kuchma's statement on the "real patriot" suggests that such attributes can be simultaneously descriptive and prescriptive. The authorities' articulation of certain sets of characteristics as "models of" and "models for" Ukrainian society could thus serve to shape the contours of citizenship and the repertoire of possible agency for the Ukrainian patriot.

The observation of concrete state practices (and especially those related to surveillance) allows us to get a better grasp of the ways in which power differentials between "ordinary citizens" and representatives of the state

came to be articulated in everyday life. Police presence was always conspicuous around the president and his entourage. Citizens often became
spectators of performances such as the president's commute to and from his
suburban residence: While driving one's car or riding public transportation
along the road leading to the presidential residence, one would first encounter traffic police officers standing at regular intervals along the highway.
Then, an officer would stop one's vehicle and ask one to pull off the road and
wait. Police would not usually answer queries about the reason for this in-
terruption. Arguing at that point would only arouse suspicion and lead to
a search of one's trunk. (A female friend of mine once confronted police:
"What do you think, that I have a machine gun in there?" "We don't know
that" was the solemn answer.) Those people sitting tight together in over-
crowded public buses would sigh, "*Kortezh* [cortege]." Once all the vehicles
were safely stopped on the side of the road and after a wait of twenty minutes or so, a police car would come through with sirens. Then, a few black
cars (one presumably containing the president), with blinking lights, would
follow at full speed. Some more police cars would then end the procession.
Traffic police would block the road for another fifteen minutes or so, and
then let traffic resume. One may argue that this sort of performance is common to most states, and that one could find one's schedule disrupted by a
similar presidential motorcade in Washington, D.C. In Kyiv, however, the
people who traveled regularly to the suburbs often planned their trips around
their president's (unpredictable) commutes: "Will Kuchma have gone back
home already?" they would wonder. As Jean and John Comaroff have noted
in the South African context, the motorcade and attendant police performances "deployed the full power of the law—the right to usurp public space
and time" (2006: 291).

In the fall of 2004, government authorities increased police surveillance,
quoting concerns about terrorism. This meant an increase in police presence and surveillance cameras, especially in the subway. Many people believed this to be a good thing, claiming that with Ukraine's participation in
the Iraqi war, they felt more vulnerable to terrorist attacks. "God forbid that
those crazy terrorists blow up our subway! Those Chechens are scary [*stras-
hni*]," said Svetlana, the teacher with whom I lived. Kyiv subways are very
deep in the ground so that the ride up and down the escalator may take as
long as ten minutes. The "captive audience" of the escalator may be treated
to music (Shostakovich was a favorite for the morning rush hour in my
neighborhood station), but was most often subjected to a recording of sub-

way regulations. "Citizen-passengers [*hromadiany-pasazhyry*]" were instructed not to run and to "maintain order." In the fall of 2004, a new message was added that instructed commuters on how to behave in case of a terrorist attack. This new concern arose after the September 2004 terrorist hostage crisis in a school in Beslan, Russia. An official moment of silence was decreed in Ukraine to honor the victims. On that day in the private school, a student told me that she did not quite understand the reason for marking this event, as "[The attack] didn't happen *in Ukraine*," but her classmate said that he understood it to be a show of sympathy for the schoolchildren who had died. When asked if a similar attack could occur in Ukraine, some students seemed to think that it could (one of them mentioned the country's participation in war efforts in Iraq), but most did not appear overly concerned because, in the words of one student, "It is Russia that is at war with Chechnya." It was indeed unclear why Chechens would wish to target Ukraine, traditionally an ally. Yet following the logic of "risk governmentality," everyday practices combined to create an atmosphere in which increased surveillance appeared to be a necessary precaution. Not everyone equated increased surveillance with the protection of citizens, however. "What are [the authorities] so afraid of?" asked a friend of mine, a university student, as we discussed over coffee the somewhat excessive police presence around the president. "Of terrorists, apparently," I suggested. He directed an incredulous look at me: "*What* terrorists? They're making this up!" He reminded me that the presidential elections (pitting a pro-government candidate against an opposition candidate) were coming up and that surely the state would put its surveillance apparatus to good use then.

Many people agreed that daily life in Ukraine had become marked by new forms of disorder, insecurity, and lawlessness visible on the streets of the capital. They spoke of transition (*perekhid*, literally, crossover) as being in large part responsible for this state of affairs. Young and old referred to their country as a mess (*bardak*), a nuthouse (*durdom*), or pure chaos (*khaos*), and engaged with the teleological discourse of transition by stating such things as "We are going backward," or "We are not moving, merely stamping our feet." Tetyana, a student's parent and 34-year-old homemaker, was driving me home from school one day. She remarked, after a car in front of us had made a U-turn across four lanes of traffic, almost causing an accident, "Look at the way people drive! There is total chaos on the road, nobody respects traffic law, everybody does as they want [*khto shcho khoche*], with no regard for others. I'm telling you, we're going toward this [making the motion of playing a drum with her hands], in the direction of the wild people. Although it seems to me there must have been more order [*poriadok*] then, you know, shortly after the appearance of man on earth."

In this example, disorder is first associated with peoples imagined as "pre-modern." For Tetyana, Ukraine is regressing rather than progressing. The image of Transition as a process that moves people away from modernity (one they may have achieved under Soviet rule) resonates with local discourses in other countries of the region. Platz (2000) speaks of transition as "demodernization" in Armenia, and Verdery (1996) of transition as a "return to feudalism" in Russia. Tetyana was also referring to people's disregard for the law (in this case traffic law) and for others. I was curious about the kind of picture of "order" she might have, so I asked her whether there had been order "earlier" (*ranishe*, code name for the Soviet period). "Yes," she replied, "because at that time, people were united around a single ideology. They had something to believe in, something to hold them together. Now, there is nothing like that, every person goes in a different direction, and of course, it results in chaos." Tetyana seemed to be pointing to the emergence of the person or individual, with his or her own will and "direction." Yet this individual's desires and actions were not (or no longer) limited by the welfare of the society or the collective. She added that it was people's economic struggle to survive that led them to be selfish and disrespectful of others, and to break the law. "Now, people live according to the law of the jungle [*zakon dzhunhliv*]," she added. What seemed to emerge from discourses such as these was a sense that society, previously held together by a single ideology, a certain set of moral values, and (implicitly) a decent standard of living, was now in some sense becoming atomized along "individual" lines. Tetyana's invocation of a new kind of regulation, the "law of the jungle," suggests that everyday life has become a new kind of struggle in which only the strongest individuals survive.

Despite widespread complaints about people's disregard for the law, or what was sometimes referred to as "legal nihilism," opinions differed on the best way to keep "disorder" in check and the role of the authorities in this process. For example, while students could state that police and security presence on the streets and in stores made them feel "safer," they would also complain about what they considered the "excessive" presence of police at youth events such as concerts, a presence that they claimed made them feel uncomfortable or unable to enjoy themselves. Their teachers had their own take on the best way to maintain order. During an English class in the public school, Vira, a teacher in her mid-sixties, asked her students if it was possible for them to purchase liquor even though they were underage. They candidly replied that they could ask an older sibling to purchase it for them, but that they could usually buy it themselves without problem. Lamenting Ukrainian people's disregard for the law, Vira looked at me and said: "We need a policeman for each person in this country."

"What for?" I asked.

"To make sure that people respect and obey the law." My host Svetlana's perception of people as disorderly veered into a nostalgic discourse about the structure and order of Soviet life. We were having cake in her colleague's classroom at the end of the school day. Reflecting on the number of people she now encountered in the subway at all times of night and day, Svetlana said: "People are so undisciplined now. I remember in Andropov's time [Yuri Andropov was General Secretary of the Communist Party of the Soviet Union, 1982–1984], there was no one on the streets during the day, no one crowding public transportation, everyone was working. It was so nice." Her colleague of thirty years, Katya, was more cynical and interrupted: "Of course, everybody *had* to work. Remember when that cop stopped you because you were at the store during work hours?" Svetlana continued, unperturbed, "Yes, once, I was done with teaching early, around three o'clock in the afternoon, and I stopped by the food store. A policeman [*militsioner*] grabbed me by the wrist and asked me: 'Why aren't you at work?' and I had to show my documents and explain myself. But still—what *order* there was then [*takyi poriadok buv todi*]!" This kind of statement (though not uncontested) underlined in some sense the need for order "from above." According to this logic, people were prone to disorder and lawlessness and needed figures of authority not only to watch over them, but also to *enforce* the law. Humphrey (2002) points to this kind of discourse in other post-Soviet countries, stating that "many people seek order not *in* themselves but *for* themselves, that is, from powers [*vlasti*] conceived as above; and therefore if the local polity does not provide order, they seek it from higher levels, culminating in the symbolic reification of an ultimate power" (29). In the Ukrainian language, *vlasti* is translated as *vlada*. *Vlada* may be used to refer to the state (more accurately translated as *derzhava*) or the government (more accurately translated as *uriad*). It is usually a reference to the executive branch of the government. However, it is best translated as "the powers." This term is all the more potent because it is vague and thus can encompass many realms while also suggesting the impossibility of attributing agency or responsibility.

The *vlada* is best defined in relation to the *prosti*, literally, the "simple/ordinary" people, but also meaning the people who are not in power, or not in charge. These terms will be examined further in Chapter 5.

Of the many threats of internal disorder invoked by the Ukrainian government, one deserves particular attention here: nationalism. Throughout his term in office, President Kuchma stated that nationalism is "bad," articulating it as a major threat to peace, law, and order. Prime minister and presidential candidate Viktor Yanukovych also treated nationalism as a dirty word, blaming "young nationalists" for a September 2004 incident that received much publicity (a student threw an egg at him and the candidate fell to the ground as though he had been shot). He also claimed in response to Western Ukrainians' active opposition to his political program that "Nationalism is a disease" (*Stolytsia*, September 29, 2004). This, of course, is not a unique way of characterizing nationalism. In many, perhaps most, Western societies, patriotism is considered "good" while nationalism is seen as at least problematic if not bad. In the European tradition, nationalism was initially linked with democracy, but in the twentieth century, it became associated with the reactionary anti-democratic forces of fascism. The Ukrainian authorities' concern with the threat of nationalism reflected to a certain extent their concern with appearing "modern" in the Western sense. In other words, authorities wanted to portray Ukraine as a civilized country, and not one prone to "nationalistic passions" (see Todorova 1997 for a discussion of the Western imaginary of the Balkans as a space of nationalist excess).

It is useful here to examine the Soviet construction of nationalism in some detail, for it seems to have some bearing on current attitudes toward nationalism as well as on representations of the nation in post-Soviet Ukraine. In the Soviet Union, modernity took the form of an overarching Soviet identity encompassing various "nationalities," and nationalism (especially *bourgeois* nationalism) was thought to constitute a real threat to the Soviet state. Kasianov (1998) defines "Ukrainian bourgeois nationalism" as "any kind of show of national consciousness, cultural, ideological, or political tendencies which did not coincide with state ideology on the nationality question and could . . . threaten [the state's] rule or become the basis for separatist tendencies" (40). Bourgeois nationalism named the possibility of both ideological and *moral* transgression. A 1938 report to the Politburo signed by Molotov and Stalin illuminates the difference between "nationalism" and "nationality." The report condemned "bourgeois *nationalist* counterrevolutionary elements . . . [that] undermined the brotherly unity of the *nations* of the USSR" (quoted in Fowkes 1997: 67; emphasis added). While "nation" (or the more widely used "nationality" [Rus. *natsional'nost'*]) was associated with the positive concepts of unity and brotherhood, the adjective "nationalist," paired with bourgeois and counterrevolutionary, has negative undertones. Bourgeois nationalism evoked the kind of exclusive, separatist nationalism detrimental to Soviet internationalism. In contrast, the Soviet nationality was considered *inclusive* in that its boundaries could be eroded for the sake of Soviet unity and fusion.[1] The distinction between the Soviet nationality and the kind of identity promoted by so-called bourgeois nationalism was in part a difference in temporal orientation. Thus, while "bourgeois nationalism" aimed at securing for itself a national future, the Soviet nationality was, inherently, a category with no future, that is, it was meant to disappear.

In the 1920s, the Bolsheviks had initially promoted *korenizatsiia*, or nativization, creating separate republics with titular nations and local communist parties, and encouraging the development of local languages (the Bolsheviks' desire to break from Russia's imperial, "chauvinist" past had kept the Russian Soviet republic from claiming its "own" communist party and other key institutions). However, this led national elites to the realization that they could build communism without being subordinated to Moscow. Faced with the threat of *national* communism, Stalin put an end to nativization. In the 1930s, Stalin recast Russia's role as "leading nation" of the Soviet Union, and Russians as "first among equals." This led, among other processes, to the Russification (in alphabet, lexicon, and grammar) of Slavic languages, and the cyrillization of non-Slavic languages (Slezkine 2000: 321). According to Stalin's 1930 formulation, the Soviet Ukrainian nationality, like other nationalities, was to be "national in form, *socialist in content.*" The national in form "tended to manifest itself in the Soviet view in terms of overt cultural forms—language, dances, folklore, and such like" (Bromley in Banks 1996: 21). The emphasis on (often decontextualized) folkloric practices ensured that the national culture would not become grounds for challenging state authority and ideology. Indeed, while elements such a national costume, food, and (selected) songs became emblematic of the nationality, elements associated with socialist ideology remained dominant. This was evidenced in the production of traditional Ukrainian crafts such as carpet weaving, in which traditional Ukrainian ornaments framed embroidered "socialist" or Soviet elements such as the *sputnik*, the atom, the dove (symbol of peace), and portraits of Lenin or other Soviet leaders (for visual examples, see *Derzhavnyi Muzei Ukrains'koho Narodnoho Dekoratyvnoho Mystetstva URSR*, 1967). In the 1960s and 1970s, Ukrainian writers (some of them dissidents) attempted to renew the concept of "nationality" by reviving various Ukrainian cultural icons. Most writers had difficulty transcending the socialist realist genre endorsed by the Soviet state, however, and thus followed a "familiar recipe of folklorism mixed with a . . . cult of Shevchenko [the Ukrainian national poet] and the Cossack myth" (Wilson 2000: 155). Nevertheless, the attempts were followed by a wave of repression under Volodymyr Shcherbytsky (leader of the Communist Party of Ukraine, 1972–1989) that had Ukrainian intellectuals arrested and sent to labor camps on charges of "bourgeois nationalism."

How did state authorities articulate nation and nationalism in the *post*-Soviet period? My data suggest that despite the new coincidence of nation and state in Ukraine after the collapse of the Soviet Union, and despite the dissolution of socialist ideology, the authorities continued to articulate nationalism (of one's own people) as a threat to state stability. Specifically, during the presidential campaign of 2004, President Kuchma and his government used the term "nationalists" to refer to people who were nationally conscious and *willing to act* on their nationalism, that is, to use it as grounds for political action, potentially against the authorities themselves. This is in stark contrast to the peace-loving and predictable patriotism championed by the president. During the 2004 presidential campaign, Yanukovych supporters repeatedly referred to PORA (or "It's Time," the group that initiated the demonstrations leading to the 2004 Orange Revolution) as "nationalists" and "terrorists" (two categories of disorder and excess) who wish to "destroy the country and lead us to civil war." In these discourses, the nationalist became the opposite of the patriot. While the patriot existed "for" and "within" the state, the nationalist existed outside and *against* the state.

Drawing in part on the work of Corrigan and Sayer (1985), anthropologists of the state have come to speak of nations, or what Benedict Anderson called "imagined communities," as effects of state power. In this view, not only does the state define the range of identities or subject positions available to people, but the citizenry is reproduced as national so as to legitimate state power (see, e.g., Coronil 1988; Borneman 1992; Nagengast 1994). Alonso (1994) has explored the tropes of substance necessary to the persuasiveness of the "nation," tropes often associated with kinship and gender that naturalize the imagining of the people through a fusion of the ideological and the sensory, the bodily and the normative. The nation articulated under Kuchma bore a resemblance to the Soviet Ukrainian nationality, to the extent that folkloric elements were prominent. An example of this is the spatial organization of Kyiv's Independence Square after the renovations of 2002, and its assemblage of characters, be they statues of Cossacks playing the *bandura* (a traditional instrument) or of the (muscular) archangel St. Michael (patron of Kyiv), or the monument Ukraina, portraying a female figure in traditional Ukrainian dress. Sites for the dissemination of national culture also included concerts on national television, holiday celebrations, historical monuments, and state-issued calendars. Although some elements (religious symbols) constituted a sharp break with Soviet representations, apolitical and benign features were still central to the state's depiction of Ukrainian culture. Wanner (1998) suggests that post-Soviet Ukrainian national culture arose as a (necessary) compromise between the Russian-Soviet orientation found in Eastern Ukraine and the Western European orientation found in Western Ukraine. However, a Ukrainian university professor told me that the resulting state-produced national culture was a culture "without teeth" or bite (*bez zubiv*).

This type of national culture allowed the authorities to position themselves in a particular way vis-à-vis "the nation." It is significant that the metaphors for the relation between nation and state put forth by the authorities were usually gendered, with the state depicted as a man, and the nation, *Ukraina*, depicted as a woman or a young girl. The most common illustration of this dynamic was the ritual greeting of Ukrainian high state officials upon their arrival to various Ukrainian regions. Every day on the news, one could see young smiling women in traditional Ukrainian dress (the style varied by region) welcoming the president or prime minister (themselves in dark suits) with the traditional offering of bread and salt (*khlib ta sil'*). The programming of the First Channel (UT-1, the official government channel) epitomized state-defined national culture, in the concerts it broadcast, in documentaries about Ukraine, or in Ukrainian "patriotic segments" between programs. These construed Ukraine (or Ukraina, a feminine name) metaphorically as a female "victim" of its history, and the adjectives "wronged" (*oshukana*) or "raped" (*zhvaltovana*) were often used. Alternatively, Ukraine was portrayed as an old destitute woman in need of being rescued. These narratives conveyed the message that with Ukrainian independence, the nation had acquired in the state a "landlord" or "owner" (*hospodar*). The state also appeared as a protector in more tangible ways. The traffic police (DAI,

Figure 2. Archangel Michael towers over a section of Kyiv's Independence Square. For a brief moment in 2003, when this picture was captured, the monument coexisted with the hammer and sickle, seen on the adjacent building. Photo by the author.

or State Automobile Inspectorate) were perhaps the most visible representatives of the state (as least for the city's drivers). In the fall of 2004, the news media focused on several stories in which DAI officers had helped women give birth on the road. These reports emphasized a relation in which the benevolent representatives of the state had helped birth the nation, portraying the officers as smiling father figures (and thus providing a sharp contrast to people's perception of DAI as corrupt, bribe-loving "bandits in uniform [*bandyty u formi*]"). A similar metaphor for the relation between state and nation could be seen on a huge billboard overlooking the highway. The billboard (presumably an advertisement for DAI) portrayed a smiling uniformed police officer with his arm around a smiling young girl of about six years old dressed up in the traditional embroidered shirt (*vyshyvanka*) and wearing a flower wreath (*vinok*). In the background stood the bell towers of the Pechers'ka Lavra monastery. The caption read: "The safety of the people is the highest law! [*Bezpeka narodu, naivyshchyi zakon!*]" In this case, the adult uniformed man appears to represent the "state," while the small girl in national gear, presumably in need of protection, seems to stand for the "nation." The relationship itself is staged "within the law" (both in its legal sense, as indicated by the caption, and in its moral sense, with the backdrop of church bells). While this type of representation shows the police protecting citizens rather than the president and his entourage, it also involves an element of paternalism. By posing citizens as children (in Ukraine, children are thought to be particularly prone to disorder), the authorities could perhaps more easily justify their role in the maintenance of order.

Nations are not limited to state projects, however, and local and individual experiences shape the nation as a concept and a set of practices. Clearly, some Ukrainian citizens did act on the basis of what we might call national self-awareness or self-consciousness. For example, I was walking with Svetlana along Andryivskiy Uzviz, a tourist-oriented street-turned-market. I noticed a stand that displayed pictures of Stalin, and as we paused to look at them, a man in his fifties walked by and addressed the seller: "Why are you selling portraits of Stalin? Have you forgotten what he did to Ukraine? Shame on you! [*Han'ba!*]" He then walked away. I asked Svetlana what she made of this, and she said that the man had been right, but was also seemingly uncomfortable with the fact that he had spoken up in such a self-confident manner. "He's for Ukraine [*Vin za Ukrainu*]," she ended up saying.

The Orange Revolution of November–December 2004 was key in reconfiguring some of the meanings around the nation. Significantly, a large section of the Ukrainian citizenry rose up against the government, the scenario most feared by the latter. The hip hop group *Tartak* of Western Ukraine composed a song that became a hit on Kyiv's Independence Square, the center of the Orange Revolution. The song entitled "I don't want to [*Ia ne khochu*]" claims that there is no point in being a hero in Ukraine, because the country "does not value heroes." It speaks of the hero who rises from the masses to go fight—but while people flood him with praise, they secretly perceive him as an "internal enemy" (a term that suggests a certain degree of popular ambivalence toward the active and assertive patriot). The song also exposes the kind of national culture that both people and government tend to reproduce in everyday life. It claims that while Ukrainians got their own state, they lost the nation. The song enjoins people to move away from superficial cultural forms and meaningless metaphors "'Language of the guelder-rose' . . . 'song of the nightingale' . . . a little more chatter and Ukraine will be annihilated [*'Mova kalynova' . . . 'pisnia solovina' . . . shche trokhy pobalakaiemo - znykne Ukraina!*]," and affirms the need for Ukrainian heroes

Figure 3. Citizens attending an Independence Day celebration in Kyiv in August 2003. In the backdrop, a poetic reference to Ukrainian as the "language of the nightingale." Photo by the author.

"without embroidered shirts or Cossack pants [*bez vyshyvanky ta bez sharovariv*]." The song arose as a challenge to existing discourses around the patriot and emerged as a call for political mobilization.

The construction of the patriot in Ukraine rested not only on a particular kind of relationship between "state" and "citizens," but also on the relationship between Ukraine and its neighbor to the east, Russia. Wanner (1998) notes that nation-building in Ukraine is based on a compromise between Ukrainian and Soviet/Russian elements. In her ethnography, Wanner examines the new Ukrainian calendar, in which Soviet, national Ukrainian, and religious holidays coexist. She claims that the civic, inclusive nationalism produced through the state calendar both reinforces citizens' attachment to place *and* fractures society by maintaining regional alliances and keeping alive nostalgia for the bygone Soviet era (1999: 106). What Wanner calls, following Kathleen Smith (1999), "dueling rituals," which may be interpreted in Soviet or nationalist terms, are indeed compatible with the reproduction of hybrid, bi-national identities (113). Based on my observations in the city of Kyiv (this may vary in other regions) the "nation" does not appear to be a given nor the category within which everything else operates. Supranational self-identification (e.g., East Slavic, including Ukrainian, Russian, and Belarusian, fused in the expression "our people") is common. Some citizens believe that Ukrainian patriotism is compatible with "brotherhood" with Russia (a country of shared history), and under Leonid Kuchma's rule, this particular version of Ukrainian patriotism went hand in hand with efforts to form a Single Economic Space (CES) that was to (re)unite Russia, Ukraine, Belarus, and Kazakhstan, making borders irrelevant and making the ruble (once again) the common currency. The former head of parliament and head of the Socialist Party of Ukraine articulated this logic when he stated in 2001 that: "To be a patriot of Ukraine today means to work for integration with Russia" (quoted in Shevchenko 2001: 2).

In classical models of nation-building, one observes the production of national "purity" at the expense of (putatively natural) "hybridity." This process is what anthropologist Laada Bilaniuk (2005) describes in her book on the nature of Ukrainian language policies and practices in the first few years after the country's independence. Rodgers (2008) frames his analysis of regional responses (and resistance) to nation-building in Ukraine in similar terms. Yet it seems that during President Kuchma's second term (1999–2004), the formulation of hybridity (harmonization, rapprochement) arose as a political project that competed with attempts at restoring national unity and specificity. The political forces behind these two competing projects each claimed to be restoring "eternal" identities.[2] Benei (2008) points out that the term "identities" conjures up the image of something "congealed" or "essentialized" (3). In contrast, the term *identification* emphasizes "the processual agency of social actors" and "leaves the way open for indeterminacy and the necessarily fragmentary character of all projects of self-formation, be they individual or collective" (3).[3] Rather than asking which of the above projects is truer to Ukrainians' "real identity," therefore, it is perhaps more useful to examine processes of identification as they both overlap with and diverge from these particular political projects. The educational setting is a key site for the negotiation of identity projects.

Remaking the Person: Ukrainians' "Return to Themselves"

Educational reform in Ukraine began almost immediately following independence, in 1992, under Leonid Kravchuk's presidency. The reforms were based on the premise that Soviet education had been authoritarian and had emphasized uniformity and collectivism at the expense of students' natural talents and individuality (Wanner 1998: 82). Catherine Wanner has noted that "the restoration of a Ukrainian cultural identity is seen as part and parcel of the process of fostering individual development" (1998: 82) and thus the new national pedagogy was to follow the principles of "individuality, nationality, and morality" (82). Courses in Ukrainian history, culture, and language were deemed central to the creation of "nationally conscious citizens and patriots"(Kuzio 1998: 63), and became compulsory (62).

At the time of my fieldwork, these educational goals were still in place, but there were also attempts at making the substance of national history compatible with Russian historiography. In May 2002, an intergovernmental commission of Ukrainian and Russian historians was created in Moscow to "harmonize" Russian and Ukrainian versions of history. The idea arose from a sense of worry among Russian intellectuals that Ukrainian history textbooks presented certain historical events in a negative fashion (e.g., some textbooks depicted the 1933 famine in Ukraine as a "man-made"[4] famine for which Stalin was held responsible) (Kuzio 2002). Comprised of both Russian and Ukrainian intellectuals, the intergovernmental commission sought to develop a non-conflictual approach to history (Kuzio 2002). These efforts eventually failed amid protest by some Ukrainian intellectuals that Russia was trying to reintroduce the "imperial viewpoint" in Ukrainian history.

In his book *Education and Science in Ukraine: Paths to Modernization* (2003), then Minister of Education of Ukraine Vasyl Kremen' spelled out some of the directions to be taken in order to bring Ukraine to the "world standard" in education (37). Kremen' emphasizes the need for a "radically humanitarian education," pointing to the "orientation toward the person" as the fundamental building block of democratic education. In fact, one of the central themes of post-Soviet Ukrainian education has been the return of the "person" as the highest value. Not only was a new principle of child-centrism (*dytynotsentryzm*) necessary (Kremen' 2003: 40), but children had to be seen in a new light: as the subjects rather than the objects of pedagogy. The new emphasis on personality and individualism dictated "Self-recognition, [recognition] of one's 'I', of one's aspirations and abilities, the recognition of how to best realize one's strengths—this new, worthy humanism is the task of education, teaching, and upbringing [*vykhovannia*]" (Kremen' 2003: 38).

While these goals were articulated (at least implicitly) against Soviet principles, it should be pointed out here that the Soviet educational system did not officially take a position against individualism, but rather emphasized the individual's connection to the larger collective. A school program adopted by the Commissariat of Education in 1918 claimed that "the individual [*lichnost'*] remains the highest value of socialist culture. But this individual can develop all its endowments only in a harmonic and solidary society of equals" (quoted in Kharkhordin 1999: 190). This logic emanated from the idea, articulated by the Soviet leadership (including by Stalin himself), that the individual cannot be truly free until the masses have themselves been emancipated (Kharkhordin 1999: 192). According to Lunacharsky (1918), socialist education, "by uniting the wish to construct psychological *kollektivy* with a subtle individualization . . . , engenders an individual who is proud of the development of all capacities in himself in order to serve society" (quoted in Kharkhordin 1999: 190).

The making of the unique (*nepovtorna*, lit. "not repeated") person in post-Soviet Ukraine was tightly bound with the making of the patriotic person (*liudyna-patriot*). Not only because nations, like individuals, were thought to have their own "personalities," but also because "The success of the whole nation is a prerequisite for the success of each person" (Kremen' 2003: 45). In addition, people who are individually self-conscious have the sense of being the "owner [*hospodar*] of their country, of being responsible subjects and shapers of the country's future" (46). That said, the new pedagogy was to be based on historical and cultural traditions rather than on "nationalism," the latter understood here as a divisive, intolerant, and potentially violent ideology. In fact, Kremen' suggests a focus on the Ukrainian "national mentality" rather than on "belligerent nationalism" (*voiovnychyi natsionalizm*) (2003: 46). Interestingly, mentality here seems to connote passivity (it is something that is already inside one and that one cannot change), especially when positioned in relation to active and aggressive nationalism. A whole set of concepts circulated in Ukrainian society that sought to avert nationalism while still evoking continuity with a Ukrainian past interrupted by Soviet rule. This included not only mentality (*mentalitet*) and historical memory (*istorichna pam'iat'*), but also the idea of the genetic code of the nation (*henetychnyi kod natsii*). The genetic code of the nation, an expression I had heard used by some Ukrainian intellectuals, expresses the fact that no matter how much different powers (and especially Soviet power) had tried to annihilate Ukrainian culture, the latter survived deep within Ukrainians, inscribed in the genetic code itself. In this primordial perspective on the nation, the national essence survives in the "underground," passed on biologically by one's ancestors. Thus the national essence can be altered neither by conquerors nor (implicitly) by oneself, which is to say that even if one became outwardly Russified, one's Ukrainian inner core would necessarily remain.[5] Another popular concept that expressed continuity with the past is the "wisdom of the people [*narodna mudrist'*]." The wisdom of the people inhered in songs, stories, legends, and sayings that had roots in Ukrainian village culture, and was a central concept in Ukrainian folklore (*narodoznavstvo*), literature, and history textbooks. A textbook designed for fourth graders and entitled "Ukraine and I" (*Ia i Ukraina*) had a "wisdom of the people" section in each chapter that showcased Ukrainian sayings such as "It is good to be a guest, but even better to be home," or (significantly) "You can choose everything in the world, son. / The only thing you cannot choose is your Fatherland [*Batkivshchyna*]." A similar slogan, this time about the Motherland, circulated in the Soviet Union.

School textbooks often described the nation as a "family" (Soviet patriotism had also relied on the image of the family, expressed for example in the family of nations, or "brotherhood of Slavs"). A class handout for eleventh graders read: "it is not a coincidence that our coat of arms symbolizes a trinity: that of person, family, and nation." One's individualism was dependent on belonging to a nation, and one's belonging to a nation made it possible for one to belong to the world. In fact, a folklore textbook entitled "Bless me, Mother" (1995) and designed for grades 5–8 claimed that "A person who gives up on their land, language, people—is an *orphan*; she does not find a place for herself in the world" (12; emphasis added).

A crucial element in the pedagogical shaping of the person (and consequently, of the patriotic person) is the *move toward interiority and self-regulation*. The emphasis on self-improvement and self-regulation was also present in the Soviet Union, but these processes were configured differently. Michel Foucault's work reveals that "the government of the individual in modernity has moved from the outside to the inside" (Jenks 2005: 67), and scholars have explored this process and its manifestations in the Russian Empire and the Soviet Union (see, e.g., Hoffman and Kotsonis 2000). In his book *The Collective and the Individual in Russia: A Study of Practices* (1999), Kharkhordin traces the rise of the individual in the Soviet Union through practices of self-transformation and self-improvement. He claims that starting in the Stalinist period (and particularly, during the purges), the practice of *oblichenie* (the condemnation of an individual's deeds) forced people to reflect on their personal features (250) and to self-evaluate in relation to the norms of the *kollektiv*. The associated methods of "horizontal" surveillance (i.e., surveillance among peers rather than by superiors) (Kharkhordin 1999: 355) developed in several institutions, including the Communist Party and youth organizations such as the Pioneers, but also came to pervade the school, with the result that self-transformation became common among children (1999: 250).

The principle of horizontal surveillance can be seen at work in a Soviet-era poster depicting a young male student (wearing the red Pioneer scarf) pointing accusingly at his male classmate, who cowers in shame. Behind him hangs the portrait of another Pioneer, Pavlik Morozov, who during the collectivization of the later 1920s and early 1930s, denounced his father to the authorities (Pavlik was subsequently killed by angry relatives). The poster's caption reads, "A Pioneer tells the truth and treasures the honor of his unit" (see Bronfenbrenner 1970 for a reproduction of this poster). Soviet children played an important role in the socialization of their peers (in this case, bringing a classmate's shortcomings to the attention of the collective in an effort to help him improve himself). Children's collectives in the Soviet Union indeed functioned as a "major source of reward and punishment" (Bronfenbrenner 1970: 50). Kharkhordin claims that "the ultimate achievement of Soviet individualization [would be] a modern subject who constantly readjusts his or her self-concept by staging internal mini-trials over his or her demonstrated deeds," and who could impose "self-order" (1999: 251). In late Soviet rule, "style" and consumption of certain goods would become new sources of individualism (1999: 342).

In post-Soviet Ukraine, the new focus on the individual's "inside" went hand in hand with the principles of self-knowledge, self-development, and self-realization (Kremen' 2003: 46) and spoke to larger efforts (e.g., by international development organizations) at undoing the "collectivization of the person" (Phillips 2008: 99). Scholars have examined attempts (in various settings) at cultivating risk-taking yet self-regulating individuals able to successfully negotiate the new market economy (see Phillips 2011, Dunn 2004, Matza 2009). In Ukrainian schools, the project of forging a self-aware and self-regulating person included a concern for the inner world of the child and the cultivation of a soulful or spiritual person (*dukhovno bahata liudyna*). On the one hand, the soul (posed in textbooks as something "everyone had") was described as a space of freedom. A study guide containing complete (ideal) exam answers for the eleventh grade humanities course made the following claim under the question, "Compare the categories of soulfulness and soullessness": "The soul needs freedom [*svoboda*], sovereignty and independence" (Bakka 2004: 19). It adds (and this kind of statement is what students are expected to learn by heart and repeat during their oral exams): "a person lives her spiritual life according to her own choices, but she guides herself according to her moral values as inner regulators of human behavior, [this] is a law [*zakon*] that exists in every person, [but] is shaped by social relations" (Bakka 2005: 11). Spiritual life is tied to values (11), so that "a spiritually developed person is a person who has self-worth, honor, and duties toward society" (Bakka 2004: 19). In contrast, soullessness [*bezdukhovnist'*] is defined as "a way of life according to which a person takes care only of her own personal interests, [and] improves her own well-being, disregarding the values and moral norms of society" (Bakka 2005: 39). Thus while the soul emerges as a space of freedom, it is also posed as a sphere of (moral) self-regulation and self-governing. In this view, freedom and choice should not arise at the expense of society's norms. The *Study Guide* states that "it is important for every person that her ideal and self-improvement not go against the ideals of the social environment in which she lives and self-fulfils as an individual" (Bakka 2004: 19).

The emergence of individuality, personality, and soul points to an attempt at producing a *governable inner world*. This project is compatible with neoliberal governmentality in that "order" is seen as the product of self-regulation. In this scenario, order comes from inside the individual rather than from "powers conceived of as above" (Humphrey 2002), as discussed earlier.[6] Yet the discourse presented in the study guide suggests that the *normativity* of society remained an important factor in shaping the individual. In independent Ukraine, one must abide by the rules and values of the *national* collective rather than the Soviet collective. These new rules and standards must in turn be reconciled with the humanistic view of the individual as the "supreme value." As illustrated above, there is considerable tension between individualism on the one hand and conformity on the other. Students in Kyiv were made intensely aware of the taboo against becoming a *bila vorona*, or white crow among black crows. "We live in a normative state [*normatyvna derzhava*]," said a teacher of Ukrainian literature to her students, "you don't want to be a *bila vorona*."

In her study of post-Soviet Estonia, Rausing (2004) claims that Soviet normativity expressed itself not only through the "modular" forms that pervaded everyday life (e.g., in the area of dress, housing, and even language), but also in people's unwillingness to draw attention to themselves. She also notes "a certain submissiveness in [people's] conformity" in Estonia (2004: 35). If the "specific Soviet kind of individual [was to be] formed in the public gaze of his or her peers" (Kharkhordin 1999: 356), perhaps so would the (developing) neoliberal subject? Fehérváry (2002) and Patico (2008) have noted the extent to which postsocialist consumption practices themselves have become "normative," so that one evaluates oneself according to what "everyone else" supposedly owns or consumes (more on this in Chapter 5), suggesting that consumerism may be one of the spaces where individualism and normativity can be "reconciled."

"I'm Not a Nationalist, but I'm for My Country"

When I began my research on citizenship education, several teachers pointed out to me that schools focused on teaching "national culture" rather than nationalism. I was on a school trip to L'viv (Western Ukraine) with Masha, a teacher of Ukrainian literature in her later sixties, and her class early in my fieldwork. We were talking about national culture and nationalism, and I asked her to explain the difference to me. She stated that national culture has to do with "the wisdom of our people, our traditions, our way of doing things." She was unable to define nationalism for me and said she would have to think about it. A bit later in the day, we were going through a L'viv underpass when some graffiti caught my attention. One read "Death to Russians! [*Smert' Moskaliam!*]" (the term *Moskali* dates from the Russian Empire and was used to refer to the inhabitants of Moscovia), while another read "Heil Hitler!" and had a swastika next to it. The teacher turned to me triumphantly: "Oh, now this, Anna, *this* is nationalism!" She went on: "You see, nationalism is like chauvinism, like imperialism." In an interview with the principal of the private school in which I worked, nationalism was also posed as something inherently negative. When I expressed interest in patriotic education, the principal immediately told me that in Ukraine, they had a different view than in America. "You cannot force students to be patriotic," he claimed. "That amounts to *nationalism*. There has been enough

bloodshed in our country's history: the last thing we need is nationalism!"
On another occasion, this same principal, who decided to devote a corner
of the school's main hall to a display of Ukrainian culture (including a
bandura [a traditional musical instrument], a traditional embroidered towel,
and a bust of the national poet Taras Shevchenko), justified himself in
front of other teachers and administrators by claiming: "I'm not a nationalist, but I'm for my country [*Ia ne natsionalist, ale ia za svoiu krainu*]." Many
educators felt the need to define themselves against nationalism. Because of
nationalism's association with hateful action against others and potential threat to peace and order, it was unthinkable to most (at least in the
Kyiv region) to have a citizenship curriculum based on it. For example, a
civics textbook for ninth graders entitled *We Are Ukrainian Citizens* (*My –
Hromadiany Ukrainy*) (2002) contains a chapter entitled "What is patriotism?" in which one may find the definitions of three key words: patriotism,
chauvinism, and cosmopolitanism. There is no mention of the word nationalism anywhere in the chapter, despite the fact that nationalism is probably
the most contested of the terms.

Students themselves were unsure of how they should stand toward nationalism. Teachers of Ukrainian routinely reprimanded them for not speaking Ukrainian among themselves in school (they speak Russian instead).
Some students confided, however, that they do not speak Ukrainian in
school for fear of appearing "too nationalistic" to others. A class of eleventh
graders pointed to one of their fellow students, saying that she was the only
one in the class who spoke Ukrainian at home, but that it was because she
had moved from Western Ukraine. The student blushed violently. Normativity did not always work in favor of the national project: in this particular
case, students posed cultural and linguistic hybridity as the norm. When I
raised the issue of patriotism and nationalism in a group discussion with
eleventh graders, opinions differed on the way to differentiate the two. One
student explained the terms thus: "Nationalism is to love only your nation
and hate all other nations, while patriotism is to love your country, to love
everything in your country. Nationalism is to hate nations that live in your
country." His colleague intervened: "But that's *fascism*! That's Nazism, not
nationalism." To which another student added: "No, nationalism means
that people should respect other nations, but have their own specificity, and
form a single community." A student suggested that "nationalism became a
bad word, but at first it was a good word, like patriotism." Most agreed that

"Patriotism is something that is not aggressive: people just love their country and enjoy their lives."

School textbooks typically defined the patriot as "one who loves his/her nation and state." Over and over in the classroom, teachers posed patriotism as something in the soul or the heart, thereby emphasizing the new educational concern with interiority. While lecturing on a poem in the Ukrainian literature class, a teacher stated: "It's a soulful [dukhovnobahata] person who can appreciate nature like this poet, a patriotic person [liudyna-patriot]. Someone who goes screaming around about their national identity, that's not a patriot." A Ukrainian history teacher once told me that patriotism is something that lives within you and that should not be expressed to others. She said, referring to a Russian colleague of hers who had stated how much she loved Russia: "Why do you need to talk about it? You have to *feel* it and that's enough." On the one hand, patriotism was posed as a sentiment that was already within the individual. Metaphors such the national "mentality" and "genetic code" reinforced this primordial view of national identity. Yet at the same time (and within the context of the "return to our national selves"), educators portrayed national identity as something that must be learned from scratch.

Schools emphasized repetition as a strategy for the reproduction of patriotism. In Ukrainian high schools as elsewhere (see, e.g., Luykx 1999, Lazar 2010), rote learning constitutes a large part of the pedagogical endeavor. It includes the in-class recitation of literary works that comprise the essence of the Ukrainian literature class, and the memorization, narration, and paraphrase (perekaz) of studied texts. It also includes repeated visual exposure to various Ukrainian cultural icons such as the national poet Taras Shevchenko, or the filmmaker Oleksander Dovzhenko, who are presented as ideals to be followed. Repetition was also present in the ritualization of bodily gestures that signify respect for one's country, or what Lazar, in her study of schooling in Bolivia, refers to as the "embodied forms of political agency" (2010: 182) taught in such contexts as ceremonies, demonstrations, and parades. Following the same principle as the performance of the pledge of allegiance in the United States, repetition is aimed at instilling lasting dispositions in students. Like the students in Benei's (2008) study of schooling in India, Ukrainian students were "phenomenologically taught to 'feel' the nation within their own bodies" (24). Most teachers are of the opinion that students must be constantly reminded of their culture, lest they "forget what is theirs," and must repeat certain gestures (for example, hand on one's heart during the national anthem) until, in the words of Svetlana, "whether you want it or not, you *do* it." This statement resonates with Bourdieu's illustration of how "obedience is belief and belief is what the body grants even when the mind says no" (1990: 167, quoted in Benei 2008: 78). What mattered here was repetition rather than intention. Not only were students taught to respect Ukraine, its state symbols, and its great patriots, but they were also taught to respect the authority of their teacher through the ritual of standing up when the teacher enters the classroom. In principle, all students should stand until the teacher tells them to be seated. The importance of this practice was made clear in the reaction of Nina, a ninth-grade teacher who had the reputation of being short-tempered, and who upon entering her class, realized that the usual troublemaker had not bothered to stand up. Her response was to yell at the student and to make him sit down and stand up several times, shouting *"Vstan'!" "Siad'!" "Vstan'!" "Siad'!"* (Stand up! Sit down!).

Teachers offered fierce resistance against suggestions by some Ukrainian intellectuals that the humanities classes do away with recitation. For Svetlana, for example, students' recitation of various poems not only reassured her that they had "learned something," but also achieved the effects of "unity," producing for her a sense of orderliness, common purpose, and perhaps (at least the illusion of) common belief. The performances may be thought of in terms of Austin's "performative utterances" (1999), that is, as utterances that *do* something not as a result of the speaker's intentions, but because of the conventions surrounding them. Svetlana believed that word by word repetition limited the range of possible opinions and discouraged "cynicism" (the latter is addressed below). She had asked her eleventh-grade literature class to read a text on self-improvement at home entitled "What makes a better person?" and the following morning, invited a student to stand up and tell the class what the text was about. He started: "Well, in my opinion, the text—" "I didn't ask for your *opinion*," Svetlana interrupted, "I asked for a paraphrase [*perekaz*]!" There existed two types of *perekaz* (or paraphrase): very close to the text, and less close to the text. These forms had existed under the Soviet system where repetition of certain formulas ensured minimal deviation from state ideology. In the Soviet "authoritative discourse" described by Yurchak (2006), the emphasis was on participation in the reproduction of the *form* (rather than constative meanings) of ritualized and speech acts. Yurchak argues that while contributing to an image of the system's "monolithic immutability," this form of reproduction did not result in the total constraining of meanings in Soviet public life. Rather, "the performative reproduction of the form of rituals and speech acts actually enabled the emergence of diverse, multiple, and unpredictable meanings in everyday life, including those that did not correspond to the constative meanings of authoritative discourse" (2006: 25).

Lazar (2010) notes of the Bolivian educational context that even those seemingly "traditional" or "authoritarian" educational methods that appeared to foster conformity in fact do not necessarily inhibit the development of students' political agency. In Ukraine, the combination of a new curriculum centered on the production of the "unique individual," and of repetition as a form that aims at creating (at least outwardly) a degree of uniformity, resulted in unexpected configurations. I sat in a tenth-grade Ukrainian literature class in the public school while each student in turn repeated the following poem:

> You know that you are—a person [*liudyna*].
> Do you know that or not?
> . . .
> Your suffering is unique.
> Your eyes are unique.
> —V. Symonenko

While the above poem could be read in the most dispassionate manner, it could also be performed with perfected enthusiasm. Students were masters in the art of performing the required patriotism. The performance of compliance is evident in a certain tone of voice, and takes the form of recitation, whereby the answer to a teacher's question (e.g., Why is it important to speak your national language?) is almost sung, without breathing pauses. Teachers, and especially the older generation trained in the Soviet educational system, generally expressed satisfaction with these optimistic and sentimental performances, and sometimes even praised them as patriotic. This does not mean that teachers were necessarily "falling for" students' emotional renderings. After all, what was required of students was not that the performance be sincere (presumably, for some it was), but rather that it be true to form. What we might call the recitation mode (and the attendant performance of affect) is such, however, that it may border on parody. On one occasion, the Ukrainian history teacher asked one of her students, "And *why* was Ukraine's territory divided among various empires?" The student answered: "Because our land is so beautiful and so rich and everybody always wanted to steal from us." The answer and the tone seemed so overdone that the teacher responded mockingly, "Oh, Natalka, what a patriot you are!" Both the student's performance and the teacher's comment suggest a keen awareness of the "pro forma" nature of this kind of patriotism. We should not conclude from this that students are unpatriotic, but rather that they may be less than enthused by the particular *packaging* of national rhetoric, especially in its pedagogical form.

On another occasion, in a ninth-grade civics class dealing with the law on Ukrainian citizenship, the teacher tested a student's knowledge thus:

"Misha, do you have the right to be a Ukrainian citizen?"

"Yes."

"Why?"

"I have Cossack blood! [*U mene kozats'ka krov!*]"

"What kind of Cossack blood, if for example you're Jewish? Tell me the *law* about citizenship. The law says *one of your parents must be a Ukrainian citizen!*"

Misha, not knowing the answer to the teacher's question, had relied on the traditional (sentimental) metaphors of the nation that circulated in the school context to make a point about the structural aspects of citizenship. The teacher clearly did not fall for this kind of national rhetoric, especially when substituted for factual knowledge.

In his 2005 book *Cultural Intimacy: Social Poetics in the Nation-State (Second Edition)*, Michael Herzfeld investigates the kinds of "creative dissent" that lie behind the "façade of national unanimity" (1). He asks, "what advantages social actors find in using, reformulating, and recasting official idioms in the pursuit of often highly unofficial personal goals, and how those actions—so often in direct contravention of state authority—actually constitute the state as well as huge range of national and other identities" (2005: 2). Ukrainian students' performances illustrate the extent to which they are able to manipulate the form and content of official idioms in order to "get through" the required schooling. In the process, they reproduce and thus constitute "the nation" as a form. Far from being simple objects of national pedagogy (one premised on a *linear*, accumulative temporality), students are the subjects of a performance in which the nation is constantly *repeated* anew in varied, sporadic, and contingent ways (Bhabha 1990). In fact, students' reproduction of the nation may be "neither about change nor about continuity, but about introducing minute internal displacements and mutations into the discursive regime in which they are articulated" (Yurchak 2006: 28). Therefore, as Benei (2008) suggests, the goal in investigating patriotic education (and its bodily disciplines in particular) is not so much to try to answer the question, "Does it work?" (25), but rather to trace "the agency *within* the internalization of socialization" (3).

Students did not perform the aspects of patriotism learned in school only to their teachers. During a group discussion, a student explained patriotism to me and to her fellow students thus: "If you have a brother or a sister, you love him or her whether or not they are pretty, right? It's the same with the country: people should love their country whether it is rich or poor—that should not matter. You should love it like you love your family." The student was improvising on the theme of patriotism as "unconditional love." Many students (in both schools) claimed to be proud of their country, as well as of their language and traditions, even though they admitted to speaking Russian at home and on the street, and to only rarely following Ukrainian traditions. Nevertheless, they sometimes openly lashed out at the kind of national culture present in textbooks. Based on my observations, discussions were rather rare in the school setting, so that students usually challenged the curriculum through jokes or isolated comments that could be either whispered or voiced more aggressively. On one occasion, a Ukrainian language teacher was reading a dictation to her students, entitled "Journey into Childhood [*Podorozh u dytynstvo*]." The narrative told of an elderly man returning to his native Ukrainian village: "It was a world made of black earth, blue sky, grass, the blooms of spring trees, smelling of clean air, the songs of birds—a world that he could have honestly, as a son, called his own, a world for which he and his people felt a deep feeling of gratitude" (based on Hutsalo, in Tykhosha, Ursulenko, and Movchun 2004: 149). The descriptions of flowers and butterflies were too much to bear for the class clown. He finally burst out: "This text sounds like a Poplavski song!" (Poplavski is a Ukrainian singer whose lyrics most students considered cheap and silly.) I once asked a group of students in that same class to define Ukrainian culture. They all started laughing. They then began reciting a list: "Bread and salt [*khlib ta sil'*]," "lard [*salo*]," "embroidered shirts [*vyshyvanky*]," and "Taras Shevchenko [the national poet]." Once again, this should not be taken as evidence that students are unpatriotic. Reflecting on young people's practices in Bolivian schools, Lazar speaks of the complicated relationship with one's own culture, noting that "although at some points during their school career the students distance themselves from indigenous cultural codes, . . . at the same time they use them, honor them, and make fun of them" (2010: 194; see also Luykx 1999). It is likely that Ukrainian students at times found the *pedagogical construction* of the patriot somewhat limiting. Not only did the school pedagogies I observed pose students as "repeaters" versus constructors of the nation, but the narrow definition of the patriot did not reflect the range of identities and loyalties (local, supranational, global) that students experienced in everyday life.

In her study of Evenki youth in Siberia, Bloch points out that young people were often skeptical of a process of cultural revitalization (grounded in "traditional" representations of culture) that "discounted their daily experience of being Evenki and did not reflect the hybrid, ever-changing processes that were influencing their identities and interactions with the community" (2004: 179). Young people in Kyiv constantly dislodged, displaced, and hybridized the identities produced for them in the school context. For example, they de-centered Ukrainian culture through the use of Russian elements. It was common to hear students correcting each other's Ukrainian grammar *in Russian* during the Ukrainian language class. They might also answer the teacher's questions in Russian. When a Ukrainian language teacher asked students to bring a Ukrainian newspaper to class for an exercise, some students would bring Russian-language newspapers, leaving the teacher frustrated. For example, in the history class, a teacher asked: "And what large entity was Ukraine a part of in the twentieth century?" And students answered "*Sovetskii Soiuz!* [the Soviet Union, in Russian]," and the teacher corrected them, annoyed: "*Radians'kyi Soiuz!* [the Soviet Union, in Ukrainian]." Teachers lectured students on the Little Russian complex and attempted to drive home the message that Ukraine cannot exist without the Ukrainian language. In some cases, conflicts arose over comments perceived as Russocentric. In one instance, a student was expelled from the class (the teacher upset to the point of shaking) for mumbling during the history lesson that Mazepa was a traitor. Mazepa is a *het'man* (Cossack leader) who joined with Sweden to wage war on the Muscovites in 1709. Soviet historiography had portrayed Mazepa as a traitor, but in the new Ukrainian pedagogy, he has been reconfigured into a Ukrainian patriot/hero. A history teacher who happened to find the scribbled inscription *Mazepa lokh* (Mazepa is an idiot, or a bumpkin) on his classroom wall said to his class, "No, Mazepa is a *hero.*" The teacher might not have been particularly well disposed toward

Mazepa, but he knew that his students' success depended on the repetition of the content of school textbooks.

It is difficult to determine whether the de-centering of Ukrainian culture through references to Russian culture was a conscious strategy on the part of the students or whether it was simply the result of living in a context in which Russian cultural referents were readily available. The use of the Russian language or other cultural forms did not imply political loyalty to Russia as a state. For example, when political issues such as dual citizenship, two official languages, and an economic union with Russia surfaced during the 2004 presidential campaign, it became obvious that most students felt that these propositions would not be in Ukraine's best interest. Statements such as the following were commonplace: "We don't need Russia," "We want to have our *own* language [Ukrainian], and only our own, as a state language," "We don't want to be citizens of a country [Russia] at war [with Chechnya]." A small minority of students thought that reunification with Russia could be beneficial to Ukraine, at least economically. The students' appropriation of Russian elements in the school context seemed to constitute an alternate (or perhaps complementary) form of belonging. Crucially, it provided the students with an opportunity to locate themselves within what they considered to be the less "local" Russian culture. In fact, students' exposure to the Russian media, and the fact that they tended to consume Western products brought through Russia and advertised in the Russian language, may have contributed to making Russia seem more "global" and closer to the world.

From Cynicism to the "Child Citizen"

While the pedagogical incarnation of the patriot encompassed some of the meanings circulating in the wider society (for example, the connection of patriotism with obedience and normativity), other factors also came to bear on the construction and negotiation of citizenship in schools. In particular, it seems that the economic transformations following the collapse of the Soviet Union had important effects on power relations in school, and especially on the student-teacher relation. The new dynamics of power in schools shaped ideas and practices around what it means to be both a patriot and a "child."

Patico (2008) speaks of the "downward mobility" experienced by Russian schoolteachers following the collapse of the Soviet Union. A similar phenomenon can be observed in Ukraine, where economic transformations undermined teachers' livelihood and social status. In the first five years after Ukrainian independence, the country dealt with high rates of inflation, reaching a peak of 10,000 percent in 1993 (Hare, Ishaq, and Estrin 1998: 179). This was accompanied by shortages of basic foods such as milk and butter. Industrial production fell consistently. Many Ukrainian state-owned enterprises were highly dependent on Soviet (especially Russian) markets, and relied on raw material deliveries from other parts of the Soviet Union, but the energy supply from the Russian Federation and Turkmenistan was now only available at market prices (181). Official employment declined, and the shadow economy grew. The economic crisis meant a sharp decline in state subsidies for schools, and there were delays in the payment of teacher salaries, especially in the mid-nineties. Parents had to contribute both money and labor in order to keep the schools operational, and students were often charged with cleaning classrooms (this is still the case, and I participated in these efforts during fieldwork). Inhabitants of Kyiv juggled state and informal jobs, and businesses such as racketeering (protecting other people's newly privatized property) were booming. Former members of the *nomenklatura* were also becoming rich thanks to privatization deals, currency speculation, and other semi-legal or illegal activities. While those citizens operating at the margins of the law were becoming richer, the teachers (or at least those who could not or would not take additional employment) were getting poorer, and as a result, their status had declined dramatically, especially in larger cities. This is compounded by the fact that as Svetlana claimed, it is now possible to "buy" an education rather than get one. In other words, the educator's role in society had been recast. Many of the New Rich, or so-called "New Ukrainians"/"New Russians" of Kyiv, view money, connections, and the willingness to take risks as more important to a successful life than a formal education. At home, parents often reminded their children that schooling was something they had to "get through," one way or another. Educators had played a leading role in the socialization of Soviet citizens, but teachers now complained that the pedagogical endeavor has lost much of its prestige. In Kyiv City, a teacher's salary (which could amount to as little as 300 *hryvnias*, or 60 dollars, a month) is often several times less than the salary of the students' parents, who are businesspeople, government officials, or lawyers. It is sometimes less than students' monthly allowance or pocket money. Teachers (especially in private schools, but also to some degree in public schools in the city) are constantly reminded of this as they look at children's designer clothes and expensive gadgets, and as they listen to their accounts of travel abroad. Patico (2005) describes a similar situation in Russian schools, where teachers are made increasingly conscious of their relative poverty in relation to students and must sometimes suffer the humiliation of students' insensitive comments on their appearance. Teachers in Ukraine claim that changes in economic circumstances are visible in students' behavior and attitudes toward authority, and especially their new arrogance and disrespect for teachers. "Nothing matters to them: their only goal in life is to get money. And money corrupts all [*Hroshi vsikh psuiut'*]," said a woman who had taught mathematics for forty-three years. "Children don't need anything from us anymore, they believe that they can succeed without studying," complained Svetlana. "Children look at us and tell us we're stupid to work for so little money" said Pavel, a teacher of civics in his late forties.

Why did teachers then go into teaching or continue teaching after retirement age, which was common? In interviews, several teachers said that their intention was to make students into decent, honest, and educated "persons," a goal reflected in the new pedagogy.[7] For teachers whose careers had been mostly spent under Soviet rule, this included elements of *kul'turnost* (Rus. for culturedness). The adjective *kul'turnyi* meant "civilized" in a Soviet way and could refer to someone who is educated, well mannered, and well behaved. Texts in schoolbooks often portrayed teachers as agents of transformation and improvement, stating, for example, "Danylo always remained grateful to his first grade teacher, who had taught him how to be a person [*liudyna*]."[8] Teachers liked to assign texts to students that underlined the skill, sacrifice, and selflessness required to be a teacher. The study guide for state exams (eleventh grade) included two texts, "A Teacher's Life," and "The Teacher [*Vchytel'ka*]" (the latter text picked as the statewide exam text for the spring of 2005). However, informal conversations with teachers revealed more practical concerns, especially among the older teachers. For example, some teachers would be unable to survive on their meager pension were they to retire, and elderly women who had lost their husbands could not stand the thought of staying home by themselves. The school could also be a source of welfare, as when colleagues from the same department (e.g., languages and literature), who were usually also close friends, pooled money to pay for a husband's operation or an elderly parent's funeral.

Teachers used various strategies in an attempt to remedy their perceived loss of status in the post-Soviet era. These strategies included putting subtle

pressure on parents to supplement the teacher's salary with gifts or sometimes money. Svetlana had a locked shelf in her bedroom in which she kept
her treasures, mostly gifts (birthday and Women's Day gifts) from wealthy
parents, including expensive perfumes and fine liquor. She was considered
an exceptionally devoted teacher, and so parents spared no expense. She kept
the gifts in order to re-gift or to use them as "currency" in case she needed a
favor from an acquaintance or bureaucrat. Parents sometimes came to the
apartment late in the night after work to deliver more substantial gifts such
as electronics. The less wealthy parents gave simpler gifts such as bath or
kitchen items. Many teachers also tutored (especially the wealthier) students, thereby adding to their income. Teachers would suggest to the parents that the student may not pass if left untutored, and parents, eager to get
their children through school and often too busy to help with homework,
would agree to tutoring sessions. Yet this strategy was not necessarily empowering, for as Patico has noted in the Russian context, children may come
to see their tutors as "domestic labor" (2005: 486).

My observations suggest that one of the ways in which teachers responded
to students' attempts at undermining their authority in the classroom was
by being stricter. "Nowadays, children don't want to study, they don't want
anything," said a woman who had taught in the same school for fifty-two
years. "How do you deal with students who don't want to work?" I asked.
"We force them [*Zmushuiemo*]," she replied. Yet as many teachers liked to
remind me, they no longer had "back up" from Soviet institutions such as
the Pioneers and the Komsomol (the Communist Youth League) or juvenile
police that could intervene if a student was out of control. Youth organizations had played a key role in the socialization of young Soviet citizens and
were an integral part of the educational system (Moos 1967: 80). Typically, a
Soviet student first joined the Octobrists, and then (around ten years old),
the Pioneers. The rules for Pioneers emphasize a child's patriotic duty and
its connection to discipline, and "embody the moral goals of Soviet education; the Pioneer promises to love his country, to study industriously, to
speak the truth, to be friendly to children all over the world, to be brave and
honorable, to keep physically fit, to honor the memory of those who died for
their country, to be careful of public property, to be always polite and disciplined, to love nature and conserve it. Young pioneers who persistently
break these rules may be brought before the group for criticism" (Moos
1967: 81). The Komsomol, meant for young people ages fifteen to twenty-seven,
was also an "instrument for preparing young people to work collectively, to

become socially responsible citizens" (Moos 1967: 80). Membership was more selective, and because it carried more responsibility, members' conduct was under intense scrutiny (82). The Komsomol's cultural, scientific, and sports activities (83) occupied most of young people's "free time" outside the school, thus minimizing opportunities to get in trouble. With the disappearance of the Komsomol, teachers must now bear the full burden of "maintaining order" [*zberihaty poriadok*]. On one occasion, a tenth-grade student expressing a view different from that of the teacher in a foreign literature class was reprimanded thus: "The teacher is always right, and in case you forget this, remember the first rule, The teacher is always right." This statement is a rephrasing of a Soviet expression used in the military: "Rule #1, the officer is always right; and in case you disagree, refer to rule #1." Presumably, teachers could have used such a statement during the Soviet period. Historian of Stalinist Russia Sheila Fitzpatrick describes patterns of authority in Soviet society by referring to the Communist leaders of the 1930s: "They cultivated a peremptory style of command, barking orders, demanding instant obedience and no backchat, and insisting on the Soviet version of the bottom line, which was to meet plan targets at all costs. Consultation or lengthy deliberation was a sign of weakness" (1999: 31). While we might be tempted to interpret teachers' authoritarian style as a simple "legacy" of the Soviet past, I would suggest that it was the erosion of their authority (i.e., its lack of ideological grounding in the post-Soviet space) that caused teachers to resort to self-referential utterances reminiscent of the statement, "The law is the law!"[9]

Teachers often framed students' deviations in terms of a new and pervasive "cynicism." On one occasion, Mykola, a teacher of civics in his mid-sixties in the private school, was explaining to his students what it means to be "equal under the law," stating that a member of Parliament cannot prevent his murderous son from going to jail. And students screamed: "But that's what they do!" And about the presumption of innocence, students said, "Why do we need that? You just have to pay the Court and you'll be found innocent. Everything can be solved with your wallet." To which the teacher responded angrily: "You're so cynical!" Ries (2002) claims that *tsinism* (cynicism) in Russia describes "a general context of moral corruption and dishonesty, where it seems that everyone is engaged, to some degree, in cheating, lying, swindling, and stealing—whatever it takes to capture one's share of the available economic resources" (276). In the Kyiv school context, *tsynizm* is the word many teachers of the Soviet generation use to describe students' unwillingness to focus on "what is beautiful and good about our country." For example, teachers often repeated that "good patriots" must love their country unconditionally. A recurrent theme in pedagogy is the idea that "We must love our country no matter what." Teachers praised great Ukrainians who could love their country with all its faults, embracing or finding beauty even in its negative elements. As a history teacher put it: "We have what we have, and let's honor what we have [*Maiemo shcho maiemo, i shanuiemo shcho maiemo*]." Svetlana and her colleagues often reminisced about life in the Soviet Union, agreeing that despite some difficulties, people have been kinder [*dobrishi*] and naturally enthusiastic. They took pride in their work and in the country, and there was none of the *tsynizm* that one now found at all levels: in students, in people, and in the government.

While the students with whom I worked were all born after the collapse of the Soviet Union, they often made deprecatory comments about Ukraine and its status in the world. This was particularly salient in the classes of history, geography, and military preparedness. "How many tanks does Ukraine now have?" the teacher of military preparedness would ask. "Two!" would be the students' "cynical" answer. Or the teacher of geography would ask, "And in the volume of its exports, Ukraine is comparable to what other country?" "Africa!" they would shout, not knowing the answer and assuming that Ukraine could only perform at the level of what they considered the "poorest" countries.[10]

While we might expect post-Soviet students to use Western European or North American countries as a "standard" against which to compare Ukraine's performance, based on my observations, it was mostly popular accounts of the powerful Soviet Union that led students to perceive Ukraine as deficient. Textbooks were usually critical of the Soviet system, and so were many teachers (arguing, for example, that the Soviet system had manipulated citizens politically through shortages). However, some teachers liked to remind their students that the Soviet Union had possessed the most advanced nuclear arsenal, that the Soviets, not the Americans, had been first in space, and that the Soviet Union had been respected in the world. Interestingly, these statements about the Soviet Union also seemed addressed in part to me, the person from "America." Students tended to feel ambivalent about the Soviet Union. In an eleventh-grade class of world history covering the twentieth century, the teacher, a man in his seventies, was talking about the formation of the United Nations, and the Soviet role in it, when a student interrupted: "You mean when Khrushchev banged the table with his shoe? That's embarrassing!" The teacher, on the defensive, immediately came to Khrushchev's defense: "What do you know about it? Maybe he was killing a roach!" upon which the class clown broke into song, delivering to the class the first verses of the Soviet anthem. In a discussion about patriotism with this same class, however, the Soviet Union arose as a kind of standard. Volodya, a tenth grader, claimed that "The Soviet Union was patriotic because everyone saw how it won the Second World War, and [citizens] felt that their country is really powerful, and that their standard of living after ten years of war was not that high, but they made it higher. In our country, we don't feel that we are powerful, that our standard of life is very high compared to other countries. And because of this, we cannot be patriotic." This statement suggests that the Soviet Union was still "present" for young people, and that just like Western Europe, it could be looked upon as a standard. Paradoxically, students' "cynicism" was fed in part by some of their teachers' nostalgic evocations of the Soviet past.

Cynicism was also the juncture at which the teachers' construction of the patriot, and students' experience of life beyond the school, met, and it opened up a (discursive and performative) space of negotiation between the school and the outside world. In fact, much of what teachers called cynicism had to do with students' smuggling of the "real world" into the classroom. They did so in a form that could be termed "real-life answers." For example, the teacher of geography in the public school once asked her students, pointing to the map of Ukraine, "Where is the Polish minority concentrated in Ukraine?" To which a student replied: "At the market! [*Na bazar!*]" This was a comment on the ubiquitous presence, especially following the collapse of the Socialist Bloc, of Polish citizens selling Polish goods in Ukrainian markets. The teacher, however, was not amused. "You think it's funny," she snapped, "You think it's *civilized* to answer like that?" Svetlana was having an eleventh-grade class read a text entitled "Businessmen need scrupulousness, knowledge, and decency [*Biznesmenovi potribni sovist', znannia, i poriadnist'*]." The text told of the life of a Canadian Ukrainian millionaire and philanthropist. He was referred to in the text as a *milioner-trudiaha*, or "hardworking millionaire." The students laughed at the mere thought of that, claiming, "We don't have those!" This was a reflection of their daily encounters with the new rich driving their Hummers on the sidewalk and otherwise flaunting their wealth.

Ries claims about Russia that through cynical talk, citizens "actively deconstruct whatever legitimizing discourses or practices are presented on behalf of the reformulated political-economic order, and thus regularly inoculate themselves against any naïve belief in state or market ideology" (2002: 277). In Kyiv schools, students deployed their cynicism both against the state's excesses (as in the unequal application of the law), and against the school's "naïve" moral claims (e.g., about "honest and hardworking" millionaires). This does not mean that they rejected both stances, but rather that they constantly weighed one against the other. In fact, their critique of state excesses signaled their awareness of, and perhaps desire for, a particular moral standard (one that schools attempted to put into place). Conversely, students' critique of the school's moral blueprint worked to validate a more "predatory" order in the realm of business and social relations in general. It pointed to students' understanding that (economic) success in life often depended on the partial or total suspension of moral principles.

What was perhaps most disturbing to teachers about cynicism is that it contributed to what Ries (2002) alludes to as the (post-collapse) blurring of the realms of childhood and adulthood. Teachers saw cynicism as undermining not only children's performance of the "good patriot," but also their performance of the "normal" child. What does this reveal about teachers' image of what a child *ought* to be like? Those teachers in the private school who taught the high-school-age students often agreed among themselves that teaching the younger children would be much easier. Young children were portrayed as more docile and obedient (*slukhniani*), they took in knowledge more easily, and were not cynical about the material. What is more, they were innocent and ignorant of the unpleasant aspects of life. Because cynicism required engagement with an alternate reality (life outside the school), it constantly articulated the gap between the school and the world. This meant that teachers were not able to pose the school as a refuge from the real world, either for themselves or for their students. The articulation of this gap also meant that their attempts at "person-making" risked failing.

The extent to which children should be exposed to the world's harsh realities had also been an issue for Soviet educators. In her book *Inside Soviet Schools* (1974), Susan Jacoby relates a conversation with a Russian teacher in which she told the teacher about a new American reader that included stories about a twelve-year-old's experience of divorce. The teacher, a woman, responded, "But you take away their childhood when you give them such things to read . . . . I don't believe this kind of realism is even interesting for children" (quoted in Jacoby 1974: 179). She went on to say that stories assigned to Russian children (fairytales and stories that dealt with the political life of the Soviet Union) shared a key element: "they take [children] into a world in which good and evil are easily recognizable" (179). This would ensure that children were not needlessly confused. These statements presuppose something about children's innocence and thus tap into the romantic discourse of childhood (also popular in the West) developed by Jean-Jacques Rousseau. Yet while Soviet children were viewed as a category to be protected and indulged, they were also charged with the responsibility to help protect and build socialism. Pavlik Morozov, the young Pioneer referred to above, who, at the time of collectivization, told the authorities that his father was hoarding grain, became one of the most popular Soviet child-heroes. He came to symbolize "youthful bravery, self-sacrifice, and willingness to challenge unjust authority . . . , whether parental or that of other adults" (Fitzpatrick 1999: 73). Morozov's influence as a child-hero waned after World War II (he came to be despised by Russian intellectuals in the last years of Soviet Union [Fitzpatrick 1999]), but his story points to the kind of agency granted to Soviet children. While the Soviet emphasis on both children's protection *and* their responsibilities vis-à-vis the system appears paradoxical, it may reflect a situation whereby children were expected to be loyal to and serve the institutions (school, Pioneers) that sought to protect them from nefarious influences (including, potentially, their own parents). In the Soviet Union (as elsewhere), children's agency indeed had to be in the service of the larger society to be recognized. Livschiz (2006) recounts the response of the Soviet authorities to the perceived excessive agency of children in the aftermath of World War II. She examines how decreased adult supervision and the loosening of social control brought by the chaos of war forced children on a path of "rapid maturity" (194), thus blurring the boundary between childhood and adulthood. The authorities issued decrees against juvenile crime and hooliganism to try to contain the postwar children who had become "more assertive, more self-sufficient and less prone to defer to adults" (194). In fact, the effort at restoring public order after the war also came to mean "the re-establishment of control over children . . . [and] returning children to their appropriate place—namely schools" (195).

While the Soviet experience may help us contextualize attitudes toward young people in Ukrainian schools today, it is important to note that the discourse of childhood innocence is newly replicated in pedagogies that aimed at constructing "nationally conscious citizens." In fact, childhood is central to post-Soviet pedagogies because it is a powerful symbol in the process of Ukrainians' "return to themselves." Texts such as "Journey into

Childhood," cited above, describes how an old man who has seen the world returns to his parents' village and the setting of his earliest memories. Like the national "essence" (whose locus is the Ukrainian village in its pre-Soviet incarnation), childhood is presented as pure and uncorrupted, a space of "rose-colored dreams." Cheney (2007), drawing on Eriksen (1997), notes that "childhood memories become symbolically linked to nationalism, in which individual life narratives become metaphors for the national narrative" (12). In Ukraine, the return to childhood is also framed as an imagined return to *pre*-Soviet "normality." As Rausing points out about the post-Soviet Estonian context, "The 'normal' . . . tended to mean not what Estonia . . . actually was, but what it should have been had the Soviet invasion not taken place" (2002: 131). Similarly, in Ukrainian textbooks authored by nationally conscious elites and former dissidents, the return to childhood appears to index a desired (though ultimately impossible) return to pre-Soviet "innocence." From this perspective, by recasting childhood (and thus the return to it) cynicism threatens the national project itself. If this is true, then the construction of the patriot must involve at least a partial "re-infantilization" of children.

Although the students I worked with were teenagers, in my experience teachers and administrators often treated them like young children who were expected to listen and obey. Students from grades one–eleven (ages seven–seventeen) were referred to as *"Dity* [children]." Frequent statements by teachers were variations on the theme: "You're too little to have an opinion [*vy zamali maty svoiu dumku*]." Even those teachers who were more liberal and keen on communicating their ideas to students could contribute to their infantilization, as with the Ukrainian language teacher who simply ended a lecture by saying to her eleventh graders: "Well, anyway, you'll understand the Little Russian complex when you're older." These practices suggested that students lacked the experience, knowledge, and discernment to understand the kind of context (cultural, economic, political) in which they lived, and their own place in it. Students internalized this to a certain extent, so that they might say of themselves, "We are too little to do [such and such]," or an eleventh grader about to graduate and enter university might write in a composition: "When I grow up, I want to be [such and such]."

These statements coexisted with students' "cynical" stances, suggesting that young people negotiated their membership in the "child" category differently according to context. In her study of children's citizenship in Uganda, Cheney notes that "for children, childhood is more than a concept;

Figure 4. "Ukraine, we are your future!" Photo by the author, 2005.

it is the social mode through which they experience the world, and thus more a practice than a state of being" (2007: 30). Ukrainian students knew full well that there were advantages to performing childhood (one of which was that you could "get away with a lot of things"). Yet they also at times wished to move away from the confining category of "childhood." Franklin notes that the "question 'what is a child?' is answered by those in authority—those who hold power in society" (1986: 8), and students sought to contest the boundaries that teachers set around childhood. For example, in a Ukrainian literature class, the teacher, a woman in her seventies, was speaking about the female protagonist of a story who falls head over heels in love, remarking: "Imagine that, a girl [*divchyna*] of seventeen!" To which one of the female students (a seventeen-year-old) sitting in the front row replied, looking at her classmate: "Seventeen? That's not a 'girl' anymore! [*Tse vzhe ne divchyna!*]."

The teachers' re-infantilization could be viewed as an attempt to effect in their students a return to personal (and, metaphorically, national) innocence. Yet it seems that in the context of new struggles within the classroom, teachers also deployed it as a means to counter what they saw as the nefarious influences of capitalism (i.e., the arrogance of newly wealthy students) and democracy (i.e., the cynicism of students who now felt "free" to express their views) that threatened their authority as educators. Re-infantilization as a tactic also worked to emphasize the need for a "parent figure," symbolized here by the teacher. The practice of framing students as "too young to understand things" served not only to discourage dissenting opinions, but also to restore the (Soviet-era) belief that the teacher is necessary *because he or she "knows best."* Thus paternalism, and attempts at constructing a relationship of need or dependency, seemed part of the equation in a context where teachers' knowledge had become devalued. Paternalism is central to the construction of authority in a variety of contexts.[11] It often marks the relationship between actors constituted as "the state" and actors constituted as "citizens." It is important to explore how it manifested itself in the construction and performance of Soviet citizenship. For example, in the "Soviet family," Russians were often portrayed as the "elder brothers" of the other nations. In her book *What Was Socialism, and What Comes Next?* (1996), Katherine Verdery explains the relation of citizenship in socialist countries as one of "socialist paternalism," or a "quasi-familial dependency" that "posited a moral tie linking subjects with the state through their rights to a share in the redistributed social product. Subjects were presumed to be neither politically active, as with citizenship, nor ethnically similar to each other: they were presumed to be grateful recipients—like small children in a family—of benefits their rulers decided upon for them. The subject disposition this produced was dependency, rather than the agency cultivated by citizenship or the solidarity of ethnonationalism" (63). Similarly, Kornai notes that in Soviet-style systems, the state and its bureaucracy stands "*in loco parentis*"

(1980: 315). Clearly, "rights to a share in the redistributed social product" produced various forms of agency marked by certain types of claims making (Verdery 1996), including public displays of gratitude to the leadership (see, e.g., Brooks 2005). Yet dependency was also part of the equation, and seems to arise most powerfully as a feature precisely at the moment of the imminent collapse of the Soviet state. A Ukrainian friend of mine, a student in one of Kyiv's universities, spoke of the emergence, during the Gorbachev era and continuing after the collapse, of a large number of feature films that had orphans' and street children's struggle for survival as their central theme (e.g., *The Thugs* [1983]; *Plumbum, or the Dangerous Game* [1986]; *Little Vera* [1988]; *Freedom Is Paradise* [1989]; *Avaria, the Cop's Daughter* [1989]; *The Thief* [1997]). My friend argued that these films had constituted an un-conscious attempt at dealing with the impending disintegration of the state. The collapse of the state would "orphan" citizens, who would be forced to survive "on their own." Conversely, some of the post-Soviet efforts at so-called "neo-sovietization" have been articulated in paternalistic forms, for exam-ple in Belarus, where President Lukashenka presented himself as a kind of *Tsar Batiushka* (or "Father Tsar") figure. Examples of the infantilization of the nation in relation to the (male) "adult" state were presented earlier in the chapter. In that case too, the figure of the child-nation served to justify the existence of a parent-state.

Yet because paternalism could not be dissociated from force (or in the case of schools, threats), students were ambivalent toward authority. They sometimes expected teachers to be more forceful, as the male student who raised his hand during a class devoted to quiet reading. "Mariia Alexan-drivna," he told the young teacher, "everybody's talking and we're supposed to be doing quiet studying, why don't you say anything?" "What, I should oppress everyone?" answered the teacher. "That's not necessary," she replied, and went back to her grading. Students often complained about the princi-pal but still admitted to needing discipline. Similarly, teachers constantly spoke of the unfairness of the principal, especially in the private school. But even those teachers who hated the principal with a passion would admit that "He maintains order [*Vin trymaie poriadok*]. If he were not there, the school would never hold together, there would be chaos."

Efforts at constructing the Ukrainian patriot in school appear tied in large part to an understanding of "order" as obedience to (paternalistic) authority. Cynicism undermines this authority in that it allows students to reconfigure and recombine the conflicting discourses to which they are exposed in novel ways. In her study of Sikh youth in Great Britain, Hall (2002) notes that teenagers in modern capitalist formations are not only subject to various projects of social reproduction in school, at home, and in the community, but are also "prime targets of the market forces of consumer capitalism and the commodification of mass culture. In this way, the central ideological forces within a social order can be seen to converge in the lives of adolescents" (2002: 35). By pulling together these different ideological strands, young people can find ways to work out some of their tensions and contradictions. Cynicism as a practice also reconfigures the child as *knowing*, thus eroding the category of childhood itself. In fact, the "defeat of innocence . . . signals the loss of childhood through the recovery of agency" (Cheney 2007: 13). By threatening "childhood as a time of innocence" (Woodhead and Montgomery 2002: 65), cynicism allows students to engage deeply with a world in which the line between good and evil is infinitely blurry. The next section traces the way young people's conception of democracy as freedom can challenge the equation of order and patriotism while paving the way for particular forms of claims making.

"Democracy Is Not for Us"

Levinson (2005) notes that "school-based programs in democratic civic and citizenship education have become one of the primary sites for the creation of new political dispositions and identities and for the consolidation of meanings about 'democracy'" (335). Based on my observations , the concept of "democracy" that students encounter in the classroom most often takes the form of a definition to be memorized and repeated. Definitions of democracy in Ukrainian civics textbooks typically emphasize the idea of popular sovereignty or "rule by the people," and "rights and freedoms" can also be mentioned. Yet despite students' mechanistic reproduction of this type of normative (if highly abstract) definition, democracy is clearly open to (individual and institutional) reinterpretation and contestation. Certain types of behaviors and interactions provided opportunities for teachers and students to reflect on democratic practice and its potential drawbacks.

A few weeks before the presidential elections of October 2004, I was in the public school attending Pavel's civics class. He had reluctantly agreed to let me in, reminding me that this was his worst group. As I sat in the last row (the most interesting things always happened there), I could see a student speaking loudly on his cell phone, while his friends sat on desks around him. In front of me, a male student had arranged four chairs so as to make a bed on which to lie down. Further toward the front, a girl had partly lifted the back of her sweater so that her female colleague could give her a massage. The noise level was very high, and students kept circulating in the class, some of them rushing outside when their cell phones rang. The teacher was barely able to make himself heard over the noise. Exasperated, he finally made the following observation to his students: *U vas vzhe povna democratia!* ["You already enjoy complete democracy!"] I asked him, "Why do you call this democracy?" to which he answered: "Well, maybe I should call it anarchy. But there's at least *some* order in anarchy, as [Nestor] Makhno [the famous Ukrainian anarchist] said." Pavel had spent most of his life in the military and had recently turned to teaching to supplement his meager pension. His years in the army had undoubtedly left him with a particular conception of order and discipline. However, his spontaneous association of chaos with democracy reflected a wider concern among teachers. In fact, many teachers found it difficult to reconcile democracy with authority. "Students are a majority in the class, so they think they can do whatever they want," Pavel told me. Students constituted a majority in the school itself, and it was likely that they had taken democracy (understood as the "rule of the majority") to the letter, and applied it to their own situation, thus demonstrating that they grasped one of its key principles. But did the fact that students outnumbered their teachers mean that they should rule, or be able to overrule the school authorities' decisions, worried the teachers. What compounded this worry was teachers' sense that they lacked the means to enforce school rules. Not only had they lost much of the prestige accorded to teachers in the Soviet Union, but the trend toward openness and democratization meant that they could no longer resort to forceful tactics (physical force or psychological pressure) to discipline students. "The problem is that today's students are not afraid of anyone or anything," claimed Pavel. According to him, in the absence of fear (generated from above), there was no incentive for compliance.

Not all teachers agreed that order could only be generated by fear, however. Lida, a teacher of Ukrainian history in her seventies who had traveled extensively after the collapse, offered her students less traditional views of the state. "The state is a chimera," she would say. "People do not need someone to rule them from above. They are capable of governing themselves," or

"Anarchy is not chaos, it has order" (the latter statement is an indirect reference, once again, to the Ukrainian theorist of anarchy Nestor Makhno).
Lida was exceptional in her articulation of "revolutionary" ideas about citizenship and the state. Other teachers' critiques of the "power from above"
model came mostly as indictments of authoritarian-type leadership. A teacher
of Ukrainian once told her students: "Some people want a president who is
going to be like the head of the family, who'll tell them 'Put your spoon back
in its place!' and they'll do it. That's just stupid!"

Pavel's concept of *povna democratiia* is especially interesting because it
constitutes a particular engagement with democracy. What are the conditions of possibility for imagining democracy in its "total" or excessive (i.e.,
uncontrollable from above) form? What made democracy prone to trans-
figuring itself into chaos, so that the two could become equivalent? It seems
that Pavel and others perceived *povna demokratiia* as the result of a particular encounter: that between "democracy" in its Western form and the so-
called "Ukrainian (or East Slavic) mentality." While most teachers did not
perceive democracy as bad or excessive *in itself,* the idea was that it could
become so when *appropriated locally* as a practice. Caldwell (2011) notes
something similar in Russia, where people tend to blame "*popular* philoso-
phies of 'democracy'" (78; emphasis added) and post-Soviet understandings
of freedom and civic responsibility (154) for problems of litter, vandalism,
and pollution (78). What this meant in Ukraine was that one could adhere
to democracy as a political system and system of values while also worrying
about its possible local appropriations and manifestations.

Schools were fertile ground for the circulation of self-stereotypes. Students and teachers would state things such as "Ukrainians never agree/can
never compromise," thereby pointing to the tension in democratic practice
between individual desires and the need for collective decisions (Catt 1999:
12). Alternately, they would claim that "It's our mentality, we don't respect
anything, anyone, any law," drawing attention to what they viewed as an
inherent tendency toward unruliness. A week before the Orange Revolution
started, an eleventh grader in the public school, a Yanukovych supporter,
told me: "I don't think that democracy is for us. Our people [in this context
meaning Ukrainians, Russians, and Belarusians] need someone strong to
tell them what to do. The Supreme Council [*Verkhovna Rada*] can never
reach an agreement, everyone wants his own thing, and they even fight
physically in parliament. It's our mentality, we need one person to tell us:
'This is what you must do!'" While the idea that Ukraine was not *ready* for

democracy circulated widely in the school context, the above statement suggests something rather different. The student was articulating the notion that the democratic way is not right for Ukrainians (nor Belarusians and Russians), who need a strong leader to guide them. "Democracy is not for us" reflected the belief that democracy in the region could only become permissiveness or license [*vsedosvolennist'*]. One is struck by the powerful resonance of this type of discourse with the ideas of such Russian thinkers as Vissarion Belinsky, who wrote, as early as 1837, "True, we [Russians] do not as yet possess rights—we are, if you like, slaves; but that is because we still need to be slaves. Russia is an infant and needs a nurse in whose breast there beats a heart full of love for her fledgling, and in whose hand there is a rod ready to punish it if it is naughty. To give the child complete liberty is to ruin her. To give Russia in her present state a constitution is to ruin her. *To our people liberty . . . simply means license.* The liberated Russian nation would not go to a parliament, but run to the taverns to drink, break glass, and hang the gentry because they shave their beards and wear European clothes" (in Berlin 1955: 165; emphasis added). Belinsky was still widely read during the Soviet period, and thus it is likely that he had an influence on the kind of discourse articulated in Soviet, and then post-Soviet schools. Another influential Russian thinker Alexander Herzen once wrote (though not referring specifically to Russians): "The liberation of those who inwardly still remain slaves always leads to barbarism and anarchy" (paraphrased by Berlin 1978: 95). The philosopher's thoughts resonated in the Ukrainian context with everyday reflections on the nature of freedom and order.

A professor of philology in one of Kyiv's universities once told me: "We were prisoners for so long under the Soviet system. When the collapse happened, we were like a bunch of prisoners who have suddenly been liberated. Prisoners don't know how to handle freedom [*svoboda*], and when they first go out in the real world, they make a lot of mistakes." Many reflections on freedom drew on the images of the "wild" and the "tame." A teacher of history in the private school, a man in his late sixties, had invited me for tea in a tiny room adjacent to his classroom after his lesson. I had asked him why many Ukrainians seemed to be attracted to strong leaders, such as Putin or Yanukovych. After fixing me a tea "just the way Stalin liked it," he proceeded to explain that Ukrainians did not really understand freedom: "If you go to the zoo, and open the gate for the tiger: will it be able to go back to living in the wild? No, because it doesn't know how. It was born in captivity. The same is true of our people."

Ihor, a man in his sixties who picked up his granddaughter from school every day, once said: "Of course, our people want to be free, but it's like with a dog—if you suddenly let him loose, he will go absolutely crazy. I saw this growing up in Transcarpathia. If you ever succeed in catching this dog, he won't be obedient anymore, he won't ever behave like a dog again, forget it." These reflections on freedom and excess are reminiscent of a cartoon by Levon Abramian, an Armenian anthropologist and cartoonist whose work adorns Anatoly Khazanov's 1995 book *After the USSR*. The cartoon depicts a smiling zoo employee opening the gate for a creature (a lion?) who looks grimly at the scene outside. Other cages have already been opened, and outside of them a crocodile has half-eaten a smaller creature, and what looks like a buffalo is only a pile of bones with birds picking at its entrails. A deer is being eaten alive by four foxes, and two monkeys are holding hands while another pair is mating. A trampled sign on the ground reads "DEMOKRATI-ZATSIIA [Democratization]." In Ukraine (and other countries of the region), democracy pictured in its local manifestations was often equated with the "state of nature." The term *povna demokratiia* seems to capture a chaotic, unregulated freedom in which everyone does as they please (*khto shcho khoche*), in a game of who eats whom (*khto koho zist'*).

The above discourses attempt to explain "mentality" with reference to historical processes. In the case of Russian thinkers, the reference point is the experience of serfdom that putatively produced obedient "slaves" with no rights and who cannot "handle" freedom when it is granted to them. In the case of post-Soviet discourses, some of them by individuals who would identify as nationally conscious Ukrainians, the reference point is Soviet authoritarianism, and the idea is that the sudden collapse of the state has produced not "free" but "feral" citizens.

We might consider my informants' representations of their "inherent" disorder (to me, to each other, and to themselves) as an example of what Michael Herzfeld (2005) calls "cultural intimacy," a form of self-representation and self-stereotyping that goes against official representations of "the people" (and in this case, against the official equation of patriotism and order) but nevertheless operates as a source of national cohesion.[12] (In fact, while some of my informants deplored the "inevitable" distortion of democracy, others viewed this local appropriation as a potential source of agency, identity, and cohesion against the advances of neoliberalism.) Yet disorder, as we saw above, is also the trope that *state authorities* use to characterize (at least implicitly) their citizenry, so that popular uses of the term could be seen as both a distancing from state idioms *and* a reiteration of the state's claims. One could perhaps argue that the Kremlin's concept of "managed democracy" (Rus. *upravliaemaia demokratiia*) arises as a response to *povna demokratiia*. Managed democracy articulates the perceived need for a strong hand for those problems "not susceptible to democratic solutions" (S. Markov quoted in Volkov 2003), suggesting that citizens are unable (at least under some circumstances) to rule themselves. Popular appropriations of "inherent disorderliness" can have certain benefits beyond cultural intimacy. As students liked to remind me, there are advantages to being children, and one of them is that you can get away with a lot of things. Surely then, a certain kind of freedom may be found in mischief and disorder. (There is a caveat, however. By performing disorder, one seemingly confirms the stereotype that reproduces the need for supervision/oppression in the first place. This reframes transgression from a challenge to power to its *raison d'être*.)

While students could participate in the reproduction of larger discourses around "mentality" and inherent disorderliness, adults (e.g., the civics teacher) perceived young people as having their *own* (post-Soviet) take on the meaning of democracy. In her study of dachas in Russia, Caldwell describes her middle-aged and older informants' claim that young people equated freedom with being able to do *whatever they pleased* (2011: 155). She adds that "according to this interpretation, freedom was an individual-focused notion that suggested freedom from constraints and freedom to act; it was not a community-focused notion that entailed freedom from the actions of others" (Caldwell 2011: 155). Similarly in Ukrainian schools, there was a feeling among adults that young people had somehow omitted a key dimension of democracy and freedom. According to some teachers, not only had students' notion of individualism strayed from the Soviet concept of "harmonious individualism" (i.e., individualism in the service of the *kollektiv*) (Kharkhordin 1999: 190), but their notion of democracy also constituted a misinterpretation of Western/global "normative" definitions.

Freedom *is* a key aspect of democracy, but Catt (1999) notes that "it is the ways in which the freedom of the individual interacts with the existence of a collective group that tie liberty to democracy" (Catt 1999: 10). In other words, traditional definitions of democracy do not pose it as a free-for-all because this would amount to taking out the "rule" portion of "self-rule" (Catt 1999: 10). Teachers' emphasis on the collective aspect of democracy is valid, no doubt. But while it may appear that young people are overlooking an important aspect of democracy when they focus exclusively on individual freedom, it is important to note that young people in schools (i.e., minors) do not typically have access to the decision-making processes that constitute "the rule portion of self-rule" to begin with. In other words, young people's tendency to "overdo" the freedom aspect of democracy may be connected to their exclusion from another key aspect of democracy, that is, participation, an issue explored in the next chapter.

Chapter 3

Seeking Rights, Performing the Outlaw

> The encounter with human rights is the encounter with
> a more real, more exalted, and more consequential self.
> (Goodale 2007: 144)

"When we are in school, we feel like slaves [*raby*], not like people," Tanya, a ninth grader in the public school, whispered to me as we waited for the morning bell. Given that humanism is the intended direction of education in Ukraine, it is surprising to hear students refer to themselves as "slaves," a term that denotes lack of rights and absence of agency. Tanya went on to say that "there is a single opinion for everyone, and the teacher is always right. You cannot diverge from this opinion; you must do what they tell you. Outside of the school, I feel like a *person*." When I asked students what exactly made them feel like persons, they agreed that it was in part the freedom they had to develop individual creative interests and engage in activities at which they excelled. For example, a male student in the tenth grade had won several wrestling awards, and a female student studied piano with a famous professor at the conservatory. Students' activities during free time also included playing computer games, cycling, reading novels, and going out with friends. I accompanied students to cafés and shopping malls, where they gossiped, joked, and taught me some of their games. In the classroom, in contrast, students felt that "Teachers want to have power *over* us. When we are with them, we have to do only what they want us to do. We feel that we are *their things*." For example, they stated that their student government (a relatively new institution in most schools) is "just for show" and that students had no actual decision-making power in school. A student who was president of her class claimed: "We [class presidents] have no opportunity to provide anything for our fellow students. And if we have ideas or initiative, it's bad, it's seen by teachers or the principal as fantasies on our part. . . . That is why I told you that our student government is not working: teachers don't allow us freedom of opinion." Students also spoke of incidents in which teachers and principals had ruled arbitrarily, threatened or humiliated them, or had simply failed to listen to them. A ninth grader in the public school recounted how he had once tried to make the principal understand his point of view: "I spoke in a calm way, she listened, and then she changed the subject. When I said 'You haven't answered my question,' she screamed, 'Sit down and shut up!' She is very angry, and everyone is afraid of her."

"The Right to Buy Ice Cream": Law, Arbitrariness, and the School as Space of Exception

Since complaints of unfairness and arbitrariness abounded, I asked students in both schools if they had some kind of booklet with school rules to which they could refer. In the private school, students told me, "Yes, I once saw this book in the principal's office. But he makes up the rules as it goes" and "The law is in his head." In the public school, the students simply said, "No, we don't have a book like that. She [the principal] is our law!" The law, understood here as a set of school rules and regulations, was imagined as residing "in the principal," and thus could not be codified. The principal appeared as an all-powerful being whose moods had concrete effects on his or her subordinates' existence. I once told an English teacher in the private school about the expression "the man upstairs" to refer to God. "Oh, we too have the 'man upstairs,'" she said, pointing to the principal's office.

While students (starting in grade 9) had civics courses [*Pravoznavstvo*, which translates literally as "knowledge of the law"] in which they learned about the laws of the country, some posed the school as special kind of place in relation to those laws. One student said, "I know my rights as a citizen, but in school, I cannot prove them." The sixteen-year-old claimed that his rights as a citizen would not be recognized in the school and that no one would even listen because the school authorities would perceive him as "only a child." Some practices contributed to making the school appear to students as a space in which the country's laws were suspended and arbitrary rules and punishments were formulated. I recall a certain Thursday in the private school, when both students and teachers ran around stressed and fearful because the principal had just returned from a holiday. He was teaching a course that day and although the class door was closed, one could hear him yelling at his students. He had already punished the students whose uniforms were not exactly as they should be, and there was talk among teachers and students of "today's victims." On that particular day, Halia, the civics teacher (she was young and very engaging), made some comments in class to the effect that "In the Soviet Union, they had unfair trials and summary executions. Now, we have the rule of law." She then interrupted a female student who was chatting with her classmate: "Stop talking right now or I'll send you out in the hallway without your *pidzhachok* [the jacket that goes over the blouse in the uniform]!" (This would amount to a "death sentence" if the principal caught her! Punishment for failing to wear the uniform properly could range from being sent home to having to stay in school all day but not being allowed to attend one's classes.) This incident illustrates the disjuncture between the *substance* of the curriculum, with its focus on the production of rights-bearing individuals, and the *form* in which the curriculum is imparted (a form that, according to students, produces "slaves"). In addition, the rules and disciplines of the school may at times conflict with the laws of the country, as when teachers (often unintentionally) violate the students' new constitutional rights to respect and dignity. It is precisely students' awareness of their constitutional (and other) rights that made it possible for them to picture the school as a kind of "space of exception" in which the laws of the country could be suspended.

The school apparently also functioned as a "space of socialization" since students claimed to have acquired knowledge about their rights in their civics textbooks. The civics textbook used by ninth graders in both schools, *Ocnovy Pravoznavstva 9* (Principles of Civics, Grade 9) (2002), organized the section "Basis of the Legal Status of the Person and Citizen" into the following subsections:

> *Civic rights and freedoms of Ukrainian citizens*: included explanations of "the right to life, respect, and dignity of the person," "the right to freedom of conscience and worldview," "the right to the privacy of correspondence, telephone conversations and telegrams," and "the right to choose one's place of living."

Political rights and freedoms of Ukrainian citizens: included explanations of the "freedom of assembly" and "freedom to join
political parties."

The right to work and rest: explained the latter and included the
"right to strike."

Constitutional social rights: included explanations of the right to "a
decent living standard," "a dwelling," and "the protection of one's
health."

Constitutional economic rights: included the "right to private
property."

The right to an education and other cultural rights: included a
section on the "rights and duties of pupils."

Constitutional duties of citizens: these included "defending the
Fatherland," "respecting state symbols," "paying taxes," and
"upholding the Constitution."

Students were thus knowledgeable about the kinds of rights they had or
would have upon reaching adulthood, and therefore were quick to identify
teachers' and administrators' "violations" of these rights. Kaplan (2006) refers to a similar logic when he notes that students in Turkish schools use the
language of democracy and rights to condemn what they see as undemo-
cratic pedagogical practices (220).

The media played an important role in educating students about the law.
For example, Channel 5 (P'iatyi Kanal, the only channel not controlled by
the government at the time of my fieldwork) aired a five-minute segment on
citizens' rights after the evening news, dealing, for example, with a citizen's
legal recourse in case of arrest. In the latter half of 2004 especially, the opposition, along with various civic groups, worked on making citizens more
aware of their constitutional rights (rights that they claimed were increasingly being violated by the government). Students also credited their parents
for making them aware of themselves as individuals deserving of respect.
All parents had been schooled in the Soviet system and thus had learned
that the social unit of significance was the collective, not the person. Yet the
collapse of the Soviet Union and the period of intense economic hardship
that followed had forced them into a struggle for survival in which *individual* talent, initiative, and knowledge of the law were essential. Many of the
students' parents had become successful businesspeople.

What emerged from different pedagogies of rights was that "if one person has a right to do something, other members of his society have an obligation to respect this right" (Birch 1993: 114), and young people felt that teachers and administrators were obligated to respect not only their rights as Ukrainian citizens, but also their more basic human rights, such as the right to equal treatment, or freedom from cruel or degrading punishment. Students' awareness of the law "out there" (the country's law, materialized in documents such as the Constitution or the Criminal Code of Ukraine) made their subjection to the seemingly arbitrary rules of the school seem all the more unfair, and produced a discourse of injustice (*nespravedlyvist'*). Students' sense of powerlessness was rooted in part in their inability to participate in making the rules to which they were subjected (Franklin 1986: 24), a situation that appears to go against democratic principles (Franklin 1986: 45). Yet Marshall points to the oft-used argument that were it to grant sufficient democratic rights to students, the school as an institution would be unable to function (1984: 108).

In Ukraine, teachers and administrators often justify the absence of students' voices in decision-making processes by claiming that children are likely to make unreasonable demands, or to "exercise their rights in a way that would damage themselves and others" (Marshall 1984: 108). How could the view of children as unfit for the "rational" exercise that is politics be reconciled with the global discourse of human rights that poses children as individuals endowed with agency and "participation rights"? As Ennew and Milne point out, young people's everyday lives are marked by the "conflict between two Western ideas: the development of individual personality, and the quarantine of childhood" (1990: 14). It is precisely the tension between these two ideas that teachers and students attempt to negotiate in school.

Students' inability to participate in decision-making in school is in part what led one student to identify as a "slave." As Marshall (1984) suggests, "if [children] are obliged to follow . . . rules [that they did not participate in making] then the obligation must be similar to that of the coerced slave" (108). Students also described themselves as being subjected to a particular form of power, one that also excluded them via arbitrary decisions, secrecy around the nature of rules, and random forms of surveillance. These tactics made it impossible for students to predict when they would be found at fault and for what transgression. This system was far from the "tangible" law of the country's legal documents (e.g., the Criminal Code, which young people

Figure 5. A student's eye view of the classroom; the graffiti on the chair reads, "Yes, Yushchenko!" Photo by the author, 2005.

were fond of consulting). At the mercy of the whims and moods of authority figures, and isolated from the country's protective laws, students could easily come to think of themselves as slaves who exist *"outside the range of the law* and the body politic of the citizens" (Arendt 1963: 107; emphasis added). Students' perception of the school as a space in which their rights under the country's laws were suspended (*allegedly* "for their own good") is reminiscent of Agamben's concept of state of exception, where an individual or group is included in the law as a category to which the law does not apply. While claiming that students experience the vulnerability of Agamben's *homo sacer* when they are in schools might be taking it too far, a parallel can be drawn between the *homo sacer* and the child to the extent that both are portrayed by power as occupying a "natural" space that is not only outside but also "prior to" politics. What is more, the category of child, like the category of *homo sacer*, is produced by power. Indeed, "the term 'child' has a connection less with chronology than with power," that is, it specifies a power relationship (Franklin 1986: 8).

Despite the fact that students valued the written laws of the country and thought of them as recourse (at least in theory) against the school's random form of power, they did recognize their own ambiguous location in relation to the larger legal order. Because of their status as children or minors (*nepovnolitni*, lit. "not of full years") students could feel marginalized in relation to the country's laws. Many of the laws and rights that Ukrainian students learned in their civics course applied only to people over eighteen. For example, after explaining some aspects of criminal law in class, Pavel, the civics teacher in the public school, told his students that as usual, some of the rights applied only to *povnolitni* (adults, or people of legal age). A female student interrupted, frustrated, "So tell us what kinds of rights we have as minors!" "Oh, I don't know," said the teacher smugly, "the right to buy ice cream?" The question was left at that.

Veloso (2008) describes children as a very specific kind of legal subjects because the law sees them both as *citizens* who have rights and as *children* meriting special protection (48). The focus on "protection rights" emerges from the perception of children's "inherent" (physical and psychological) vulnerability. Yet as Lansdown has pointed out, this perception can obscure the extent to which vulnerability is produced by children's *lack of civil status* (1994: 35). Children's legal vulnerability has been conceptualized in terms of "permanent exclusion *as a child*" (Franklin 1986: 45; emphasis added), that is, it is only when one ceases to be a child that one can be included (1986: 45). In attempting to conceptualize the place of the child in relation to the law, Ennew and Milne (1990) refer to the status of children in eighteenth-century Europe, noting that children appeared in the French Declaration of the Rights of Man as a "residual category of persons, lacking full human rights" (12). In England during the same period, the child's body was not considered to be inhabited by a legal person, so that if one stole a child whose body was not clothed, it amounted to stealing a corpse (1990: 12). According to Ennew and Milne, not much has changed in children's legal status since that period, so that "just like a corpse, which lacks the ability to act because it has no biological life, a child lacks the ability to act because it has no legal life" (1990: 14).

Perhaps it is not so much that children face outright exclusion as that they are included in the legal and political system *as "potential" citizens*, or as the "future" of the nation. Therefore, we might want to think of the child's relation to the legal order not through the metaphor of the corpse, but rather through the image of the naked, corpse-like body of the neophyte in what Turner (1967) describes as the liminal stage of a rite of passage. The body that lies temporarily "betwixt and between," excluded from the law

insofar as it exists outside the rules guiding either its previous or future social status nevertheless holds the potential for inscription. It has become a
tabula rasa upon which society may inscribe its law, thus preparing it for the
transition to a new status. Clastres (1974) states that the body as a "writing
surface . . . suited for receiving the legible text of the law" (149) "mediates
the acquisition of a knowledge" (151). This image speaks to John Locke's
conception of the child as *tabula rasa*. According to Locke, the child's body
and mind must be disciplined and shaped by adults so as to produce a rational, self-controlled, and responsible citizen (Woodhead and Montgomery
2002: 64) and one who can be properly included in the legal order. The logic
of citizenship education itself is one of inscription, including inscription on
the body via disciplines and routines.

Rights as Obligations

When, in the course of a group discussion, I asked students in the private
school what kinds of rights they felt they had within the perimeter of the
school, they answered: "None," "Maybe the right to breathe! [*pravo na
dykhannia*]," "The right to study," "The right to go downstairs at 12 and eat
lunch in the cafeteria," or "The right to use the bathroom after the third period." "We have no rights, only duties," added one student. Students posed
some of their rights in school in terms of allowance for biological necessities:
the need to breathe, to eat, to go to the bathroom, and so on. These rights
were in turn constrained by the particular regime of the school, with its strict
schedule. The "rights" to which students cynically referred were in some case
both obligations and (bodily) disciplines. Childhood, according to Rose
(1989), is "the most intensively governed sector of personal existence" (145);
"the child's body is organized temporally in terms of its ablution, nutrition,
excretion, exercise, etc., and all of this is homologous to the drilling that oc-
curs in the armed forces and the specialization and division of labor on the
factory floor" (Jenks 2005: 68). Thus the obligations and disciplines that
teachers identified as "rights" in fact reproduced a certain kind of order particular to the school and other institutions (e.g., the prison). Students indeed
associated rights in the school with order *rather than* with freedom. As for
the "right to study [*pravo na navchannia*]," teachers constantly reminded
their students that they should appreciate their right to an education. At the
same time, teachers posed studying as a duty, sometimes even as a patriotic

duty. A teacher of history in the public school once told her students, in a wave of patriotic fervor: "Don't ask what your country can do for you, but what you can do for your country!" A female student asked eagerly, "So what *can* we do for our country?" "Right now, your only duty as a citizen is to study, study, study," she replied. The student lowered her eyes, disappointed.

Many teachers' views of rights reflected former Soviet entitlements (for example, "the right to work" or "the right to a dwelling") and thus had a lot to do with obligation and/or patriotic duty. In fact, the Soviet Constitution of 1977 stipulates that "Citizens' exercise of their rights and freedoms is inseparable from the performance of their duties and obligations" (Article 59). In fact, while one was entitled to a job in the Soviet Union, one did not have the right *not* to work. I remember a long cab ride from the suburbs of Kyiv during which the driver, a man in his mid-sixties, reminisced fondly about the "order [*poriadok*]" of Soviet life. When I asked him what he had in mind exactly, he said, "Well for example, everyone worked. And if someone didn't show up for work for more than two days, a policeman [*militsioner*] would ring the bell, warn the person, and force them to go back to work." Article 40 of the Soviet Constitution of 1977 stipulates that "Citizens of the USSR have the right to work (that is, to guaranteed employment and pay in accordance with the quantity and quality of their work, and not below the state-established minimum), including the right to choose their trade or profession, type of job and work in accordance with their inclinations, abilities, training and education, with due account of the needs of society." Article 60, however, poses work as a duty: "It is the duty of, and a matter of honor for, every able-bodied citizen of the USSR to work conscientiously in his chosen, socially useful occupation, and strictly to observe labor discipline. Evasion of socially useful work is incompatible with the principles of socialist society."

The association of rights with obligations was not limited to those teachers who had spent most of their lives under Soviet rule. During a geography lesson in the public school, the teacher, a young woman in her late twenties for whom the students had great respect, referred to some of the rights of Ukrainian citizens, as defined in the Ukrainian Constitution of 1996: "For example, you have the right to work [*pravo na pratsiu*]." "Or not to work!" shouted a male student enthusiastically, from the back of the class. The teacher was usually very calm, but this answer clearly annoyed her: "Yes, of course, if you want to sit with a bottle [*sydity z pliashkoiu*] all day, you can!" she snapped. In this case, "sitting with a bottle" means doing nothing, or being a "lazy bum." The young teacher associated the "right not to work" (a post-Soviet concept) with selfish indulgence so that this right was posed as a (morally rep-rehensible) privilege. The Ukrainian Constitution (1996), like the Soviet one, guarantees the "right to rest and leisure." The formulation in the Ukrainian Constitution, however, is "Everyone *who is employed* has the right to rest" (Article 45, emphasis added). The civics textbook used by ninth graders in both schools had the following quote next to the text explaining citizens' constitutional "right to work and to rest": "Only work gives [one] the right to an enjoyable life" (M. O. Dobroliubov quoted in Usenko et al. 2002: 135).

The Soviet Constitution of 1977 also guaranteed the right to (state-allocated) housing (*pravo na zhytlo*). Soviet citizens had been bound to their dwelling by the so-called *propyska* (or record of one's place of residence) that made it virtually impossible to move, another example of a right being tied to an obligation. The Ukrainian Constitution of 1996 also guarantees the right to housing, stating that "The State creates conditions that enable every citizen to build [or] purchase a property, or to rent housing." The *propyska* system still exists in Ukraine, and access to social services such as medical care, or the allocation of pensions, is still tied to one's permanent residence. However, citizens now officially have "the right" to move and live wherever they want.

A textbook for fourth graders entitled *Ia i Ukraina* (Ukraine and I), published in 2004, contains a section entitled the "Rights and Duties of the Citizen" in independent Ukraine. These rights are essentialized in the form of a poem written by a student, Hanna K., from the Zhytomyr region.

> I want to live, it's my right [*Ia maiu pravo*].
> I have the right
> to rights.
> I have the right to magazines,
> newspapers, comics,
> and books.
> I have the right
> to well-being [*zhyty v dobri*].
> . . .
> I'm—a child [*Ia—dytyna*].
> . . .
> I have the right
> to a dwelling,
> to parents, education,
> And friends! (in Baybara and Bibik 2004: 59)

The text goes on to describe the rights guaranteed by the Ukrainian Constitution of 1996, stating that every person has the right to: education, life, rest and leisure, living with one's family/with one's parents, special protection and assistance from the state, the use of different sources of information, humane treatment, and protection of one's health (Baybara and Bibik 2004: 59).

Most of the above-mentioned rights figure in the Soviet Constitution of 1977. Yet despite the very similar wording, rights such as "the right to a dwelling" have lost their component of obligation. A notable exception is the "right to an education." Article 53 of the Ukrainian Constitution stipulates that "Everyone has the right to education. Complete general secondary education is compulsory" (Article 53). Of course, the compulsory nature of secondary schooling is not unique to Ukraine, and neither, for that matter, is the more binding dimension of citizenship and rights. For example, in response to the 1989 UN Convention on the Rights of the Child (and its focus on children's provision, protection, prevention, and participation rights), the African Charter on the Rights and Welfare of the Child (1990) emphasizes both the rights *and responsibilities* of the child. These include the child's duty to respect and assist his parents, superiors, and elders, and to fulfill his obligation to the national community by putting his intellectual and physical abilities at its service. Lancy (2008) points out that responsibilities should not be interpreted necessarily as burdens on a child's life because contributions (e.g., helping to raise younger siblings) can be a source of pride and self-respect for children. Yet what comes across in school practice in the Ukrainian context is the idea of *everyone being equally obligated* (rather than possessing equal rights), a notion that brings us back to the teacher's statement about Ukraine as a normative state in which there is no room for "black sheep" (*bila vorona*) (see Chapter 2).

Many teachers perceived students as unappreciative of their rights. In the private school especially, the students and their families were largely independent from the state. That is, they were not tied to the web of entitlements (and therefore of duties) that had held society together during the Soviet period. Many of the students' parents were businesspeople, and this meant not only that they could ensure their own livelihood, but also that they could "buy" things previously obtained through the performance of duty. I had heard of the practice of paying to avoid military service, but according to my informants, even an education (i.e., a high school or university diploma) could now be "bought." The wealthier students in the private school relied on their parents to relieve them of some of the burdens of citizenship *and* to secure their future in the form of employment and dwelling (a former prerogative of the state). Svetlana often reminded a male student whose family was very wealthy that he needed to study anyway. "Now you don't care about doing well in school, you don't want to do anything, but God forbid something happen to your dad [the provider of the family]! What would you do? How would you live?"

When I asked the teacher of military preparedness in the private school about students' view of citizenship, he said immediately: "They want to have everything from the state but don't want to give anything back!" He went on to tell me how his generation (he had just turned 71) had conceived of their duties to the (Soviet) Motherland as honorable. He said that at the time he was drafted for military service, there was a belief that no girl would even look at a man who had not served, and only the invalid and psychologically ill could escape the service. He added that now, the male students had parents at the top ("*vyshchi*"), and that parents would intervene (i.e., pay the right people) so that their sons could escape being drafted. When I spoke about this with the oldest students in the private school, they confirmed that they had no interest in serving in the military. "Why not?" I asked. "Because we're peace-loving hippies!" replied the class clown, punctuating his statement with a peace sign. His colleague replied more seriously: "We don't want to be the older guys' slaves, cleaning toilets with a toothbrush for two years [the duration of the service]!" The tenth and eleventh graders' behavior in the military class reflected their lack of interest for the subject. A "marching class" I attended in the schoolyard had tenth graders saluting with the wrong hand, kicking and tripping one another, marching in line in monkey-like postures while the teacher was looking away, and counting in German "*Ein! Zwei! Ein! Zwei!*" (a thinly veiled reference to excessive Nazi discipline) over the Russian-language prompts of the teacher. While the students at the private school and most of the students in the public school were confident that they would not have to serve, I heard of students who were less lucky and had to use different strategies for avoiding the service. This included, in one case, having someone break their arm on a toilet bowl in order to be disqualified.

In questionnaires distributed to teachers in both schools, I asked how they thought students perceived their rights and duties as citizens. Although many teachers were positive about students' increased confidence and knowledge of their rights (a change with their generation), many pointed out that students did not have a strong sense of duty. "Their rights, they know, but their duties [*oboviazky*], that's another story," wrote a teacher of fifty-two years in the private school. "They know their duties but they don't fulfill them," argued another teacher. A young teacher wrote that "[Children] don't fulfill their duties as students [*oboviaz'ky uchniv*] very conscientiously; they just have fun [*beshketuiut'*]. That's children [*Tse dity*]." In her study of dachas in Russia, Caldwell (2011) notes similar discourses about youth and rights. She quotes the author of an article on littering as stating that "Freedom [*svoboda*], which our party and government proclaimed for many years, has one negative nuance: many people seem to think that it means that freedom liberates them from obligations. Therefore even youth now have one hundred times more rights than obligations" (Burilov 2005: 5, in Caldwell 2011: 155). This concern is legitimate to the extent that "the *social* character of rights is an essential aspect of the concept. The existence of rights always implies obligations on the part of other citizens and frequently implies obligations on the part of the person or group holding the right" (Birch 1993: 114). Yet while teachers liked to remind students about the obligations that come with rights, they did not seem enthusiastic about their own obligations vis-à-vis rights-bearing students. This is in part because being obligated to students (e.g., legally compelled to respect them) implied that students were "equal," a principle that seemed to undermine the hierarchies of the school.

Some teachers wrote indignantly of the way students invoked their rights. "Imagine," writes a mathematics teacher of forty-seven years, "students are now saying 'You cannot shout at me because I'm a *person*.' This would have never been possible earlier [meaning, during the Soviet period]." The teacher was right in asserting the latter to the extent that the social unit of value in Soviet schooling was not the person, but the collective. Thus, claims to rights *as an individual* would have been misplaced. Teachers were also shocked to hear their students assert things such as "You cannot touch me: I have rights, you know." Some teachers stated that they were happy to see that today's youth, unlike their own generation, had become more confident in themselves (*samovpevneni*). However, a civics teacher who was young and open-minded confided in me that she was simply floored when a female student told her in class, "You're wrong [*Vy ne prava*]." Teachers emphasized the process whereby the new generation of post-Soviet students had extricated "rights" from the realm of *duty* (and "order") only to perform them as *excess* (i.e., as the freedom bordering on disrespect). Teachers were fearful that students would go overboard if they were granted rights, and that they would become superior to their educators (a superiority that was already being felt at the material level). Birch (1993) states that "there is always a problem about whether rights are absolute rights, such as to publish whatever you please about anything [as in the right of free speech], or whether they can be properly limited in this way or that while preserving their essence" (122). Because rights have the potential to be interpreted by students as absolutes, teachers often treated young people as in need of protection from the rights they did have. What is more, teachers feel compelled to protect students from the very dynamics that have produced those rights, that is, democratization and marketization. It is these processes (and the discourses and performances around them) that students in turn cannibalize in their effort to "fight back" and fashion themselves into rights-bearing citizens.

The "Bandit Repertoire"

How did students deal with their perceived lack of rights within the school? Students' strategies for dealing with this situation included "keeping quiet" so as not to cause problems for themselves. I was in a student's home sitting at the kitchen table with his mother when he started telling her about some injustice he had suffered at the hands of the principal. She advised him not to try arguing with the principal, who, he should remember, had the power to expel him. She gave me a defeated look and said: "The whole country is afraid of their bosses, they live in the fear of being fired. It's the same with me, I try to keep quiet at work." She advised her son to keep a low profile so that he could get through his schooling. Other ways in which students dealt with their perceived lack of rights included the use of humor, irony, and cynicism. Students could also subtly challenge official school hierarchies, as when they performed the military salute in addition to standing up when a teacher entered the class.

In response to teachers' and administrators' perceived unfairness (*nespravedlyvist*'), students also performed what I will refer to as the "bandit repertoire." The bandit repertoire is characterized by an aggressive and insolent stance borrowed from the media, including feature films or television series portraying gangsters, and music glorifying prison life. Although American films dubbed in Ukrainian or Russian offered models of the bandit hero, the style of dress, hairstyle, slang, and bodily signs performed by students tended to bear the characteristics of the figure of the bandit presented in the Russian media.

An analysis of the "bandit" portrayed in Russian productions reveals the following characteristics: The bandit is rough (Rus. *grubyi*) and aggressive (Rus. *agressivnyi*). He does not speak much, but when he does, it is in Russian mixed with prison slang, or "*fenya*," the slang born in the Soviet gulag. He is often shown in a threatening stance, and usually spits between words (he is everything but "civil"). The bandit is also portrayed as immune from certain feelings: he is fearless, kills without second thoughts, and does not feel remorse. As Svetlana's son-in-law explained to me, "Bandits don't think. They just kill automatically, without any feelings, like wolves in the forest [*iak vovky v lisi*]. Their law is the law of the jungle [*zakon dzhunhliv*]." Women and children are marginal to the life of the bandit: they must come to him, for he will not seek their company. Women, when present, are often portrayed as prostitutes and tend to die violently.

In what ways can the bandit be posed as a hero? I would argue that the bandit's status as a kind of hero/informal role model has everything to do with his relation to the state (the latter usually represented by the police). For example, the film *Bumer* (2003) [*bumer* is Russian slang for BMW] tells the story of four St. Petersburg bandits who steal a BMW and escape eastward with it, toward Siberia. The film is filled with physical violence (including a scene in which children rob and beat a man to death with a baseball bat), and the language is very coarse. One of the scenes shows the bandits being pulled over by traffic police. The police officers open the trunk of the BMW, and upon finding nothing unusual, plant a small pouch containing marijuana. Following their "discovery," they rough up the leader of the bandits, extracting all the money from his wallet (the distinction between bandits and police becomes blurry at this point). What the police officers do not know (but realize only when it is too late) is that the leader had discretely extracted that same money from their police car while they were looking away. In this instance, the bandits' heroism lies in having deceived the state. At the end of the film, three out of the four bandits are killed by police, and the fourth one escapes, swearing to avenge the others.

The Russian television series *Brigada*[1] (The Gang, 2003) was less violent because it was shown on prime time in the evenings. There again, the post-Soviet bandit hero is portrayed as "better" (more clever than, and in some ways morally superior to) the state, represented by his adversary the police officer. The hero himself claims that he never lies to fellow gang members, and that he is loyal to them: he keeps his promises and fulfills his obligations. He is portrayed as more open and honest than the sneaky, secretive state. In reality, bandits and state representatives often collaborate, as when criminals are hired out by government officials to perform certain tasks related to "security." In his book *Violent Entrepreneurs* (2002), sociologist Vadim Volkov posits a rupture between the Soviet "thief" (*vor*) and the post-Soviet "bandit" (*bandyt*), arguing that the thief distinguished himself by his opposition to the authorities (collaboration was severely punished by the community of thieves), while the bandit is usually well connected at the top. What comes through in most bandit stories, however, is that the *state* is the "bigger mafia" (i.e., there are no limits to the state's corruption: it is completely "rotten"). Therefore, it could be argued that while post-Soviet Russian bandit stories are not about Robin Hood–type characters, they are tales of *relative* morality.

Many teachers deplored the popularity of bandit films. A teacher of Ukrainian history told me that she was shocked at the brutality of the life depicted in the media. She blamed the Russian media for dumping on the Ukrainian market television series and films that glorified violence. The students I worked with, regardless of age, were exposed to these types of movies. That is to say, while a Russian television series such as *Brigada* might appeal primarily to the male students in the ninth grade (they admitted to finding it *klasno* [cool]), many eleventh grade female students reported watching it as well (along with such shows as "Beverly Hills 90210" [dubbed in Ukrainian], and a Russian take on the sitcom "The Nanny" entitled *Niania Vika*). Some students found bandit movies "stupid," but claimed that there was nothing else to watch on television. I asked the more enthusiastic students why they were attracted to the figure of the bandit. They told me that as a bandit, you are "cool," "You can get a lot of money," "You can have a good car," "You can *be somebody*," "You're tough," "You rule by force," and "Everybody is afraid of you." Zhenia, a student with whom I often discussed power relations in the school, said that students are attracted to bandit culture "because of the money, because it's cool. You know, 99 percent of the people in our country are *bydlo* [lit. cattle, but meaning in this context, ignorant and destitute], they have no money, they don't know *anything*. To be a bandit for them is the only way to escape this." In the same vein, a female student in the eleventh grade said that students are attracted to bandits because they want "to be somebody, to have a good life. Why would you spend your life being a *nobody*, earning a small salary from your small job, if you can make good money without working?" Others claimed that because bandits were "tough and mean," they were able to survive, and even succeed, and that many people admired them for that.[2]

The figure of the bandit performed in the media was also performed on the streets of Kyiv. The so-called New Rich (or *kruti* in slang) had become highly visible, and the men, usually around 40 or 50 years old, sported very short haircuts, wore black suits and shirts, and often had tattoos. They could be observed talking on their cell phones, their black Mercedes or Hummer (with heavily tinted windows) parked prominently on the sidewalk in front of banks or casinos. Some of the wealthy students' fathers fit this description. A father who picked up his young daughter from the private school one afternoon sported a tattoo on his hand depicting a skull whose eye sockets had been stitched through the skin. Some of the students' parents, especially in the private school, participated or had participated in semi-legal business activities following the collapse of the Soviet Union. I knew of at least two students who had lost a parent to shady deals gone wrong. A few students lived on the outskirts of the city, in mansions surrounded by high brick walls protected around the clock by closed-circuit cameras and security guards (*okhorona*). The bandit-type dress and demeanor was not reserved for the New Rich, however. There was a tendency among the younger generation (twenty to thirty years old) to dress in the style of what Volkov (2002) calls "violent entrepreneurs." In the Ukrainian case, this meant, once again, the very short haircut, as well as very tight-fitting clothes that were meant to show one's top physical form. (Volkov [2002] explains how the 1990s saw the emergence of special sports clubs frequented by those men newly engaged in providing "protection" services.) I never once during my fieldwork encountered anyone wearing the loose-fitting clothing associated with African American, and now increasingly global, "gangsta culture." Bandit-style masculinity in the post-Soviet context was displayed according to a different logic: rather than dissimulating his body in garments that mimicked prison slacks, the violent entrepreneur showcased his muscular body. (An element that was increasingly shared with African American gangster culture, however, was the wearing of "bling" or oversized golden jewelry.) The style of dress was combined with an aggressive stance, signaling readiness for violence. The young men performing this were informally (and jokingly) referred to as *patsany*, the prison (originally gulag) slang for "guys."

How did students appropriate the figure of the bandit performed in the media, on the streets, and sometimes even at home? What I call the "bandit repertoire" was a situational and malleable array of performances marked by arrogance, disrespect, and an aggressive stance. It must be emphasized that the students deploying this repertoire were *not* actual criminals or delinquents. While they *at times* broke school rules, this was not a necessary condition for performing the bandit. Part of the aggressive stance characterizing the bandit repertoire involved the use of prison slang and swear words (*fenya* and *blatniak*) and bodily demeanor that included signs originally used in the Soviet prison setting. A specific style of dress (a leather jacket and a very short haircut) was also common but was not essential to the bandit repertoire. This repertoire, while used primarily by male students, was also available to female students. Their male classmates were sometimes astonished at their rudeness and command of *blatniak*. "They are even worse than us," a male student once told me.

The bandit repertoire was highly visible and recognizable. In fact, teachers (talking to one another or to me) commonly used the term "bandit" to refer to students: "Nowadays, kids are all bandits." "Oh, 11b: it's my bandit class." "What kind of patriots can kids be, if they all behave like bandits?" The term "bandit" in this usage referred to unruly children rather than to actual criminals. That is to say, the term "bandits" suggests that students were "outside" of their teachers' understanding of what constitutes order and civility (and consequently outside of their teacher's definition of the obedient patriot; see Chapter 2).

Teachers often point out that students have become very disrespectful of authority. The performance of disrespect toward teachers was expressed by terms such as *khamstvo* or *nakhabstvo*. *Nakhabstvo* translates as impudence, insolence, or impertinence, while *khamstvo* translates as boorishness or rudeness. Both these terms denote disrespect, insensitivity, lack of civility, and disregard for the person. According to many teachers, students were *nekul'turni*, a Soviet expression used to refer to a person who is uncultured, or not properly brought up.[3] A whole array of student behavior was subsumed under the terms *khamstvo* and *nakhabstvo*, and thus considered "bandit-like": students defending themselves from verbal attack by teachers (i.e., "talking back" when reprimanded), refusing to obey when asked to perform a task, answering cell phones in class, walking out of class without asking permission, coming late to class without apologizing, lying, making "cynical" comments about class material, laughing while the teacher addresses a serious topic (e.g., the 1933 Famine or the Chornobyl' explosion), or differing in opinion and saying it out loud. Interestingly, what appears to teachers as flagrant disrespect for authority also includes students' defense of what we might think of as "legitimate" rights, for example, their right not to be physically punished or verbally humiliated by teachers or school administrators. When I asked young people what kinds of rights they thought they should have in school, the answers ranged from the right to express themselves freely in class, to the right to be respected by teachers, to the right to make their routine in school more interesting by having a say in the organization of their schedule, to the right to exit the school during breaks (this was not allowed). As we will see, the boundary between civic freedoms and excessive freedom could be blurry.

Teachers who had spent most of their career under Soviet rule often told me how students' *nakhabstvo* would have been unimaginable "earlier" (i.e., during the Soviet period). The encounter between the Soviet-generation teachers and the first generation of post-Soviet students can be summed up by this teacher's exasperated question to her student: "*Koval'chuk, koly ty stav takym khamom?* [Koval'chuk, when did you become such a boor]." Students in turn claimed that it is their lack of power in school that forces them into *nakhabstvo*. One student stated that "[Teachers and the principal] put our opinion down, 'Ah, you're only children.' They think that they are all so *right*. And that is the reason for our rudeness." The student identified rudeness as a form of self-defense against oppression from above rather than as something inherent to "disorderly children" in general or to the "new generation" in particular. Even if this appears to be simply an instance of "blaming" the adults, it is important to note young people's own take on the matter of their insolence because the perception of "injustice" is what ultimately fuels their quest for rights in school. In addition, the student's perspective resonates with Jenks's (2005) suggestion that we move away from seeing children's transgressions as "disruptions" to a properly normative life, and instead "employ their disruption as a source of critical examination of our dominant means of control" (150).

The bandit repertoire that students mobilized to claim rights was flexible (i.e., one could move in and out of it at will) so that even the best students or the class pet who recited poems with all the right intonations could become rough and use prison slang when needed. Zhenia told me how difficult it was to *avoid* performing this kind of roughness in the school context: "Most people in the class were brought up well at home, but in school, they use swear words, because it's very difficult to resist doing this when you are in such an environment, it's hard to be a white crow [*bila vorona*, or black sheep] among black crows. Most people, myself included, don't want to do it, but I myself use bad words. If not, others will just crush me, destroy me." In some sense, students performed the bandit repertoire not only for teachers and administrators, but also for one another. The following incident illustrates this.

One morning in a tenth-grade Ukrainian literature class in the public school, students were being tested on a poem that they had had to memorize the night before. The student at the top of the class (he was expected to graduate with a gold medal), sitting in the first row and wearing a suit, stood up and recited the assigned poem, with all the appropriate intonation and without any mistakes. "Very good," said the teacher. She then pointed to another student: "Zhora, please." Zhora was wearing tight-fitting jeans and a short leather jacket, and sported a very short haircut. We all watched as he stood up slowly and defiantly, assuming a bandit-like pose (torso propped up and hands clasped in front of him). He started reciting in a monotonous voice, looking straight ahead of him: "Spring, oh golden spring, how much joy you bring me. The cherry trees bloom, etc., etc." The scene seemed to me full of irony. Here I had a fifteen year old known for his use of prison slang and for bullying others. His clothes, hair, and whole demeanor corresponded to what could be observed in all the bandit films showing at the time. And yet, he was reciting (from memory, in Ukrainian) one of the literature curriculum's most maudlin poems about spring. His voice showed resignation—his body, defiance.

When I recounted this incident to Svetlana's son-in-law over dinner, he said, "Ah, the double standard [*podviinyi standart*]. He performs one thing for the teacher, and another for his classmates, trying to show them that he's cool." And indeed, the "bandit repertoire" was such that it could also be performed in conjunction with another "repertoire," that of the Ukrainian patriot in its pedagogic incarnation. Zhora was indeed performing for two audiences, doing a fine job of complying with the teacher's demand without losing respect from his peers.

Zhora's performance of national stereotypes signifies his participation in the school as an institution, and is required for a "good grade." Yet he appropriates national stereotypes in such a way as to make them compatible with the more rebellious repertoire of the bandit. Inculcation in this context becomes a lively engagement in which the patriot is simultaneously repeated and de-centered. The ability to perform both the bandit and the patriot also points to the flexibility of the bandit repertoire itself. For this is indeed a "repertoire": it has not congealed into a "subjectivity," nor into a habitus, because it does not constitute a *durable* set of dispositions (Bourdieu 1977). I have indicated that bandit-like behavior is highly recognizable. Yet it is only so *while it is being performed*. Herzfeld (1982) claims that the *kleftes*, or Cretan sheep thieves, do not constitute a "discrete category of people," but can be seen in terms of a "category of *performative role*" or "broad behavioral continuum," so that "when they are not out on a raid, they are not *kleftes*" (64). Similarly in the school context, students may move in and out of the bandit repertoire as required, displaying some of its attributes in the history class but not during the geography lesson.[4] Some students performed the bandit more consistently in the school context and on the street, but not at home. In fact, some of the parents attending parent-teacher meetings were surprised to hear from the teacher that their children were "lazy" and "rude." This disjuncture could be attributed to (especially the older) teachers' lower level of tolerance for insolence. Conversations with parents revealed that they often felt a certain pride in their children, whom they considered more self-confident (*samovpevneni*) than *they* had been as children growing up while the Soviet Union was under Brezhnev's leadership (1964–1982). Parents realized that their children would be more likely to succeed in a newly competitive world if they were assertive or even slightly aggressive. Of course, there was a measure of ambivalence as to the limits of this assertiveness. Svetlana's phone often rang late at night as parents called, sometimes in a frenzy, to ask her advice. Their teenager was hysterical (*v isterytsi*), or otherwise out of control; had got into a fight on the street, or had disappeared for two days after borrowing money from parents to attend a rock concert. Svetlana would usually promise the parent that she would have a word with their child the next day. Between lessons, she would take the student aside and explain, calmly but sternly, that they were causing much pain to their parents and that they should think of their future rather than gamble with their lives. Parents' reactions to young people's attempts at pushing limits varied widely. Some parents had very little tolerance for it and would yell at their teenagers, while others would withdraw and even confess to being afraid of their child. As a teacher of mathematics told me, some of the students were so rich and "spoiled" that they feared nothing and no one. "They're holding God by the beard," she claimed. In student households that included grandparents, the situation was somewhat different as the latter often played the role (much like Svetlana) of keepers of discipline. Many schoolteachers blamed the parents, claiming that they were never home, and that when they were, they spoiled their children with material things. Other teachers claimed that parents were simply too lenient and that as a result, children grew up like weeds on the side of the road (*burian na dorozi*). When Svetlana called a female student's home after she had not shown up for school, parents often said such things as, "Oh, she had a headache this morning so I let her sleep." Teachers often reminisced about the way they had been punished by their own parents after missing school. One of the school guards, a man in his late sixties, recounted to me how as a boy his father had hit him so hard after finding out that he had missed school to hang out with friends that he had thought twice about skipping school again. According to him, today's kids were *rozpushcheni* (lit. left uncared for, let loose). Yet a teacher of folklore once warned a recalcitrant student who lived in a village on the outskirts of Kyiv: "I talked to your father on the phone about your disobedience and he said to me: 'You have a pointer [*ukazka*, a heavy wooden stick]? So use it!'" Clearly, parents had different conceptions of discipline and of the way to enforce it.

It appears that the simultaneous performance of patriot and bandit is something that would most likely have been praised by parents as a kind of adaptability essential to success. On the one hand, the parents I spoke to felt that their children had to be able to comply with the school's requirements (however "useless" or "stupid" the latter might sometimes seem). On the other, it was important that children develop the assertiveness required to fend for themselves.

The Informal Hierarchies of the Classroom

While for most students, bandit-like behavior and demeanor remained a repertoire that could be accessed at will, for a minority of students, it represented a more permanent way of being and doing, a more entrenched set of dispositions in the school context. In the public school, there existed in some classes what one student called an "informal hierarchy." Not every class had this informal hierarchy. I did not find evidence of this type of hierarchy in the classes I interacted with on a day-to-day basis in the private school, but observed it closely in three classes (two ninth-grade classes, and one eleventh-grade class) in the public school. Several students told me that this phenomenon was prevalent in other schools (especially the ones in poorer areas of the city), and I had occasion to observe a similar hierarchy when visiting a public high school in Western Ukraine. The hierarchy in question was comprised of *students only*. There was an informal class leader, "higher" than everyone (*vyshchyi za vsikh*), his powerful buddies (two or three guys), and the lower people, who comply because they prefer to, or because they have been "defeated" by the gang. The leader (unlike the class president) is not elected by the student body. Rather, he comes to power and rules by force. He is rough (*zhorstokyi*), and he pushes others around (*obizhaie*), imposing his dominance through verbal humiliation and/or physical abuse. Leaders changed from time to time, but that was always the result of a power struggle involving physical confrontation. Students told me that this hierarchy usually begins to manifest itself in the ninth grade (i.e., what would be considered the first year of high school in the North American context). However, even when a ninth grader became the "leader" of his class, the eleventh graders could still easily pressure him or beat him up. In other words, the hierarchy within the class was still subsumed by a larger hierarchy based on seniority (this is reminiscent of the hierarchy found in the Soviet army, and the particular form of bullying [referred to as *dedovshchina* in Russian] present among conscripts).

Zhenia, a ninth grader who often shared with me his perspective on the way power was wielded in the school context, recounts his attempt to move up the class hierarchy:

> *Zhenia:* I was getting to the top of the class, and that's when the problems started for me, because the highest (*vyshchi*) didn't want the competition. They prevented me from accessing the cafeteria by sitting on the steps, and my only way out was to fight with one boy. Now I'm in the middle . . .
>
> *AF:* What kind of power do you have in the middle?
>
> *Zhenia:* None! One day I tried to do like them, to use a lot of swear words, to say something bad to the lower people in the class, but it was terrible. It was only for one day and that's it. [. . .] I'm not very muscular, so I want peace, not war. But the higher ones are rude, it's a constant competition. Actually, it's a war for more power. It's like a game, and also like an addiction: you always want more and more control over your people.
>
> *AF:* Why do you think things are this way?

Zhenia: It's what we have in Ukraine and Russia, even at the level of
our government, it's the same. We must have power or we will
not survive.

The kinds of hierarchies associated with bullying exist in schools around
the globe. Yet what is interesting about the Ukrainian context is that based
on my observations, students drew on certain elements of bandit and prison
culture in the articulation of their own power struggles. The "prison culture" on which they drew was not monolithic, but rather a multilayered
construct that included Soviet, post-Soviet, and global elements. For example, many Ukrainian citizens have experienced gulag or prison life, and
grandparents still tell jokes from their time in Siberia. Finkelstein states that
between 1917 and 1987, about one in every six Soviet citizens served time in
a prison camp (2001: 2). Romanticized versions of life in the Gulag are also
disseminated through Soviet-era songs (e.g., the ones by Russian artists Vys-
sotsky and Kobzon). The language, practices, and hierarchies of the prison,
this time enhanced with post-Soviet elements, are also central to Russian
big-budget films and television series that depict the lives of bandits. These
films and series are in turn very popular among schoolchildren. In addition,
students are increasingly exposed to global "gangster culture," and although
they do not, as far as I could see, imitate the style of dress associated with
that culture, I noticed some use of American prison slang. This was hardly
surprising since some students were avid listeners of so-called "gangsta rap"
(e.g., the music of DMX and 2Pac, Tupak Shakur).[5]

Perhaps students' everyday exposure to prison culture came to bear on
their performance of power in a variety of contexts. It is also possible that
there was something particular to the school as an institution that led students to include prison culture elements in their bullying hierarchies. Although students never explicitly referred to the school as a prison (at least
not in my presence), they often perceived the time spent in school as time
spent in captivity. The principals' prohibition on exiting the school during
breaks (a rule enforced by uniformed guards) only exacerbated this feeling.
Perhaps then an implicit parallel was being drawn between the struggles of
prisoners and students' efforts at gaining maximum power (as well as a certain kind of freedom) in an institutional setting in which they were compelled by law to spend most of their time. There were clearly alternate ways
of gaining power within the school setting. One could, for example, be
elected president of one's class. The president's duties were often limited to

helping the teacher, however (bringing him the grade book, running errands, etc.). One could also gain respect by performing well in school and becoming a gold medal contender (pictures of the contenders in each grade were posted on corridor walls). The informal hierarchy differed in that it was power gained in relation to school authorities and in relation to one's classmates.

I was in the schoolyard with a group of male students at the end of the school day, when one of their classmates walked by. They pointed him out to me as the bully of their class, saying, "He's the *pakhan* [prison slang for the "authority" in a cell, prison, or prison colony]!" I was attending the history lesson in a ninth-grade class one day and this same individual, the one students called by his last name ("Yaremchuk"), was in attendance, sitting in the back as usual. Unlike the other informal leaders, he wore his hair long, and nothing about his clothes revealed his "status." At some point during the lesson, his cell phone rang. He had set his phone to ring to the same tune as the (bandit) protagonist's phone in the cult Russian bandit film *Bumer*. After answering and speaking briefly on the phone (over the history teacher's definition of "Constitution"), Yaremchuk kept on humming the *Bumer* tune.

I administered a questionnaire on the informal hierarchy to two ninth-grade classes (a total of 47 students). In the questionnaire, I asked students about their friends and enemies in the class, about conflicts among students, and whether there was anyone they considered an informal leader ("*neformal'nyi lider*") in the class. If so, what did he/she do as a leader? Would the respondent like to be a leader? Answers to the two last questions were most revealing of the kind of power possessed by the leader. Students' description of the actions of the leader included statements such as: "He beats everyone up [*Vin usikh bi'e*]" (most respondents connected informal leadership to the wielding of force), or "He rests [Ukr./Rus. *Vin odykhaie*]," or "He sits in class and drinks beer!" The use of violence, the refusal to work (the ninth-grade leader "Yaremchuk" always sat in the back, and others took notes for him, if absolutely necessary),[6] and illicit activity involving drugs and alcohol were thus central to informal leadership. In answer to the question, *Would you like to be an informal leader? What would you do as a leader?* most students denied any ambition for this kind of leadership, and even considered it bad to have an informal leader. "No, I don't want to," wrote a female student. "Because when there is a leader, there are people who are of a 'lower level' [*nyzhchyi riven'*] than him. I don't agree with this.... The leader should have *knowledge*, or a talent of some kind through which he can engage with other students." In contrast, another student whose colleagues had in majority identified as the informal leader of the class wrote (rather crudely) in response to whether he would want to be an informal leader: "Yes! Everyone would have to suck my dick [this was written in Russian (gulag) prison slang: *Vsim za shchichku davav!*]." In prison settings around the world, this act exemplifies submission to the leader. Even if the student meant this as a joke, it does tell us something about his understanding of "informal leadership" and its privileges, that is, what "power" might mean for the leader under conditions of "captivity" (the prison, the school). Let us now turn to power as it was exercised in relation to school authorities and in relation to classmates.

Informal leaders were defiant when they refused to work, or when they smuggled alcohol into the classroom. What characterized their relationship with school authorities, however, was their use of force. The principal of the public school forbade students to exit the school during breaks, claiming that they might get into trouble with drugs. Every time the bell rang for the break, however, students would rush down the stairs to the main hall toward the doors, trying to get there before the security guard, a man of around sixty, could lock it and physically block the way. They never got there early enough, and so various tactics were used to get out, including begging the guard, lying to him about having to go home, or trying to buy him off by promising to get him cigarettes or ice cream outside (tactics that *mostly* failed).

These kinds of negotiations could be observed from a sitting area adjacent to the door, while waiting for student informants or for the bell. Sometimes the guard would resort to quizzing those students who wanted out, and history was his favorite subject. "What was the date of the Pereiaslav Treaty?" he would ask, playing riddles like the Sphinx in his improvised checkpoint. If the student answered correctly, he or she could go through. The "highest guys" of the eleventh grade (whom classmates referred to as "bandits") had a different strategy for exiting the school, however. They threatened the guard or simply physically pushed him aside. The guard might in turn threaten them weakly or show them his fist. But he let them through because, in the words of one student, "He's afraid to be beaten up." The guard himself told me that today's kids "know their rights. We [meaning, people of the Soviet generation] don't know anything, but they know their rights. They tell me I can't touch them. Well I'll *show* them a thing or two! They can bring me to court, I don't care!" The fact remains that he let the "bandits" through, the ones for whom the principal had created the rule in the first place.

The students indeed "knew their rights," and especially the right not to be physically punished by school authorities, a right entrenched in the constitution. Adopted in 1996, the Ukrainian constitution stipulates that "Any violence against a child, or his or her exploitation shall be prosecuted by law" (Article 52). In 2002, the Ministry of Education and Science of Ukraine also passed a law on the "Rights of the Student" that was to apply to every school in the country. The law stipulates that "Pupils have the right . . . to protection against any form of exploitation, psychological and physical force [*nasyllia*] that break the law or undermine [*prynyzhuiut'*] their honor or dignity; to protection and safe conditions of education, upbringing and work." These principles were made available to students in their civics textbook, *Foundations of Civics (Ninth Grade)*: "The law stands on the side of the rights of pupils, [and of] students, guaranteeing them protection from any form of force, undermining of honor or dignity by teachers, professors and other workers in the educational sphere" (Usenko et al. 2002: 160). Crucially, students' *rights* had become teachers' *duties*. In fact, according to the 2002 law, teachers were obligated to "maintain pedagogical ethics, morals, [and] respect the dignity of students; protect students against any form of physical or psychological force [*nasyl'stvo*]." Clearly, these principles constituted a legal limit to the guards' (or others') use of force against students. Yet such knowledge, especially in the hands of the informal leaders, could become powerful ammunition in the power struggle between students and authorities. Even when they were breaking school rules, the leaders would remind the guard that he could not touch them. "Get your hands off me or I'll sue you," once said the "leader" of an eleventh-grade class when the guard, following the principal's orders, attempted to prevent him from stepping outside. Yet the informal leaders had no qualms about using force themselves against the guard, paying no heed to the principle that "your right stops where you infringe upon another's." In addition, they converted "negative liberty," or the idea that one is free from external constraints (in this case, the right of the child to be respected by adults), into "positive liberty," or the ability for an individual to do what they want (Birch 1993: 10). The bandit leaders deployed the notion of "rights" itself in order to gain the upper hand in their power struggle with the authorities. They were not looking for a relation of equality or mutual respect, but rather, for dominance. Thus the law of the country, in their hands, became a tool for intimidation, or a weapon of sorts. Sarat and Kearns note that "rights can become vehicles through which persons try on, invent, and imagine new identities and new ways of being in the world" (1997: 8). In this case, the leaders were definitely engaging with liberal ideals, but without wholly subscribing to them. The students' claims are a good example of "social actors . . . us[ing] 'the law' to legitimize self-interested actions" (Herzfeld 2005: 2). We could argue here that the principals' flexible appropriation and arbitrary application of school rules served this same purpose of intimidation. But perhaps both sides' use of the law as a "tool of oppression" (Wanner 2005) was symptomatic of the new power struggle in which they were engaged. In addition, by invoking rights that limited the authorities' power (and especially the use of physical force or pressure tactics), the leaders consolidated their monopoly over force in the school context. Why monopoly? In the private school, a faded photocopy was taped to the wall above a plastic plant in the teachers' lounge. Published by the Ministry of Education and Science of Ukraine, the document listed the "don'ts" of teaching, enjoining teachers not to use physical punishment or the verbal humiliation of students. It is no wonder that teachers could perceive students as usurping their power (or at least the power grounded in force). Several scholars (e.g., Ries 2002, Humphrey 2002, Hobsbawm 1969) have pointed out how the collapse of the state (and especially, the weakening of its coercive abilities) may leave room for the bandit element to emerge, resulting not so much in chaos as in a violent order, or what Nazpary (2002) refers to as a "chaotic mode of domination."

The informal leaders invoked rights to achieve monopoly over force, and this monopoly in turn allowed them to enjoy even more rights, including the "right" to walk out of the school when they felt like it. A female student claimed about the informal leaders that "They have *all the rights* [*Vony maiut' vsi prava*]." And yet rights in this usage connote privileges, or freedoms based on desires (a long way from the teachers' understanding of rights in terms of duties). The rights enjoyed by the informal leaders were secured through force rather than the force of *law*. In fact, perhaps the informal leaders possessed "rights" not enjoyed by other students precisely because their use of force positioned them above the law or in this case, above school rules. The idea seemed to be that freedom could only be enjoyed when one was beyond (or no longer subjected to) school rules. This points to the challenge, for students *and* their teachers, in conceiving of freedom as *civic* freedom, or freedom *within* the rules rather than outside of them. The notion of "rights" itself reflected this imaginary.

Undoubtedly, the informal leaders presented to their fellow students an alternative to the formal school hierarchy and the possibility of individual noncompliance. In addition, they could also lead collective disobedience since they were usually the ones who, by virtue of their confidence and authority over others, felt at ease in challenging the teacher in all kinds of ways. They were also usually the ones initiating mini–class rebellions, whereby students simply refused to comply with any of the demands of the teacher. Through their actions, they staged a particular kind of freedom in relation to authorities. Although the informal leader or *pakhan* bore elements of the rebellious hero, however, he also inspired fear in his classmates. Not surprisingly, in a ninth-grade class in the public school, students told me that they were more afraid of the *pakhan* than of the teacher. As we saw above, the *pakhan*, unlike the teacher, had the ability to administer physical punishment, and this, in or outside the school setting.

While the student hierarchy constituted an *alternate* hierarchy, in reality, only those two or three students at the top of the class hierarchy had power (conceived primarily as coercive power over others). In other words, students were performing an alternative distribution of power, but it was not a *democratic* alternative. The informal leaders were not revolutionaries, for while their hierarchy was one that arose against authority, it mirrored to a large degree the formal hierarchy of the school. Just like the latter, it was based on coercion. Students at the top of the hierarchy tended to reproduce within their own hierarchies the kind of unfair, arbitrary power against which they struggled.

Young people in the school were ambivalent about the informal leaders. The latter seemed to rule arbitrarily, but at the same time produced a kind of "order" (grounded in force) felt to be lacking in the school context. A friend of mine, a university student in her late twenties, responded to my query about what attracts youth to bandit culture by saying: "They want to escape the disorder [*bezporiadok*] of society [resulting from the collapse of the Soviet Union]. You know, in the *zona* [the "zone," or prison camp] everything is well organized, the prisoners' hierarchy is clearly defined, the division of power is clear. Everyone knows their place." In some sense, the informal leaders in the school may have acted as guardians of order (e.g., through physical punishment) in the context of the weakening of school authorities. As a class president in the public school explained to me casually: "There is a hierarchy in class. It's like in the country: there's a president, prime minister. . . ."

In class we also have the higher ones and lower ones. The higher ones smoke, drink, take drugs; the lower ones are trying to show that they are cool, but they are nothing. They know that they are lower." In fact, the informal hierarchy gave a sense of predictability even to the students who were lowest within it. It became a part of their school identity, as I realized when students were introduced to me by their peers first by nickname, then (if non-Ukrainian or non-Russian) by nationality, and then according to their place in the hierarchy. This could go something like, "This is Flathead, he's Kazakh, and he's the *shestiorka* (a term used to identify the "lowest of the low" in the gulag/prison hierarchy), he gets beat up a lot."

This kind of discourse presents us with an imaginary of the world in which there are only bandits who rule by force and "slaves" (or *shestiorky*) who comply. Students indeed seemed to view power relations in the school setting (whether between students and school authority or among students) in terms of only two alternatives: being a *slave* (as students claimed to be in school) and thus having "no rights," or being a *bandit*, and thus enjoying "all rights." Both the slave and the bandit are categories that are beyond (beneath or above) the law.

Why is it then that students seem to engage with rights primarily *through the repertoire of the bandit or outlaw*? What were the challenges of imagining rights and freedoms *within* the law/within regulation in the school context? We have seen how school authorities tend to define young citizens' rights in terms of duties or obligations. In addition, teachers often interpret students' assertion of their rights (i.e., their association of rights with freedoms) as "excessive," that is, as a threat to their authority. This perhaps gives the message to students that one can only enjoy rights and freedoms once one is (powerful enough to be) above the law. In addition, the repertoire of the bandit allows students not only to articulate their "legitimate" rights (e.g., the right not to be verbally or physically harassed by teachers or administrators), but also to enact some of their desires, as well as test limits. In fact, it is often difficult to draw the line between rights and privileges or excess. Chapter 1 described a ninth-grade history book in which students had transformed the major figures of the French Revolution into famous pirates. While both revolutionaries and pirates are in a relation of exteriority to the law, one could argue that their aims are somewhat different. While the revolutionaries' actions were framed by a concern for social justice, the pirates' freedom was sustained by random pillaging. Where are we to position the students' bandit-like behavior in relation to these? As previously mentioned, the informal leaders of the class were not revolutionaries in that they did not seek to break with established models of authority. They did not have an "ideology," and their concerns were not those of Hobsbawm's social bandit. They were more like pirates in that they ruled by force (a force not ideologically sanctioned), and their freedom resided in their relation of exteriority to the law (understood here as school rules).

From "Small Bandits" to "Big Bandits": Narratives of Capitalism

As mentioned above, students drew largely on media images in their construction of the bandit repertoire. In bandit films and television series, the bandit appeared mostly as an *outlaw* hero. Yet during the period of my fieldwork, many people spoke of an erosion in the boundary between the bandit (as outlaw) and the state or government (as guarantor of the law). Young and old described a process whereby common criminals and outlaws had become involved in government at the highest level. They stated that this had gradually changed the composition of Ukrainian elites. Immediately following Ukrainian independence (under Kravchuk's presidency, 1991–1994), the Ukrainian political elite had been comprised mostly of former dissidents. Many of them had spent several years in Soviet labor camps for "political crimes." The dissidents tended to share the vision of a Ukraine based on humanism, patriotism, religion, moral values, and integration into the European sphere. Yet starting in the mid-1990s, a new class had emerged, a class that my informants referred to as the "new Russians" or "new Ukrainians," and whose wealth was acquired mainly through economic activity in the unregulated post-Soviet market. These activities ranged from currency speculation to the illegal sale of state assets. As the story went, most of Ukraine's so-called oligarchs had first started out by organizing protection rackets in local markets or selling illegal goods from Poland. The Ukrainian oligarch Rinat Akhmetov, who allegedly began his career as a racketeer, is now the richest man in the country. When I came back to Ukraine in 2003 after a five-year absence, a Ukrainian friend warned me: "There are no small bandits anymore." He was referring to what he saw as the entanglement of the criminal element with the country's government, a process that produced "big bandits." The so-called big bandits became a political force that could compete with the former dissidents (although in some cases, the latter were said to have "defected" to their side). The result was the coexistence of the former political prisoners' values (political freedoms, humanism), and values based on toughness and force as a source of power, profit at all costs, and so on. While former dissidents had sought to become part of Europe through a focus on shared civility, peace, and tolerance, the "new rich" at the head of the country had also engaged with something "Western": capitalism. At times, however, their performance of capitalism appeared to be based on the *Soviet* representation of American capitalism, that is, brute force, selfishness, backstabbing, and complete absence of morals (thus the need to be "tough and mean"). What connected these two elite groups was not only their attempt to engage with what they perceived as "the West," but also their experience of the prison or *zona* (the dissidents as political prisoners, and the "New Rich" as perpetrators of fraud or other crimes). Yet the two groups had a different take on the meaning of "freedom." Would freedom be found in humanism and social justice or in the power and prosperity born of "wild capitalism"?

To Be a Person or to "Be Somebody"?

Let us come back for a moment to the student's bandit-like recitation of poetry in the Ukrainian literature class. Perhaps Zhora's *simultaneous* performance of the obedient patriot and of the arrogant, fear-inspiring bandit revealed a deeper tension within post-Soviet societies. When Svetlana's son-in-law used the expression "dual standard" to describe this performance, could he have been referring to two coexisting standards in operation within the larger society? The subjectivity of the "patriot" emerged as part of a conscious project (defined primarily by former dissidents), that of person-making and nation- and state-building, as seen in Chapter 2. The repertoire of the "bandit," in contrast, was not officially promoted by the state, yet was ubiquitous in the media and on the streets. It seems that in a newly competitive economy, students must constantly negotiate the tension between "being a [civilized] person" (and thus a good citizen), and "being *somebody*" (i.e., being assertive, shrewd, and crafty enough to survive).

Students clearly found advantages to performing both the patriot and the bandit. They wrote long essays about the importance of being a good person, of caring about others and not thinking only of oneself, of respecting one another, and so on. Many students claimed to be living by these values and were intent on becoming good patriots. Yet as we have seen, the subjectivity of the patriot *in its classroom incarnation* was often incompatible with the kinds of rights and freedoms sought by students. From the students' perspective, the relation between the bandit and freedom (at least in the school context) was much less "virtual" than that between the patriot and freedom. The bandit or outlaw thus became a point of entry for discourses and practices around rights. Since students could not obtain the kinds of rights they wanted within the "arbitrary" set of rules of the school, they had to position themselves outside of these. This positioning in turn allowed them to invoke "rights" along the continuum of civic rights (guaranteed by the constitution) *and* freedoms associated with desire and excess.

Chapter 4

The "Bandit State": From State Force to the Violent Pedagogies of Capitalism

In November 2004, I was visiting the Western Ukrainian city of L'viv with a class when students pointed to a peculiar graffiti in Ukrainian (Cyrillic alphabet): "KUCHMAFIYANUKOVYCH." The inscription was a visual representation of what many citizens saw as the entanglement of government (President Kuchma and Prime Minister Yanukovych) and bandits (Mafia). Citizens also used the metaphor of the "bandit government/state [*bandyts'ka vlada*]" to refer to Leonid Kuchma's administration, and this kind of language came to be central to mass mobilization around the Orange Revolution. The concept of "bandit state" seems counterintuitive given the traditional view of bandits as existing in a relation of antagonism to state authorities (see, for example, Hobsbawm's [1969] depiction of the "social bandit"). In his work on the Sicilian mafia, however, Blok (1974) notes that "violent entrepreneurs" may have a more ambiguous relation with state authorities. Some scholars have pointed to similarities between the *tactics* of mafia and state, including the routinized extraction of resources and the consolidation of a monopoly over the use of force (Blok 1974), as well as the fulfillment of discipline and punishment (Ries 2002: 309).

Studies of the post-Soviet context suggest that following the collapse of the Soviet Union, bandits came to "substitute" for the state in certain areas, filling a power vacuum in the field of economic regulation (Varese 2001) and political functions (Volkov 2002). For example, Ries (2002) argues that in Russia as a place of weak governance, bandits (or mafia) maintain "order" where the state cannot, for example by taking over state functions such as the protection of private property (racketeering). Volkov (2002) states that the Russian bandit, urban and well integrated into commercial activity but armed and always ready to resort to violence (59), is well connected to local authorities and considers cooperation with the latter unproblematic (61). This suggests that bandits are moving from the margins to the "center" of the state. The shared characteristics, substitutability, and collaboration between state and criminal realm all contribute to the emergence of the local category of "bandit state" as a device for making sense of post-Soviet power.

While some analyses of post-Soviet power speak of the entanglement of "bandit" and "state," each term tends to remain conceptually separate from the other. During the second half of Leonid Kuchma's presidency (1999–2004), however, Ukrainian citizens understood the boundary between bandits and state to be so blurred that they were often at pains to describe and analyze the kind of power they were experiencing. In this context, the "state" becomes difficult to pin down (but equally difficult to evade). The previous chapters focused on the state as it is apprehended through the everyday routines of the school and implementation of the curriculum. However, young people's experience of the state cannot be fully explained with reference to these "intentional" manifestations and interventions. Moving to the streets as a site of informal learning allows us to capture the inadvertent effects on young people of the (sometimes staged) chaos associated with the "bandit state." Just like educational settings, the streets produce their own disciplines, and in Ukraine, the latter come to be interpreted by citizens as violent pedagogies.

From Fate to State

Following the collapse of the Soviet Union, bandits became the source of much anxiety and rumor. The apartment doors in most buildings were bullet-proof, and I had specific instructions *never* to open the door to strangers. Svetlana, the teacher with whom I lived, exchanged stories with neighbors and colleagues of unlucky people who had been robbed, attacked, or killed by bandits. One story in particular struck me. Svetlana had heard it from a colleague and related it to me one night after dinner: A fourteen-year-old girl was coming back from school when she noticed an elderly woman struggling with her shopping bags at the entrance of a building. The woman hailed the girl, asking her if she could help with the bags. Eager to be of assistance, the girl carried the bags up the stairs to the woman's apartment

door and was on her way down when the woman unlocked the door and
asked the girl to bring the bags over the threshold. The girl was hesitant but
did as she was told. Once she had stepped inside the apartment, a man (the
woman's relative, or someone else?) appeared. He attacked the girl brutally
and did "whatever he wanted [*vse shcho vin khotiv*]" with her. "Imagine
that," said Svetlana, shuddering, "a young girl who knew nothing about the
world and was just trying to help." The story is chilling precisely because in
it, an honest girl willing to help is victimized. However (and I will return to
other aspects of this story later), one of the characteristics of such stories is
that they did not in fact happen to *everyone*. Bandits struck *randomly*, and
thus such instances were "unfortunate events [*neshchasni vypadky*]."

Students recounted another story that circulated at the time (I will limit
myself to the essence): One night in September 2000, the young journalist
Heorhiy Gongadze took the trash out to the bin outside his building. He
disappeared. A few weeks later, his headless body was found in the woods
outside of Kyiv. Gongadze had been a harsh critic of President Kuchma, and
the SBU (Ukrainian security services) had warned him several times. Following the incident, government representatives had immediately blamed
Gongadze's death on a random act of violence: "bandits" had been after his
wallet, or alternately, his death was gang-related.

For those telling the story, the government's use of the "bandit explanation" served the purpose of "covering up" a "state" deed. Blaming a political
assassination on a random act of violence may indeed divert attention from
the authorities and clear state representatives of responsibility. Bandits are
particularly useful as scapegoats because they are traditionally seen as operating in a realm *opposite* to that of the state, that is, outside the law. Therefore, state authorities may easily distance themselves from the actions of
bandits, thugs, or hooligans, that is to say, they may easily *dis*own them. Yet
in this particular case, it may be that the power of Gongadze's death also
hinged on having citizens believe that the state (*vlada*) was somehow involved.
The state authorities' reference to bandits accomplished in some sense the
melding of the *randomness* of the bandit and the *intentionality* of the state.
It produced a kind of governance in which *state* effects and *fate* effects
became one for citizens.

Throughout my fieldwork, discourses circulated about state activities
being by nature shrouded in secrecy. For example, whenever things seemed
to be looking up for the opposition, the latter's supporters would say, referring to the *vlada*, "They will think of something [*Vony shchos' prydumaiut'*]."

When government-controlled media reported on the accidental death of a (usually pro-Western) prominent political figure, some people might claim: "This is not a coincidence/this is not by chance [*Tse ne vypadkovo*]." Others would say, "There are no coincidences in this country." True, based on newspaper accounts and people's narratives, the road accident in particular seemed to reveal a kind of "script": a Kamaz (a truck weighing several tons) usually drives slowly on the right side of the traffic lane on a two-lane highway, and as the car containing the "target" attempts to pass it, the truck suddenly veers to the left, causing a (usually deadly) collision. (Presidential candidate Viktor Yushchenko escaped alive from a similar scenario during the 2004 elections campaign.) There are lots of Kamaz trucks in circulation, however, and accidents are frequent: I can attest to many near misses, some involving Kamazes, while on the road with locals during my stay. To me, it remained conceivable that important people could die in genuine accidents. However, there was, for many, this sense of a kind of *state script parading as chance* that constituted the geography of everyday life for ordinary people (*prosti liudy*, connoting people who are not in power, and therefore innocent of the authorities' machinations). Nothing was by chance, and everything was bound in some way to state power and its maintenance. These kinds of statements and explanations had been present during the Soviet period, especially (but not only) among members of the intelligentsia, whose ideological transgressions made them the target of intimidation, deportations, or prison sentences. Thus this profound distrust of state authorities is not new. What *is* new is the type of uncertainty experienced, and the degree to which a profound feeling of vulnerability seems to spread from "dissidents" to the whole of society in the wake of the collapse.

This discourse was prevalent not only among people who had spent most of their lives under Soviet rule and who had experienced some form of political repression, but also among high school students, who often articulated ideas about their state that seemed akin to "conspiracy theory." "Everything is fixed," they would say. Or, "Those at the top will find a way to stay in power," or, reflecting on the upcoming presidential elections: "The richer candidate will win." The latter statement in particular is revealing of the new and mysterious power attributed to money. In fact, the encounter with capitalism itself seems to alter local notions of causality. For example, money seems to magically appear, and people in turn magically disappear because of it (Wanner 2005). As Nazpary (2002) argues about Kazakhstan, "The breakdown of social trust and the sudden emergence of the *random and invisible logic of the market forces* accompanied by the alienated and alienating greed for accumulation of capital, bolstered by the enormous use of force, create the experience of a very radical ontological disruption" (5; emphasis added). Taussig writes of terror that is "dissolve[s] certainty every bit as much as it prey[s] on one's heartfelt desire to find its secret order" (1992: 9). One could perhaps argue that similarly, political and economic chaos produced a longing to uncover its hidden structure and logic.

Many students in both the public and private schools became fans of a television documentary series that sought to go "behind the scenes" of the encounter with capitalism and to chronicle the actions of the "invisible hand of the market" (Verdery 1996) and the equally invisible hand of the state in its entanglement with market activities. The weekly series *Zakryta Zona* (Forbidden Zone) was hosted by an investigative journalist whose mission it was to document the involvement of top government officials in criminal activities, including illegal privatization, blackmail, and assassinations. This show aired on the Fifth Channel, the only opposition channel on Ukrainian television (although the channel was not available everywhere in the country, most people in Kyiv had access to it). The show clearly framed the *vlada* as criminals whose disorder left visible traces, from corpses to pillaged and ruined factories, to Swiss bank accounts, to multimillion-dollar mansions in the Carpathian mountains. The stated objective of the series was to deliver the truth to citizens, and to many people whose sympathies lay with the opposition, it seemed a godsend given the general situation with the media. Yet after watching such an episode, one could only conclude (and, based on my observations, many did), that "everything was fixed," and that the *vlada* "would stop at nothing" to maintain its power. Students who had watched the show discussed it among themselves in school in the morning, often appalled by its "revelations." Thus (and notwithstanding the intent and the courage exhibited by the journalists involved) it seems that the effect of the series was to simultaneously shed light on *and further mystify* the activities of the *vlada*. In his study of rumors in Haiti, Perice (1997) argues that rumors could be seen both as a form of resistance against the authorities (a way to break the silence, a way to communicate information) and as a form that reproduced accounts of the authorities' excesses and thus bolstered their power. While the accounts broadcast on the Fifth Channel may not have belonged (entirely) to the realm of rumor, it seems that they might have had similar effects. The media's articulation of the state's "disorder" might make arbitrariness and chaos more bearable and give citizens some sense of control. Yet if citizens come to believe that "everything is fixed," they are more likely to be constantly on alert. They may become complicit in their own subjection insofar as they exercise a form of self-surveillance and self-regulation.

Chance may be defined as "something that happens unpredictably without discernible human intention or observable cause" (*Merriam Webster* 1993: 190). Yet the blurring of intentionality and randomness in everyday experience, or what we might call "state effects" and "fate effects," resulted in chance (as a realm of the everyday) seemingly losing its autonomy. Apparent in everyday discourses was the erosion of chance as a realm independent of state power. Chance as a space of alternate configurations thus became colonized by state representatives who invoked it, and by citizens who could not shake the state out of it. The conditions of possibility for interpreting the unusual as real chance or coincidence were thus partially suspended. Chance became suspect. Newly bearing the seal of intention, script, or plan, chance became thought of as *fate* (or *dolia* in Ukrainian). Fate, in contrast with chance, is compatible with plan. However, in the Eastern Orthodox tradition, it is understood as *God*'s plan, not a plan depending on human intention.[1] What arises from the melding of state effects and fate effects is the idea of the state sharing in God's power, and thus in some way willing citizens' fate. While fate implies some sort of intent or structure, it remains, to those living it, secret, unknowable, yet unchangeable. The randomness and unpredictability associated with fate in turn shapes subjects in particular ways. Here, fate as an "antecedent of authority" (Herzfeld 2001: 224) combines with the "rational" state to produce certain kinds of subjects.

The *Catholic Encyclopedia* (2003) states that divine providence, "more than a mere vision or knowledge . . . implies the active disposition and arrangement of things with a view to a definite end. . . . Providence as expressed in the created order of things is . . . called Fate." In his essay on governmentality (1991), Foucault quotes the following statement by Guillaume de La Perrière: "government is the right disposition of things, arranged so as to lead to a convenient end" (93). Though the ends may differ, the particular disposition of things is where fate and government meet. Foucault (1991) defines governmentality as a set of strategies and tactics (or even laws used as tactics) aimed at molding conduct so as to maximize the welfare of the population. Perhaps the latter part of the definition (the goals) would convince us that the concept of "governmentality" is ill-suited in this case. Yet it all depends on how one understands "welfare." Yurchak (2002) speaks of "entrepreneurial governmentality" in postsocialist Russia as what makes it possible to "relate to different aspects of the world—people, relations, institutions, the state, laws—in terms of symbolic commodities, risks, capital, profits, costs, needs, demands, and so on," and to know "who and what can be acted upon in an entrepreneurial way" (279). The ultimate end here may be to dispose and intervene upon individuals in such a way as to enhance the chances of surviving capitalism. Though the term "surviving" is used here, the category of needs, and thus of welfare, can be expanded to include luxury goods, as will become apparent in Chapter 5. Perhaps the goal of this particular form of governmentality is to partake in capitalism's "normality," however defined. Everyone might be engaged, to some extent, in this process, for example, creating certain types of networks that enhance one's chance for a "good life." (Students themselves hoped for a "good life" and were becoming aware of the kinds of struggles necessary to achieving it.) Yet when those individuals who have at their disposal brute force or other coercive means exercise power over those who do not have such access, various popular discourses of conspiracy and injustice are likely to arise.

In his book *Post-Soviet Chaos: Violence and Dispossession in Kazakhstan* (2002), Jacob Rigi, under what he later reveals to be the pseudonym "Joma Nazpary" (2007: 27), suggests that popular notions of chaos can be translated not as "meaningless anarchy," but rather in terms of a "chaotic mode of domination" (7). The latter is characterized by the (intertwined) "over-centralized arbitrariness of state officials" and "anarchic arbitrariness of the members of different informal networks of influence [including criminal networks]" (7). Rigi argues that the actions of those in power are "hidden" from the population through the staging of spectacles (e.g., military invasions) that "compensate the lack of transparency in power mechanisms" (2007: 45). Yet some displays of power in Ukraine seemed, in a sense, to "do justice" to post-Soviet insecurity and chaos, and could perhaps be thought of as "spectacles of ambiguity." The melding of chance and intention could be seen on the everyday terrain of governance in the country.

In early April 2004, President Kuchma had called for a "civic forum" to take place in one of the convention centers of the city. The forum hosted more than 3,000 representatives of Ukrainian civic organizations that supported government-initiated reforms to the Ukrainian constitution. A special resolution of the forum claimed: "We are sure that [the constitutional reform] will to a large extent boost the prospects of the socioeconomic development of our state, the establishment of civic society, the observance of human rights, and Ukraine's role and place in the European community" (RFE/RL 2004).

Because President Kuchma himself was attending the forum, roads had been closed and traffic rerouted. Cordons of uniformed police officers ensured that no one could approach the building within a radius of four hundred feet (standard procedure in the United States as well). That day, I was on my way to the nearest subway station. The station had some entrances blocked, with signs informing citizens of (sudden) "repairs [*remont*]." Inside the station, in the passageway leading to the ticket booths and on either side of me stood rows of men (and only men) leaning against the walls with about two feet or less distance between them. Approximately fifty of them stood in the short corridor, and then about fifty more through the doors along the wall with the ticket booth. The men were approximately the same height and weight. They were all dressed in a similar fashion, in clothes that I would call, for lack of a better term, "civilian uniforms," consisting of black clothes and black caps, with no badges or visible traces of the state. They appeared not to know each other. Most significantly, they stood there in *nonchalant* poses (civilian poses that said, "I'm just here waiting for somebody") of those who are up to no good. The men's postures were of the kind one would encounter in a dark alley. They signaled readiness for violence but without the discipline or restraint in body and face shown by the police officers positioned around the building. It was like choreographed and aggressive nonchalance, an "orderly disorder" of sorts. For me, the uncanny: I recognized the military part of the performance, as well as the civilian (yet somehow hostile) part, but in this case, the men performed both or perhaps neither.

Both the adults and young people I later spoke to about this encounter told me that "everyone knew" these men were connected to the government (*vlada*) in some way. One of my student informants suggested that I had encountered "Kuchma's goons," an expression that did little to demystify the arrangement. No one could explain to me the exact nature of the connection between these men and the state, and theories abounded. Maybe the men were secret police or a "special unit" on the state's (regular) payroll? Perhaps they were former Soviet security services employees who were now working in the private security sector but had been hired to assist with the event? Alternately, perhaps the men were hired thugs or criminals who had been recruited for the day?

Why did the authorities choose such a display of security? Why not place *uniformed* police officers inside the subway station, just as they had done outside? Perhaps they feared that too many uniformed officers might appear excessive (too much like a police state). This is a plausible explanation in a country that foreigners tend to perceive as "postauthoritarian." (As we saw, this understanding of Ukraine is also disseminated by some teachers in their classes.) The presence of different kinds of security in different kinds of spaces is also interesting. Presumably, the audience of the civic forum (including international representatives) would be exposed to the "normality" of the police force deployed around the building. Yet for the citizens going about their everyday business in the "underground" space of the subway, a special kind of security force was at work: one whose intentions were difficult to discern and whose connection to state authorities appeared more tenuous.

It is common in countries around the world to position *undercover* (i.e., unnoticeable or less noticeable) agents at strategic points in such circumstances. Yet the men described above did not simply watch citizens, but themselves came to stand as visible symbols of power. Because the exact nature of their connection with the state was unknown, they could be seen and sensed as a form of power that is "simultaneously of and not of the state" (see, for example, Sanford 2004 on the paramilitary in Colombia).[2] The military- or policelike order they displayed (the fact that there were only men, their sheer number, their similar physical proportions, their black attire, the military-like distance between them) was inseparable from their casual yet aggressive civilian postures.

To attribute the "orderly" elements to the state and the "disorderly" ones to bandits would be to reproduce the traditional view of the state as a bulwark against violence. The overlap between the repertoires of state and bandits seem to reveal instead something about the state's intimate connection with violence (even in its excessive forms). Taylor (1997) points out that governments may seek to appropriate or mirror the tactics of those who lie outside the state and the law (e.g., criminals, subversives, terrorists). In this way, the state may position itself simultaneously within and outside the law. The power of this performance (whether it was actually "staged" by the government, or whether it is simply a visible effect of the increasing privatization of sovereignty) seemed to lay precisely in the impossibility for the citizen to completely disentangle bandits (thugs, goons) from state, thus making the limits of state power impossible to apprehend.

The blurring of "state" and "civic" realms in the domain of security is something that existed under socialism as well. In *The Book of Laughter and Forgetting* (1978), Milan Kundera describes a particular scene in socialist

Czechoslovakia. A man has been followed to his former girlfriend's apartment by men in plain clothes whom he knows to be police. When he points to them, his former girlfriend asks him: "So now you think everyone is persecuting you?" He wonders to himself how she can be so cynical and tell him that the men staring at them with such insolence are only there by chance. She plays their game, he thinks, and the game consists in acting as though the secret police did not exist and no one was persecuted. Yet when he leaves, one learns that she knows and understands the danger he faces, yet has wanted to hide the truth from him, as well as from herself. Thus the simultaneous performance of "state" and "civic" realms, of intention and coincidence, allows for only temporary denial. Perhaps the blurring of the "us" (civilians) and "them" (state) performed by Kundera's plain-clothes yet conspicuous police officers was meant to enshrine in citizens the belief that "everyone is watching"? (The entanglement of state/civilian realms reached its apogee during Stalin's purges, when citizens were encouraged to watch and inform on neighbors, friends, and family. Slavenka Drakulic [1993] makes a similar point about socialist Yugoslavia in her article "Our Little Stasi," in which the familiar secret police can be taken to refer to the citizens themselves.) Yet what I have described is a performance that is essentially *post*-Soviet. To come back to my encounter in the Kyiv subway, I was not merely observing the melding of state and civilian repertoires typical of secret police activity around the globe. I was witnessing the performance of "bandits"/"goons" who had become a popular symbol of the chaos and violence of the *perekhid* (transition), an element which presumably contributed to the effectiveness of the performance. Young people of the post-Soviet generation exposed to such performances came to understand that "things may not be as they seem" and that intention (e.g., the "democratic forum") and randomness (e.g., "illegible" security) could coexist, drawing together the rationales of "democracy" and "bandit capitalism" in ways that could only be accounted for through cynicism (see Chapter 2).

Coincidence is traditionally seen as the exception to the rule, but perhaps the perceived merging of intention and randomness produces a form of power in which the exception threatened to become the rule. Citizens' fear is that in the "bandit state," everyone is potentially "unlucky," just like the young girl in the story related above. Chapter 2 examined state representations of the nation as a "female child," but this symbol can also be appropriated by the citizenry to represent itself. Because the (female) "child" conjures up images not only of weakness and innocence but also exclusion from power, it can become a potent symbol of political vulnerability and victimhood. Thus the story of the helpless girl produced during the electoral campaign could be interpreted as the metaphor for a dreaded form of citizenship (the latter term understood here as the relation between government and governed).

Like the innocent girl, the ordinary people (*prosti liudy*), still innocent and moral, were thought to be at risk of being tricked and raped, especially if the so-called "bandit" Viktor Yanukovych came to power. Yanukovych had been governor of the Donetsk region in Eastern Ukraine until President Kuchma appointed him as prime minister in 2002. He then became a major contender in the presidential race of 2004. Rumors circulated among his opponents that as a young man, he had been convicted twice, either for theft, murder, rape, or a combination of these. While no one was able to prove this (the criminal records had apparently disappeared), for many, the persona of Yanukovych came to be defined primarily in terms of his criminal past. When I mentioned the name Yanukovych to students during recess one day, they all positioned their fingers to form a "#," as though this explained it all. I made this sign "#" with my fingers and asked them what this meant. They said it was the symbol for prison bars, and told me, "He's a *zek* [convict]!" A girl went on to explain to me that "he [had] raped someone."

Excerpts from poems written during the Orange Revolution (and reprinted in the Kyiv newspaper *Stolytsia,* November 15, 2004) express political vulnerability using the language of sexual violence:

> Ukraine, don't let yourself be raped!
> Let's tighten ranks so that we won't live in a *"zona"* [prison camp]
> Freedom for the people, and bandits behind bars!
> Rapists' place is in prison!
> [*Ne day, Ukraino, sebe zhvaltuvaty!*
> *Shchob buty ne v "zoni," iednaiemo riady.*
> *Narodu – svobodu, bandytiv – za hraty!*
> *Hvaltivnykam mistse v tiurmi!*]

There is no direct reference to the *vlada* (state or government) in this excerpt. The term "bandits" has come to stand for the state. The poem's author identifies himself as "Les' Ukrainets" (a masculinized [and somewhat humorous] version of national poet Lesya Ukrainka's name). *Ukrainka* is the feminine form of "Ukrainian," and *Ukrainets* the masculine form, and thus the surname underlines national belonging. Chapter 2 provided examples of representations of the (masculinized) Ukrainian state, and the (feminized) Ukrainian nation. The author's taking on of a female identity might point to the pervasiveness of a feeling of vulnerability (i.e., everyone is feminized and thus vulnerable to rape as a form of violence exercised by the state).

The reference to rapists could also be interpreted as a reference to Viktor Yanukovych's supposed rape conviction. Rape itself may have different meanings in this case. While it can be seen as an act of violence and excess, it is also about lack of consent (i.e., something unwanted by one of the parties and thus taken by force), and thus it is injurious because it implies *lack of reciprocity*. Perhaps rape stands here as a metaphor for what citizens perceive as the lack of reciprocity in the state-citizen relationship, a feature that became especially salient after the collapse (I will explore this further in Chapter 5). Related to this is the perception of rape in terms of economic plunder (*pohrabuvannia*). Nationalist historiography is rife with depictions of Ukraine as a "ravaged nation," with various empires encroaching on its territory and stealing its natural resources (I have shown how students may reproduce this kind of discourse in the context of the school). What comes across powerfully is the idea that it is the whole of Ukraine that is threatened with rape. The "collective body," imagined through tropes of femaleness, comes to represent citizens' heightened sense of vulnerability *as a people*. Violent transgression is no longer perceived as something reserved for the unlucky few.

Zona: The Country as Camp

How did young people conceive of the so-called "bandit state"? As pointed out earlier, many students were attracted to the image of the bandit that they encountered in the media. Yet in the media, bandits appeared mostly as outlaw heroes. How did students react to what many adults characterized as the erosion between state and bandits (or state and mafia)? I once asked Pavel, the teacher of civics in the public school, why he thought that students were attracted to the figure of the bandit, and he said: "They see their prime minister [Viktor Yanukovych], who sat [in prison] twice, and who has no education, but who made it to the top of the country anyway."

It became clear that Yanukovych enjoyed little support from the student body in either the public or private school. While students referred to Yanu-kovych as a "bandit," they were enthusiastic about his political opponent, Viktor Yushchenko, whom they defined as "honest [*chesnyi*]," or "non-mafia [*nemafiia*]." (Young people's vision of the world as divided between crimi-nals and honest people [or good and evil] can perhaps be attributed to their exposure to the structure of the fairy tale and/or the Hollywood film.) Zhe-nia, the ninth grader to whom I referred in the previous chapter, pointed out to me that "Even the class bandits [meaning, the informal leaders] are for Yushchenko." And indeed, I witnessed the informal leaders of ninth-grade classes participating in a new student game called "Finding Yanukovych supporters and beating them up." The leaders would gang up during recess and throw themselves on Yanukovych supporters until a teacher intervened. One of these fights resulted in a student losing a front tooth. These sorts of fights among boys had been present before and continued after the elec-tions, but it seemed that political rivalry gave them additional zest.

Why would "class bandits" support Yushchenko to the point of defend-ing him physically? Could Yanukovych not be thought of as a kind of "role model," as the teacher of civics had suggested? Why did the students not support a candidate whose demeanor and slang they knew well because they performed it themselves? Students (especially the ninth graders) had often told me that being a gangster or bandit was cool, so if they perceived Yanu-kovych as a bandit, why was *he* not cool? I asked a class of ninth graders, when we got talking about the elections: "You watch bandit movies, you lis-ten to gangster rap, like DMX or 2Pac. Why are those people cool, but not Yanukovych?" A boy nicknamed "Hulk" because of his imposing stature re-plied calmly: "Because they are not running for Ukrainian presidency." This suggests that while students could perform the bandit repertoire in their own struggles, they recognized that bandit behavior and demeanor might not be appropriate in other contexts.

Many students were concerned about Ukraine's image. They told me that having a convict as a president would mean "banditry at the highest level," and that Ukraine would become "the shame of Europe." Students perhaps saw the bandit as a hero so long as he was positioned *against* higher authority (e.g., producing an alternate hierarchy). If the bandit became a le-gitimate authority (e.g., the country's president), then perhaps he no longer posed an alternative to authority and could engage in limitless oppression.

According to this logic (examined in more detail below), he would remain unconstrained by the law, yet somehow also the bearer of the law.

Viktor Yanukovych's supposed "criminal biography" was repeatedly invoked by students to shed light on how the country would be ruled if he was elected. I asked some eleventh graders, "If it is true that Yanukovych has a criminal record, why are you unwilling to see these crimes as a thing of the past, for which he has served his time?" They answered that someone who had been to prison was, in a sense, "marked for life" by his experience, and that they were scared that the presidential candidate would draw on his knowledge of prison life to rule the country. Pro-Yushchenko supporters speculated, half jokingly, that Yanukovych had been a *pakhan*, or the informal leader of a gang of prisoners, and that his prison nickname had been *kham* ("the boor"). Therefore, students feared that he would rule according to the informal "law" of the prison or prison camp (*po-zakonu zoni*). These concerns echoed popular discourses circulating at the time. Citizens' fear that violence and lawlessness could become the "norm" under Yanukovych's presidency gave rise to the metaphor of Ukraine as a potential prison camp/labor camp, or *zona* (literally, an area surrounded by barbed wire). The Soviet state itself had been pictured as a *zona* because Soviet borders, like the perimeters of the Gulag, were surrounded by barbed wire and heavily guarded *from inside* to ensure that no one could escape. Applebaum (2003) describes how prisoners in the Gulag referred to the camp as the *zona*, and the rest of the country as the "big zona" (Rus. *bol'shaya zona*) (164).

Young people understood the complexity of political realities and attempted to grapple with them in their conversations. On one occasion during recess at the public school, Alexiy, the vice president of his ninth-grade class and a very good student, pointed to his friend, telling me: He is for Yanukovych!

With him, we would have *discipline* [Rus. *distsiplina*]! replied the friend.

It would be a *zona*! said Aleksiy.

I asked, What happens in a *zona*?

Bandits rule—they beat everyone, they kill everyone, replied Aleksiy.

One can clearly see the tension between the *zona* as a space of order and the *zona* as a space of chaos. Would living in a *zona* mean the imposition of discipline and a sense of security and stability over the existing chaos (itself brought by the local encounter with capitalism and democracy)? Or would the advent of the *zona* destroy peace and discipline and impose or establish chaos as the norm? Young people framed their society as presented with different alternatives, but were divided over which one would produce the "order" they were seeking.

The concept of "stability" was central to Yanukovych's political campaign, and television ads showed young men and women saying, "I am for stability [*Ia za stabil'nist'*], I am for Yanukovych." The presidential candidate's persona and imposing stature seemed to convey the notion that he would be disciplined and get things done. Some of his supporters among students described him to me as a "self-made man" who had reached the top despite post-socialist economic and other challenges, thus pointing to the value of self-realization. Some eleventh graders told me that they accepted that he might have made mistakes in his youth, but given that he had served his sentence, they thought he deserved a second chance. Yanukovych's opponents viewed the matter altogether differently. The concept of the *zona* as a space of chaos was made explicit in one of the anti-government posters circulated by PORA ("It's Time"), the civic youth group credited for initiating the Orange Revolution. The poster's caption read, *Yanukovych, tse stabil'nist'* (Yanukovych, it's stability). It showed a map of Ukraine covered with crosses like a cemetery, a kind of visual depiction of the state as a space of death and devastation. (This is the idea, articulated by Merry [2007] in another context, that "within the state of exception, violence becomes an unending normativity in itself" [53].) What the PORA poster conveyed, with a touch of black humor, was that the production of stability could come at a price. This kind of stability conveys a sense of chaotic structure described by many anthropologists of the state (e.g., Taussig 1992, Green 1999, Poole 1994). And in fact, new anthropologies of the state have pointed out that disorder underlies order in most regimes, including neoliberal ones (see, e.g., Buck-Morss 2002 and recent writings on structural violence [Farmer 2004]). Yet Yushchenko supporters tended to believe in the possibility of a "decent" capitalism, or at least a capitalism whose disorder would be more tolerable than the chaos of the *zona*.

The PORA poster suggested that inhabitants of the *zona* were in some sense disposable. The expression *Ioho prybraly*, or "[They] disposed of him" (*prybraty* is to clean), was common in daily usage during my fieldwork. It meant either the government (*vlada*) has sacked him, has jailed him, or has killed him. This expression existed in the Soviet period, where it could refer to people being sent to prison camps for ideological transgressions. However, there was a sense that this process had somehow been more discrete in the hands of the Soviets. A friend of mine, a university student in his thirties, commented cynically during the presidential campaign: "At least in Soviet times they [government] disappeared people first. Now, they just beat or kill them openly." Mila, a teacher of world literature in her sixties, told me, "During the Soviet period, of course, you had to watch what you said, stick to the ideology, but at least then my soul rested easy. It's not like now, with all those bandits and oligarchs, whatever you do, you can never feel safe." For her, a person who had lived relatively well under Soviet rule, the feeling of vulnerability had been dramatically enhanced with the emergence of seemingly reckless actors who openly engaged in violent, profit-maximizing activities.

The imaginary of the *zona* was grounded in everyday representations and often personal memories of life in the Soviet Gulag (this accounts for people's familiarity with prison jargon). The dissidents who comprised the first independent Ukrainian government in 1991 had themselves often had first-hand exposure to the language and ethos of the prison. Young people heard stories from some of their relatives and could also supplement these with the accounts of the Gulag presented in documentaries on national television or found in their history textbooks.

The Gulag was first set up as an emergency measure during the Russian Civil War (Applebaum 2003: 13). Decrees for the creation of "special camps" marked its emergence on Soviet territory in 1919 (Applebaum 2003: 10). These special or "extraordinary camps," unlike the regular prisons for criminals run by the Commissariat of Justice, were controlled by the *Cheka* (a short version for the All-Russian Extraordinary Commission for Combating Counter-Revolution and Sabotage) (Applebaum 2003: 9). The term "extraordinary" here points to the fact that the *Cheka* (it was to become the GPU, the OGPU, and finally the KGB) was not bound by the rule of law, and thus did not need to consult with police, courts, or the Commissar of Justice (Applebaum 2003: 8). Humphrey (2002) speaks of a "tendency of Bolsheviks to reject the whole idea of law," with the latter seen as "a bourgeois invention devised to protect the institution of property rights" (103). Thus the political prisoners (e.g., kulaks, priests, White Guards, anarchists, Mensheviks) interned in the extraordinary camps, if convicted at all, had been convicted by people's courts according to revolutionary consciousness rather than knowledge of law (Solomon in Humphrey 2002: 103). The special camps were outside the jurisdiction of other Soviet institutions (Applebaum 2003). In 1929, Stalin had the idea to use forced labor to accelerate Soviet industrialization, especially in northern regions (Applebaum 2003: xvi). That same year, "the Soviet secret police began to take control of the entire penal system, slowly wrestling all of the country's camps and prisons away from the judicial establishment" (Applebaum 2003: xvi). The camps remained under KGB control until the collapse of the Soviet Union. Despite its official designation as a space of rehabilitation through work, prisoners often spoke of the Gulag as space without accountability, or of being in some sense "already dead" upon being admitted (see Applebaum 2003). "And fate made everybody equal / Outside the limits of the law. . . . Branded as traitors everyone," claims a poem by former Gulag inmate Alexander Tvardovsky (quoted in Applebaum 2003: xv). The Gulag's primary purpose was economic, and prisoners were treated like "cattle," as "Guards shuttled them around at will, loading and unloading them into cattle carts, weighing and measuring them, feeding them if it seemed they might be useful, starving them if they were not . . . Unless they were productive, their lives were worthless to their masters" (Applebaum 2003: xxxvi). Soviet prisoners could be shot at will by the guards, could die from cold cutting trees in Siberian forests or mining in Kolyma, from starvation in punishment cells, or from diseases left untreated (Applebaum 2003). While this produces a particular sense of being disposable, my findings reveal that Yanukovych's presence on the political scene evoked for his opponents a particular dimension of the exercise of power in the Gulag. The post-Soviet Ukrainian imaginary of the country as *zona* is grounded *not so much in the relation between the prison administration and the prisoners, as in the relation between the informal bandit leaders (pakhany) and the other prisoners, especially the political prisoners.*

In the Gulag, the prison guards remained *to some degree* accountable if only because they had to fill out reports that their superiors verified and sent out to officials outside the *zona*. This meant that if a prisoner was shot (for whatever reason), the guard had to enter a log to justify this in some way (e.g., "attempted escape"). It is well known, however, that after dinner, the prison guards retire and the *zona* is entirely in the hands of the *pakhany*. Thus it is precisely "after dinner" that the law becomes truly suspended. The *pakhany*, unlike the guards, are not accountable to anyone. The rules they follow allow the *pakhany* to plunder, punish, maim, and kill with impunity.[3] While these rules remain unwritten, they are "understood" by everyone, thus the expression *zhyty po-poniattiakh*, or literally, to live "by understanding." The rules of understanding instill in those who are not part of the bandit elite a deep visceral knowledge that they are disposable and that in the *zona* after dinner, "anything goes." For many Ukrainian citizens, the emergence of the so-called "bandit state" signified the formalization of the informal rules regulating prisoners' relations *to one another,* and the use of those rules in the exercise of governance. What Yushchenko supporters feared was precisely that Ukraine/*Ukraina* would be transformed into *Urka-ina,* where *urka* means bandit, a space in which open violence becomes the norm, and where the possibility for the state of law ceases to exist. During the presidential campaign, small stickers designed by the pro-Yushchenko civic organization "Clean Ukraine" (*Chysta Ukraina*) claimed: "Ukraine is not [i.e., should not become] a prison camp [*zona*]; the president is not a prison leader [*pakhan*]." Here, vulnerability is associated not only with the Gulag inmate, or *zek* (a short version of *zakliuchenni,* lit. "locked up"), but more specifically with the figure of the *shestiorka,* the lowest of the low in the informal prison hierarchy.

Young people made an instant connection between "citizenship" and status as an "inmate." I had asked a ninth-grade class in the public school, "What do you think of Yanukovych's idea of dual citizenship (*podviine hro-madianstvo,* with Russia)? Do you think it's a good idea?" The "bad girl" of the class answered, belligerently:

We don't want to be *zeky* [inmates]!
Why inmates? I asked.
Because he [Yanukovych] would make [our country into] a *zona!*
What's a zona?
A prison! [*Tiurma!*] they all screamed.
We want to be free! added a boy I knew for his exuberant patriotic
    feelings (he was Jewish, and at least one of his teachers kept
    questioning his Ukrainian patriotism). "Freedom or Death!"
    (*Volia abo Smert'!*), he added.
You're ready to die for your freedom?
No! Maybe, he said, embarrassed.
What's freedom for you?
It's when nobody oppresses you! (*Tse koly nikhto tebe ne prytyskaie*).

Students did not want to experience citizenship as a hierarchical rela-tionship in which everyone would be oppressed by the leadership, and against this, they articulated the democratic concept of "negative freedom," or freedom from the constraints of others/the state.

While the imagined oppression experienced in the *zona* was understood to be grounded in lawlessness and chaos, it was also seen as structured around a particular (and particularly brutal) hierarchy. Drawing on Gramsci, Rigi (2007) claims that the post-Soviet "chaotic mode of domination" he describes is the result of a crisis of hegemony and that during such a crisis, domination replaces the "intellectual and moral leadership" associated with hegemony. In other words, the ruling classes do not give up without a fight, and rather than ruling through consent, they reorganize their forces, exercising "coercion in forms less and less disguised and indirect" (Gramsci 1971: 60). Force plays the final role in the chaotic mode of domination (Rigi 2007: 45). Poulantzas (1974) states that in the exceptional state form that arises from a crisis in authority, "Law . . . no longer regulates: arbitrariness reigns. What is typical of the exceptional state is not so much that it violates its rules, as that it does not even lay down rules for functioning. It has no system, for one thing, i.e. it lacks a system for predicting its own transformations" (322). In the case of Ukraine, a powerful popular discourse existed according to which the Soviet ruling elite had given way not to total arbitrariness or lawlessness, but (at least partially) to a new set of "rules," that is, the informal rules that reproduced the prisoner hierarchies within the exceptional space of the camp. This suggests that the model of exceptional state referred to above, or the concept of "state of exception" as developed by Schmitt or Agamben, cannot fully convey the reality of the *zona*.

The informal rules of the camp gained new prominence in the context of the local encounter with capitalism. In the early 1990s, Ukrainian citizens faced the disintegration of the state and the absence of laws regulating the new business transactions made possible by the collapse. As my informants liked to remind me, people's survival depended on the fashioning of a system of rules that could take the place of the "law." These rules of *poniattia* (understanding) migrated from the prison camp to the business sphere, where they acted as a new form of regulation, the basis of what Yurchak (2002) terms "entrepreneurial governmentality." Clearly, this kind of order had been adaptive shortly after the collapse of the Soviet state. After the successful ascension to power of those operating *po-poniattiakh*, however, these rules gained prominence over the codified laws of the country, which is what Ryabchuk alludes to when he claims that in Ukraine, "life is still governed by the spoken, rather than the written, law and . . . the government is still the main speaker" (2004: 4). Rigi refers to the "extra-legal nature of the chaotic mode of domination" (2007: 55) in the post-Soviet space. In a similar vein, *poniattia* may be understood as existing "outside" or "against" the law. Yet my student informants associated *poniattia* with "the *law* of the strongest," "the *law* of the jungle," or the "*law* of the market" (the latter described in terms of the "who eats whom [*khto koho zyist'*]" of Marxist-Leninist discourse). Clearly, disorder had a particular relationship to the "law," a structure and system that emerged as a result of the threat or exercise of brute force.

In their volume *The Practice of Human Rights* (2007), Goodale and Merry draw attention to the relationship between the law and nonlegal normativities. They claim that "human rights regimes that have emerged over the last fifteen years increasingly coexist with alternative, and at times competing, normative frameworks that have also been given new impetus since the end of the Cold War" (Goodale and Merry 2007: 3). These frameworks include social justice, citizen security, and religious law, among others (Goodale and Merry 2007: 3). It might be useful here to think of the "law of the jungle" as a certain kind of normativity (a violent one, not unlike other normativities) that competes with both state law and the discourse of human rights. Viewing *poniattia* as a type of standard with its own definition of social order allows us to see how it comes to define (as a "diametrical opposite") the discourse of human rights in Ukraine. In addition, focusing on the informal rules of the prison as normative prompts us to examine the *pedagogies* associated with them, and, ultimately, the effects of these pedagogies on students' lives.

A couple of days after the Orange Revolution began in Kyiv, opposition television Channel 5 interviewed an Eastern Ukrainian man who had been an election observer in the Donetsk region. The man had a huge black eye, and proceeded to recount that he had been beaten by Yanukovych's thugs (additional footage from hidden cameras aired on the opposition channel seemed to reveal other such instances of voter intimidation). What was striking was the metaphor the man used to describe his wound. "I have the seal of the state [*pechatka vlady*] on my face," he claimed. This indicates that he recognized the wound inflicted by "thugs" as a *state* effect. It also suggests that he regarded this kind of violence as a mode of bureaucratic inscription. The *pechatka* (stamp or seal) is a powerful bureaucratic tool in post-Soviet Ukraine, as elsewhere. No document, however insignificant (a sales receipt, for example), is valid without a *pechatka*. The election observer's face, "stamped" by the state, is perhaps strangely similar to the passport picture (with its particular angle and lighting, absence of shadows, and the seal of the state in its corner) in that it aimed at making the citizen's face *legible*. By posing his black eye as the state's stamp, the election observer may have pointed to the way in which he was produced as a citizen by being put (through violent means) "in his rightful place," in this case perhaps marked as a *shestiorka,* the lowest of the low in the prison hierarchy. He was being "taught a lesson" in the language of new, violent pedagogies.

Perhaps in a *post-*hegemonic context where direct violence is more prevalent (see Rigi 2007) citizens are being produced in part through the "pedagogy of pain" (Das 1995)? Durkheim (1976) and Clastres (1974) have addressed the way in which the normativity of society may be internalized through the inscription of pain on the body. As Das argues, in the initiation rituals described by Durkheim and Clastres, "The mark becomes an obstacle to forgetting—the body thus becomes memory" (1995: 179). The mark is what Clastres refers to as the law written on the body (1974: 160). Indeed, "pain is the guarantee given to the individual that he belongs" (Das 1995: 182). The Ukrainian election observer was clearly "in need" of pedagogy since, by witnessing and documenting what went on at the polling station, he had defied the informal rules of the prison that severely punish informing on the *pakhan* and his allies. Though not a permanent marking on the body, the wound may have come to mark the man's inclusion in the bandit order as the disposable *shestiorka.*

Young people were constantly exposed (in person or through rumor) to these violent practices, and these fostered feelings of insecurity and vulnerability. In late October 2004, a week prior to the first round of the presidential elections, I went on an excursion to Western Ukraine with a class of eleventh graders. In the city of L'viv, I shared a room with Lida, who headed the excursion. On the first evening of our stay, we watched some television. The news (on the opposition channel) showed excerpts of a press conference recorded earlier in the day in which Viktor Yanukovych had said: "Those of you who are laughing at me there in the back. I will settle scores with you [*Ia z vamy rozberusia*]. I will put you through the sieve [*cherez syto*]." The following morning at breakfast, several of the students expressed shock at the way Yanukovych had threatened Yushchenko supporters. They reminded me that a few weeks earlier during another press conference, Yanukovych had called Yushchenko supporters *kozly. Kozly* may be translated literally as "goats," but in prison slang, *kozly* are the equivalent of the prison term "bitches" in English. Yanukovych had basically referred to Yushchenko supporters as "bitches who prevent us from working." When I asked students what this had meant exactly, a male student explained shyly that it is like in prison, when the bandit leaders (*pakhany*) play cards (a serious business), and the "bitches" disturb them with their sexual attentions. The opposition was thus feminized, connected with the figure of the "passive," "subordinate" partner in the prison setting's homosexual encounters.

Later in the day, we visited public gardens with the students and were separated from the teacher and tourist guide for a while. Some of the girls began expressing their worries about Yanukovych's plan to establish dual (Ukrainian-Russian) citizenship. I asked them why they thought this would be a bad idea, since a significant portion of the population of Ukraine (especially in Eastern Ukraine) considered itself both Ukrainian and Russian. They said they were afraid that upon reaching the age of eighteen, their male classmates (friends, boyfriends) would be drafted for the war in Chechnya. They would hate to be citizens of a country at war, they added.[4] What compounded their anxiety was what they saw as the takeover of Kyiv businesses by investors from Donetsk who had followed Yanukovych to Kyiv following his appointment as prime minister in 2002. Students also told me, half jokingly, that if Yanukovych became president, Kyiv would end up with only one radio station: *Radio Shanson*. This is a Russian radio station that is very popular in Donetsk because it airs mostly music "*pro zekiv*" (about prisoners), as the students explained. *Shanson* is indeed music that chronicles prison life and tends to glorify the criminal world (the songs of Soviet artists Vissotsky and Kobzon are often aired). Most people were familiar with this style of music for having traveled in Kyiv's privately owned minibuses, a more pleasant, if slightly more costly, alternative to public bus and tram services. Many of the minibus drivers had come from Donetsk (the easternmost *oblast'* [region] of Ukraine that shared a border with Russia), where *Radio Shanson* was very popular. The captive audience of the minibus sat listening to Russian songs peppered with prison slang. The students' comments thus revealed not only a concern for peace and security, but also with maintaining a certain level of "culture."

While earlier chapters addressed the extent to which the figure of the bandit was admired and came to be incorporated in young people's power struggles in school, what emerges from students' encounters (direct or indirect) with violent practices is that students felt worried and vulnerable in certain ways. What compounded their anxiety was the perception that

Figure 6. A school in Western Ukraine. Photo by the author, 2004.

violent practices (e.g., Gongadze's murder) reflected badly on Ukraine and isolated the country from Europe's democracies.

Plunder

Students felt strongly about what they referred to as the state's "pilfering," and often complained that the bureaucrats with whom they interacted (especially in connection with obtaining a driver's license) were requesting "extra funds" to "build their dachas." Rigi speaks of predatory forms of state as an element of what his informants in Kazakhstan called "wild capitalism." Local narratives in Ukraine described how former Soviet elites had reorganized their power in the post-Soviet space so as to maximize their profits at the expense of other citizens, illegally privatizing state assets, delaying or cancelling salaries, and racketeering. According to my informants, two forms of "plunder [*pohrabuvannia*]" had become particularly salient during the period of the presidential campaign.

The most visible representatives of the "state" during my fieldwork were police officers, and especially the traffic police, or DAI (State Automobile

Inspectorate). DAI officers' love of bribes was legendary and had earned them the title of "bandits in uniform [*bandyty u formi*]." Citizens often mispronounced DAI so that it would sound like DAY (the equivalent of "gimme"). There were the anticipated DAI checkpoints on the highway, where a few officers watched vehicles closely and decided which ones to stop (there would always be tension in the car at that moment. Did everyone have their papers? Did anyone have small bills?). In addition, on forested highways such as the one leading to the president's residence (and to the suburbs), the officers could suddenly appear from behind the pine trees and flag down a car, improvising a checkpoint. When suddenly faced with DAI, motorists tended to fear more for their wallet than for their safety. Attempting escape was not advisable, as the officers would simply radio their counterparts down the highway and have you arrested there. These improvised checkpoints caused surprise and fear, much in the same way as brigands emerging from the forest and stopping one's coach might provoke horror. In this instance, the officer asking for one's driver's license would often point out an infraction (something "not right" [Rus./Ukr. *ne polozheno*] with one's car, license plate, or driver's license) and, at times creatively interpreting the law, fine the driver. Drivers recognized that some of the officers were honest and were simply trying to do their job. Other officers, for whom "fines" meant bribes, tried as best they could to supplement their meager state incomes.

Well-connected people had little to fear: they could afford to pay the fine, and often had but to "name names" to be immediately released. Traveling on a tour bus with a class from the private school, we were suddenly stopped by traffic police on a country road. "Children, pretend that you're sleeping so we won't get into trouble," ordered the teacher in charge of the excursion. There were some transactions with the bus driver, and after about fifteen minutes, we were on our way again. I later asked students whether they had felt afraid when the police had stopped us. "No! We know what they want!" "And what is that?" I asked. "Money, of course!" they replied. The new elite (the so-called New Ukrainians) could buy a license plate with the initials "AP" (*Administratsiia Prezydenta*, presidential administration), which guaranteed that they would be left alone. Alternately, well-connected people could acquire license plates with special police numbers. A tenth grader in the private school whose father was well connected drove a car with "purchased numbers." The student told me proudly, as I sat next to him in his history class one afternoon, how he would take his parents' car for long rides. DAI officers would invariably salute from the side of the road as he drove by, unable to distinguish the person at the wheel (because of the dark tinted windows) but also unwilling to take a chance. The "façade" of power he displayed on his car made him "illegible" to traffic authorities.

The story was somewhat different for people with no such connections. I was in the car with a female friend of mine in her early thirties. She had just driven by a group of DAI officers on the highway without being hailed. She looked at me triumphantly and proceeded to instruct me, "just in case," on the script of the bribe. "You have to leave a ten-*hryvnia* (two-dollar) bill in your driver's license permanently," she said, in a pedagogical tone. "When the policeman finds it while rapidly leafing through your license, and asks, Is this yours? you should say, No! Do you want it back? he will ask. No. Okay, you may proceed." The production of such a script aimed at easing some of the uncertainty around negotiations at checkpoints. In addition, its masterful staging of the money finding itself in the driver's license "by chance" protected both driver and officer from accusations of bribery. Although people referred to the money they gave to DAI officers as bribes (*vziatky* or *habari*), they were in fact paying the officer to refrain from "causing them problems [*zrobyty problemy*]."[5] Although my informants usually spoke of the "predatory" practices of DAI, their interactions with the officers (at least as these were related to me) revealed a certain degree of flexibility. In fact, there were situations in which drivers knew that they had committed infractions, and where negotiations with a DAI officer allowed them to pay the officer an amount that was much less than what should have been paid according to the law. Thus the officer and the driver could establish a more personal relationship in which the officer might appear to be on the "same side" as the ordinary citizen, taking the money and in turn defrauding the state that he putatively represented.

Foucault claims that governmentality is "a question not of imposing law on men, but of disposing things . . . of employing tactics rather than laws, and even using laws themselves as tactics—to arrange things in such a way that, through a certain number of means, such and such ends may be achieved" (Foucault 1991: 95). Scholars of Ukraine have tended to focus on state authorities' manipulation and appropriation of the law for their own use (see, e.g., Ryabchuk's model of the "blackmail state" [2004], or Wanner's [2005] characterization of the law in Ukraine as an "instrument of oppression"). We saw in Chapter 3 how young people themselves used the law as a weapon in their struggle for power in school. In the context of the encounter with capitalism, perhaps *everyone* attempted, to some extent, to position themselves so as to maximize their chances of survival (which is not to say that everyone could do so successfully). The DAI officer's ability to wield different "personas" (bandit/police officer/fellow citizen), and the possibility of going back and forth between laws and tactics, provided the kind of flexibility necessary to survival.[6] Yurchak points out that entrepreneurial governmentality "is directed not so much at personal enrichment at any cost as at building a meaningful personal reality in different spheres of everyday activity and within different and quickly changing regimes of power" (2002: 311). In the context of daily struggles for survival, meaningless rules could exacerbate suffering, and thus were sometimes ignored both by citizens and representatives of the state. Thus while citizens' discourses about DAI always revolved around plunder, in *some* cases, the reality was perhaps closer to mutual accommodation.

The kind of citizenship experienced by a new generation of young people was marked by the existence of "duplicity" (both that of citizens and representatives of the state) that enabled subtle negotiations of power. This is not unlike the duplicity or "double standard" (bandit/patriot) exhibited by students to their teachers as a way of "muddling through" curricular requirements. What students also learned from these encounters was that negotiations with representatives of the state would be far more successful if one had money (the appropriate bribe, the right license plate). What money could buy was a basic democratic right: freedom from state intervention. This speaks to the widespread idea that the wealthy could enjoy not only the freedom grounded in "excess," but also more basic civic rights.

Scholars of the post-Soviet region have traced the emergence of *new* strategies of power connected with the government. For example, Ryabchuk (2004), following Darden (2001), identifies blackmail as a tool of state domination under Kuchma's presidency. Darden argues that many of the Ukrainian state's capacities "are exercised through informal mechanisms of control that have until recently been hidden from view. . . . The new evidence suggests that pervasive corruption, combined with extensive surveillance and the collection of evidence of wrongdoing [referred to as *kompromat*], provided the basis for the Ukrainian leadership to use blackmail systematically to secure compliance with its directives" (2001: 42). According to Ryabchuk, one of the features of the blackmail state is political oppression through *economic* means, as when the tax police shuts down an opposition television channel on grounds of tax irregularities (2004: 3).

As the 2004 presidential elections approached, opposition media broadcasts and conversations began to resonate with the word *adminresurs*, a term that translates literally as "administrative resource" but signifies the *use* of state-controlled resources for political gain. Allina-Pisano (2010) defines the term as "political actors' use of bureaucratic hierarchies and the material resources of public institutions to win electoral contests" (374). For example, bureaucrats under central command could instruct their subordinates for whom to vote (Wilson 2005: 73). What is more, material resources still under state control (e.g., heating, gas, salaries, health care, stipends) could themselves be granted *or withdrawn* as a tactic for ensuring political compliance. It is the fact that resources can be withdrawn that grounds "administrative resource" in fear, with the individuals, communities, and enterprises still dependent on the state finding themselves most vulnerable. Allina-Pisano points out that even when positive incentives are used, they may be "offered as a replacement for goods that previously had been regarded as *entitlements*" (2010: 374; emphasis added), for example, "the restoration of public transportation service" (2010: 376). The tactic of *adminresurs* is what I would call "sporadic privatization," because it allows the authorities the flexibility to appropriate public resources for their own political uses *whenever* they need them, and for more or less lengthy periods of time. During the Orange Revolution, one of my informants, a man in his mid-fifties, claimed: "Our government is such that it may one day cut off our water supply entirely, and then promise it back during the next electoral campaign just to get re-elected." The underlying idea here is that having produced chaos (*khaos*), the government would then campaign on the principle of the restoration of "order [*poriadok*]" and "stability [*stabil'nist'*]."

During the electoral campaign, Yushchenko's supporters accused Yanukovych of attempting to secure political support partially through "buying" votes (with money or food) and through threats of withdrawing basic resources. For example, some university deans had allegedly threatened students who participated in pro-Yushchenko demonstrations with the loss of their stipends. In Kyiv, people feared job loss as a result of political noncompliance (e.g., failing to sign documents in support of Yanukovych's candidacy). Some teachers told me that they had been strongly encouraged, for example, to participate in certain pro-Yanukovych meetings, but those teachers and administrators who supported Yushchenko usually found ways around this, such as sending their teacher's aide instead. The fact that having a stable job had been a basic right during the Soviet period exacerbated for some the sense of unfairness or injustice (*nespravedlyvist'*). People referred to this pressure "from above" as *admintysk* (administrative pressure). While many types of threats seemed to target *collectivities* that had demonstrated (or were expected to demonstrate) support for Yushchenko (e.g., student bodies of certain universities, inhabitants of certain villages, scholars at a particular scientific institute), the threats could also be individualized. A student in the public school had a grandmother who had worked in a shoe factory in Western Ukraine for twenty-seven years. Her grandmother had categorically refused to sign the letter of support for Yanukovych. Despite the fact that Yanukovych was extremely unpopular in her city, she was the only one at the factory who had taken a stand. Her boss was now threatening to sack her without pension.

Shortly before the revolution, my host Svetlana interpreted a temporary electric power failure as punishment for Kyivites' mass involvement in pro-Yushchenko rallies. It is significant that apparent failures in state services could suddenly be interpreted (whether this interpretation was accurate is irrelevant) as a *political tactic* rather than as general inefficiency, another indication that "chance" had become suspect. During the revolution, Svetlana worried that the Kuchma government would turn the power off to the whole city if protesters continued to occupy Independence Square (*Maidan*). "Anna, how will we *live*," she asked me. "I know this government is ready for anything just to hold on to power. They are ready to have us live like animals [*skoty*]." For her, the fact that the practice of "administrative resource" was geared at basic necessities meant that an (undeclared) state of emergency could be brought about at any time, potentially plunging a prosperous modern city into pre-modern conditions. Because it threatened the few entitlements that remained after the collapse and that guaranteed that people remained people (and not animals), "administrative resource" perhaps played on the fear of what Humphrey calls the "descent into the wilderness of having no entitlements at all" (2002: 27). What also emerges from citizens' anxieties is that the *zona* may be a space marked by both political *and economic* vulnerability, a topic addressed in the next chapter.

Many citizens believed that the law had been remade, through violence, into the "law of the jungle" (one that drew on different "chaotic orders," including the market and the informal hierarchies of the Gulag). The sense of vulnerability produced by this kind of law led not only to new imaginaries of human rights and social justice, but also to attempts at "recovering" the state by restoring citizenship as a *moral* relationship. Young people became key actors in the articulation of this reciprocal relationship between people and state.

Chapter 5

Citizenship Between Western
and Soviet Modernities

Shortly after the Orange Revolution of November–December 2004, I asked high school students in the public and private schools to write their thoughts on what it meant for them to be citizens of a European country. I wanted to get a sense of their understandings and expectations of European citizenship. In their essays, students claimed that to be a citizen of a European state means "to live in a democratic country, where human rights are more important than anything [*ponad use*]; where people will receive decent wages and pensions that allow them to live like people [*zhyty po-liuds'ky*]." Another student stated that "It means to live well [*dobre zhyty*]: protected and in security, having a large spectrum of freedoms and being part of a democratized society." Another student claimed that Europe is "a symbol of welfare [*blahopoluchchia*], blossoming, social protection and the guarantee of rights and freedoms of citizens." Young people put the most emphasis on the social dimensions of citizenship and the role of the state in ensuring the well-being of its citizens. To understand what led to the focus on care and protection in articulations of citizenship, we must examine the kinds of pedagogies and claims making that marked the mass demonstrations around electoral fraud in late 2004.

The Orange Revolution was hailed by many as a sudden and quasi-miraculous democratic breakthrough. This perception of the revolution seemed to rest on analysts' assumption of it as (1) a manifestation of people's desire for the "Western/global" model of democracy (with its focus on freedom of speech, freedom of association, and the like), and therefore, (2) an instantaneous and radical move away from the "Soviet past." The revolution did constitute a break with the Soviet order in many respects. Mass participation in protest over rigged elections under conditions of intimidation and physical hardship points to a powerful rupture with certain aspects of Soviet citizenship, and scholars have focused on this rupture in their analyses of the rise of civil society (e.g., Arel 2005, Kuzio 2006, Diuk 2006). The revolution indeed appeared to be grounded in a desire to partake in Western European normality. Some accounts of the revolution went as far as to pose it in terms of a "clash of civilizations," with Yushchenko supporters aiming at Ukraine's integration into European structures, and Yanukovych supporters aiming at the country's (re)integration with Russia. The fact that young people (university students and members of youth civic groups) were the ones to initiate the pro-democracy demonstrations also seemed to suggest a Western orientation. It has been pointed out that observers of the post-Soviet world often expect young people there to be "open to the new [and not] directly formed by communism" (Diuk 2004: 59), or to "inevitably embrace a new [post-Soviet] reality" (Topalova 2006: 24).

Much of what went on during the Orange Revolution supports the claim that it was "about Western-style democracy." In order to get a more complete picture of Ukraine's Orange Revolution, however, we must ask to what extent the revolution signified a move away from Soviet citizenship (including the relationship between citizens and what is construed as "state power," official and popular interpretations of rights and civic responsibilities, and particular forms of claims making and political mobilization). This is not to imply that Ukrainian citizens may in some ways still be "stuck in the Soviet past," or bound to so-called Soviet "survivals." The question is rather, whether *selected* elements of Soviet citizenship, *reconstituted* in such a way as to be relevant to post-Soviet challenges, could have played a role in youth-led political mobilization during the 2004 elections. Scholars have examined forms of youth engagement with Western consumer goods in Russia and elsewhere (e.g., Pilkington 2002, Blum 2007) and have presented a complex picture of the way young people include these global products in their local worlds. It is also essential to examine how young people deploy Western/global notions of democracy and rights in the context of collective action.

Mapping the Revolutionary Moment

The discourses of powerlessness put forth by Yushchenko supporters during the presidential campaign were striking. Yanukovych would win because, according to students, he "had the most money," or because Eastern and Southern Ukraine (Yanukovych's strongholds) were more densely populated than the pro-Yushchenko Central and Western Ukraine. Parents and teachers often stated that Yanukovych would win because "the elections were already fixed," or "the results had already been decided." People would go vote, but this would have "no impact on the final outcome." Every day, people declared themselves defeated. A friend of mine explained that this was part of "Ukrainian fatalism." "By expecting the worst," she said, "people feel safer. Then if something good happens, they will be happy. It's bad luck to expect something to go well." By acknowledging defeat, people perhaps also protected themselves from intrusive gazes.

The fact is that people's everyday practices in no way corroborated discourses of defeat. In many small and subtle ways, Yushchenko supporters of all ages got involved in politics and showed, as well as articulated, that they cared about who would win, and that they were conscious that they might make a difference. For instance, teachers at the private school often supplemented their incomes by tutoring students in their homes. A teacher of mathematics used this opportunity to explain to her students why it would be better to vote for Yushchenko and why there was no future with Yanukovych. Although students were not of voting age, the hope was that they would be able to relate this information to their parents, who might then change their minds about a candidate. When visiting a teacher in her home in mid-September 2004, I noticed a small portrait of Yushchenko on the billboard at the entrance of her building. Every building has a caretaker, and in this particular building, the caretaker was an elderly woman of about seventy, whom I saw tending to this image in the most caring fashion, wiping it with a piece of cloth after finding some unsightly spots. Students in classes fashioned their own "Yushchenko" notebooks and agendas with pictures cut out from magazines or newspapers, adding ribbon and colorful stickers. Because official pictures or political ads depicting Yushchenko were practically nonexistent in Kyiv, it seems that his supporters took it upon themselves to "show" him, to make him visible, while at the same time anchoring him in the domain of the familiar.

Toward Neoliberal Governmentality?

It was the official announcement, on November 21, 2004, of Viktor Yanukovych's victory (exit polls suggested that Yushchenko was the winner) that brought hundreds of thousands of protesters to Maidan Nezalezhnosti, or Independence Square, in downtown Kyiv. Demonstrators erected a tent camp on Khreshchatyk, the main street adjacent to Maidan, and buses filled with protesters from all over the country were parked so as to create a kind of barricade, blocking access to the forces of order. Despite disruptions to everyday life caused by the revolution, schools never closed, and rumor had it that the government mandated that they remain open because it did not want schoolchildren to swell the ranks of protesters on Maidan. Many parents and teachers agreed that politics was a "dirty business" and that children, who were by nature innocent of political machinations, should be kept home. As a result, on some days, teachers taught classes in classrooms that were practically empty. Those children who did not stay home would simply take the subway from school to Maidan with their friends, with or without their parents' consent.

The new disciplines and pedagogies of the revolutionary moment had profound effects on the high school students who were exposed to them, as will be discussed in Chapter 6. Perhaps the most striking element of the revolution was the self-restraint and self-discipline shown by the demonstrators. There were no reports of violence on Maidan, either among the protesters, or between Yushchenko and Yanukovych supporters. We might argue that Ukraine's Orange Revolution (and especially, its "peaceful" character) was the result of exposure to a new transnational form: that of the post-communist democratic revolution. Serbia and Georgia had already experienced democratic revolutions (in 2000 and 2003, respectively). The particular disciplines of this kind of collective action had circulated from Serbian and Georgian youth civic movements (Otpor and Kmara) to PORA, their Ukrainian counterpart, through visits and training workshops. There, PORA had learned to brief a large crowd on tactics of nonviolent resistance. Western donors had also contributed to fostering people's awareness of their civic rights by sponsoring some democracy training in Ukraine, much of which was done by local NGOs. This included "carrying out independent exit polls . . . , encouraging people to vote, publishing and distributing literature explaining people's rights, and supporting human rights organizations in monitoring violations and prosecuting violators" (Sushko and Prystayko 2006: 134). Thus it appears that the transmission of the new set of disciplines associated with postcommunist revolutions and Western democratic pedagogies was partly responsible for the peaceful character of the Orange Revolution.

Another factor that contributed to the self-discipline on Maidan was the protesters' acute awareness (especially after the Western European media had established itself permanently on Maidan) of Europe's (and especially Western Europe's) gaze. There was much at stake: people's behavior under such circumstances would determine whether or not they were "Europeans." I found this to be especially important for the high school students who took part in the demonstrations. They felt that they already belonged to Europe in so many respects (their everyday consumption of European music and fashion only exacerbated this feeling), and so longed to be recognized as fellow-Europeans and no longer as a backward or disorderly population at the margins of Europe. In fact, many of the young people I spoke to on *Maidan* were eager to point out that the Orange Revolution itself showed European democratic principles in action in Ukraine. Claims to European-ness abounded. Presidential candidate Yushchenko positioned himself unambiguously, claiming that Ukrainians, "along with the people of Europe, belong to one civilization." The sense of belonging to Europe was also apparent in novel usage of local expressions referring to Europe. For example, in the post-Soviet space, the term *evroremont* (or Euro-repair/ Euro-renovation) refers to the process by which one can improve and modernize one's living space according to European aesthetic standards. During the revolution, this term was transposed to the realm of politics, as a banner in the tent camp on Independence Square claimed: "Our Ukrainian people are doing the Eurorenovation of our state: we apologize for the temporary inconvenience."

Given the above, one is tempted to argue that the disciplines on *Maidan* were part of an emerging neoliberal governmentality characterized by *self-regulation*. For example, Dunn (2006) has argued that the new disciplines of Western companies partially succeed in creating self-regulating subjects in places such as rural Poland. Similarly, Ukraine has seen the "promotion of key neoliberal values" and with it the "privileging of various techniques of the self," including self-reliance and self-possession (Phillips 2011: 237). Yet it appears that the peaceful character of the Orange Revolution was also tied to another crucial element, that is, the protesters' wish to separate themselves, though their behavior, from the "bandit state" whose power is grounded in open violence. Their deliberate nonviolence allowed the protesters to adopt a moral (and morally superior) stance. In fact, the practices on Maidan (kindness, generosity, compassion) were consciously at odds with the selfishness and rudeness associated with bandits and "bandit capitalism." The

Figure 7. Demonstrators around the "tent city" in Kyiv during the Orange Revolution. Photo by the author, 2004.

peaceful behavior exhibited on Maidan seemed to constitute a bodily manifestation of the kind of "order [*poriadok*]" the protesters wanted restored in the country (more in next section). As will become apparent, this "order," based in goodwill (*dobro*), included a form of social justice, and thus was compatible with selected elements of Soviet modernity.

The children and teenagers who participated in the revolution learned about "order," but not of the kind encouraged by the authorities. By refusing to heed the state's advice to "stay home," young people were moving away from being passive citizens sitting on the sidelines to active participants in a larger political struggle. Topalova (2006) points to the assumption that participation in the Orange Revolution led to the recognition, in Ukraine and Russia, of the adolescent as a "self-conscious political actor" (24). While it is debatable whether this recognition had lasting effects, in the context of mass demonstrations, young people got to reframe the tension between their portrayal as agents with voices and their portrayal as beings "quarantined" into childhood. When probed about the reasons for letting children accompany them to demonstrate, some parents claimed that "it is, after all, their future being played out." Some young people (teenagers and university students) were heard saying that they would rather die than continue living under an oppressive regime, and this willingness to sacrifice oneself for one's people suggests a willingness to fulfill the ultimate civic obligation. The situation was precarious, with a mixture of troops, riot police, and (later) snipers deployed to protect one side or the other in case of conflict, and demonstrators had hung small posters on streetlights addressed to the forces of order that said, "Don't shoot!" No one would have denied that having children in the crowd was risky. In an interesting twist, however, the presence of children may have had an impact on the peaceful outcome of the revolution. In fact, members of the Ukrainian special forces stationed on Independence Square were heard saying in television interviews: "How can I shoot if my own children are on *Maidan*?"

Through the "peaceful" pedagogies of the "democratic revolution," young people learned about their nation (for example, some claimed to have learned the national anthem during the revolution) in a context other than the classroom. They were also exposed to various forms of claims making (some deployed by university students, and others by older adults) through political slogans, songs, and graffiti. Whereas in schools, students tended to come up against adults' definition of rights as obligations, in the context of political mobilization, there appeared to be more overlap in articulations of rights. Clearly, children cannot be viewed as "sponges" who indiscriminately absorb political knowledge from adults (Cheney 2007: 135). In the context of collective action, however, there was a noticeable meshing of adult and child discourses of rights. To illustrate the extent of this overlap, this chapter presents adults' and young people's discourses together.

Articulations of Order

Based on the data I collected during fieldwork in Kyiv in the period of the Orange Revolution, it seems that for many, the revolution was about restoring "order [*poriadok*]." In the early days of the revolution, observers, some of them critical of the event, had described it as a "carnival." In the following days, some protesters' signs read: "We have not come for a carnival!" A young woman from Kyiv, a student in her late twenties, told me on Maidan: "This is not a carnival. A carnival is the reversal of order. In this case, it's the opposite: the government [*vlada*] is the carnival and we are trying to put things back in order."[1] An engineer in his mid-forties who had come to

Maidan from L'viv echoed this feeling. When I asked him why he thought people had come to Maidan, and what it was that they wanted, he said: "You understand what order [*poriadok*] is, don't you? This is what people want. They want to live in a normal country."

The idea that order should be restored in the country had been circulating for some time. In the months preceding the elections, people told me repeatedly: "You'll see, when Yushchenko comes to power, he will restore order," or "Yulia will become prime minister and finally there will be order." Politicians themselves campaigned using this kind of language. As early as 2001, Yulia Tymoshenko claimed in an interview that "it [would] take two years to restore order in the country" (see www.tymoshenko.com). This expression was one she would use in a variety of contexts (see, e.g., *Moscow Times*, May 17, 2005).[2]

What was the content of this order for which so many longed? I discovered that order could be filled with a wide range of (sometimes contradictory) meanings, which probably accounts for its power in mobilizing masses of people with very different interests. During the Orange Revolution, I asked Yushchenko supporters across generations what they understood by order, and got answers such as, order is "when the government doesn't steal," or "when salaries are paid on time, like they used to be." Order is when "there are no bums on the street," or when "one can start one's own business without problems." There were two remarkable aspects to these comments. First, some definitions of order referred (directly or indirectly) to the Soviet past, while others referred to "Western" order, and second, order was strongly tied to economic stability and welfare.

I conducted 32 semi-structured interviews with Yushchenko supporters on and around Independence Square during the revolution. Some of my interviews were conducted in the lineups to food tents and medical dispensaries, others in cafés around Maidan (where one could escape the cold), and yet others while walking with informants from one protest location to another. Most people began by telling me that they had come to Maidan to protest against the fraud. Many expressed the feeling that the rigged elections had been the "last drop [*ostannia kraplia*]" for them, and that they had felt compelled to take action against an unfair (*nespravedlyvyi*) government. When I asked them about their vision of the future, the majority articulated, in some form, the idea of restoring order (some called it normality). Fehérváry (2002) states that the term "normal" as articulated in the post-Soviet region can be understood to mean "according to norms, standards,

what is customary, normative, ordinary, and average; in addition, what is
nice, natural, healthy, dependable, rational, sane" (372). She adds that normality is associated with what is Western and typically defined against
things Soviet. As will become apparent, however, in the context of the Orange Revolution, normality was not deployed solely as "Western." In fact,
the term "order" allowed for the coexistence of elements borrowed from
different modernities and thus different normativities.

The most common articulation of order had to do with the idea of
an honest, accountable government. Thus, Olena,[3] a candy factory worker in
her twenties, could say, "Order is when the government doesn't steal." Several people said something to the effect that for there to be order, "the government has to respect the laws of our country, our Constitution." Order
was posed in contrast to the perceived lawlessness in government, the sense
that when one is in power, "anything goes [khto shcho khoche]." This is what
the young student who had called the Kuchma government a "carnival" had
in mind: the sense that there were no limits to the government's deprava-
tion, and that therefore the government was an inversion of what it should
be, that is, grounded in and subject to the rule of law. Thus, order could signify legality. Many people associated order with cleanliness (chystota), and
corruption with dirt, as with the billboard stating, "Let's clean Ukraine
from dirt! Yushchenko." Related to the absence of corruption was the
understanding of order as accountability. Mykhailo, a fifteen-year-old high
school student, told me: "Look at Europe: there, the government works for
the people, and not the opposite." Others reminisced about Soviet accountability. Pavel, a civics teacher in his forties, told me about the kind of order
present during the Soviet period: "Then, if someone in the local government
did a bad job, you knew you could go to his superior and complain, and his
superior would do something about it, this person would get a warning, or
could even be fired. Now, nobody pays attention to you, or worse, you could
lose your job."

Some manifestations of order seemed tied directly to an imaginary of
Western European standards. Valya, a lawyer in her thirties, associated
order with Western economic laws when she said that order was when "one
can start one's own business without problems [i.e., bribes at every step], like
in Europe." Other respondents also referred to order as the absence of political pressure through economic means: "Now, they [the tax authorities] can
decide to tax your business for political reasons, and make the taxes so high
that it forces you to close your business," claimed Sasha, a young engineer.

Although order could be tied to freedom of enterprise, it could also mean economic security or predictability and be tied to the state. A young woman in her early twenties studying in a technical college told me that for her, order was "when salaries are paid on time, like they used to be." It is significant that references to the Soviet past were not limited to those people who had experienced it, something I will explore further when I address high school students' discourses. Young people's direct and indirect references to elements of Soviet citizenship challenged the assumption held by many that "once the 'old [Soviet] generation' dies out, Soviet discourses and practices will die out with them." Other articulations of order were reminiscent of Soviet experience, as when Svitlana, a food store clerk in her forties, told me that order would be restored when "everyone has a job [a former Soviet entitlement] and can make money honestly."

For some, the restoration of order also meant leveling the economic disparities between the very poor and the very rich. The polarization of wealth had become highly visible, for example with the increased presence of the homeless on the streets of Kyiv, as well as the open conspicuous consumption of the city's "New Rich" (or *kruti*, in slang). (The New Rich who lived in the neighborhood adjacent to mine would make their presence felt even late in the evening [on weekends *and* weekdays], when they would set off fireworks from the roofs of their tall buildings, waking the children for miles around.) Lida, a retired schoolteacher in her seventies told me: "Earlier [during the Soviet period], there were never any bums [*bomvzhy*] on the street.[4] This government, those oligarchs, stole so much from the people that now, you have people starving, living on the streets. Bums are everywhere, in the park, in the Metro, and they bring disease, tuberculosis. When Yushchenko comes to power, he will bring economic improvement [*ekonomichne pidvyshchennia*], and there won't be any bums anymore." In the same vein, Natasha, a translator in her fifties, explained that there could be no order while the rich and corrupt bandits were "on the streets or in the government, and not in jail." The restoration of equity or social justice would in some sense "disappear" the categories of very rich and very poor, and thus be more like what Natasha invoked as the simple, orderly life people had led during the Soviet period, when "everyone was the same [equal] [*vsi buly odnakovi*]."[5]

These comments illustrate how order may be associated with such values as honesty and accountability, security, predictability, and legality (rule of law/ moral law). The economic component is apparent in people's articulations of order, whether it is articulated through concerns with securing livelihood, restoring human dignity, or implementing economic laws.

Many accounts of order during the revolution referred to elements present in both Soviet and Western European models of citizenship. In both systems, there is a degree of government accountability and efficiency, as well as provisions for social welfare. In revolution-time imaginaries of order, where does the socialist Soviet state begin and the Western European welfare state end? These accounts of order seem to arise essentially from an *engagement* of Western standards with Soviet elements, so that the two models become entangled and impossible to distinguish. The fact that this entanglement could be obscured by the use of a single word, "order," is not so much a sign of poverty of language, which forces people to use the same signifier to express a variety of signifieds. It is, rather, evidence of a multiplicity of meanings, of what Bakhtin (1996) has called dialogics, whereby the word in a language becomes "one's own" as each speaker appropriates it and adapts it by populating it with his/her own intentions.

It is useful to contrast the idea of "engagement" with the model of "transition" that has dominated scholarly thinking about change in the region. Transition implies progressing from one clearly defined stage to another (e.g., planned economy to market economy, collective to private property, and authoritarianism to democracy). It is premised on the eventual *replacement* of Soviet by Western structures and norms. We might want to look at change instead in terms of an engagement, or what I would call a "double becoming" of Western and Soviet modernities. I borrow the term "becoming" from Deleuze (1987). Applying the double becoming model to the countries of the former Soviet Union means looking at change on the ground as the result of a dual process: as local populations adopt what they perceive as "Western" practices, concepts, and standards, the latter also become transformed or localized. (Thus local populations are not only being transformed *by* but are also active transformers *of* new models.) The double becoming has no direction: it is simply a constant engagement. It is a double becoming that is in fact a single process, or "single becoming" (Deleuze and Parnet 1987: 3). In contrast to the transition model, with this model nothing disappears, nothing is ever totally left behind. In addition, this engagement does not produce "hybrids," but rather new forms that are *both* and *neither*. For example, in people's understanding of order, we see how elements of Soviet and Western modernity coalesce so that they may become impossible to disentangle. And yet what is formed through this entanglement is also new.

Perhaps the double becoming is made possible by similar quests (Western and Soviet) for modernity (see Buck-Morss 2002). Although the means for achieving modernity differed somewhat, this similar quest produced the conditions of possibility for engagement. We might argue that during the Cold War, these two modernities became, to a large extent, mutually constituted. This double becoming (and the Orange Revolution itself) also rests on the condition of *direct contact* and *dialogue* with Western concepts and structures, beginning under *glasnost'* and developing after the collapse of the Soviet Union. It is the result of flows of media and consumer goods, travel and work abroad, and so on. However, the particular overlap of (selected) elements of Western and Soviet modernities that we see on Maidan is also made possible by the post-Soviet emergence of the "bandit state." The "order" invoked by demonstrators on Maidan is one that is defined against (and as an alternative to) the government's "chaotic rule."

"We Are Not Slaves"

The revolution was the symptom of what a majority of Ukrainian citizens pictured as a deep divide between Us (the people) and Them (the government), itself exacerbated by state practices that produced a sense of increasing economic vulnerability. During the election period, the term "slave" became a way of talking about Us, and the term "bandit," a way of talking about Them. Yushchenko supporters altered Yanukovych's campaign posters to show him in prison slacks, and held signs and banners claiming, "We don't want to live 'by understanding' [*My ne khochemo zhyty po-poniattiakh*]," that is, according to bandit law vs. according to the rule of law. "We will not give Ukraine to bandits! [*Ne viddamo Ukrainu bandytam!*]" read stickers plastered all over the city. The Yushchenko campaign team did their share in reproducing a morally charged dichotomy between people and authorities. Yushchenko reaffirmed it when he stated on the eve of the elections: "The greatest divide in Ukraine is not that between East and West, or that between Orthodox and Catholic: it is that between bandits and honest people [*bandyty, i chesni liudy*]" (UT-1 State Television, September 14, 2004). This sharp dichotomy between bandits and honest people is to a certain extent a fiction. In fact, in societies in which government officials engage in corruption, citizens are likely to be involved as well (e.g., giving bribes). Therefore, the idea that society will be cleansed of corruption once all bandits are in jail, while compelling, is somewhat unrealistic. As an informant explained to me shortly after the revolution, Ukrainian citizens must adapt (and this is a difficult process) to functioning in a society in which the rule of law, rather than corruption, is the norm. In addition, we should not assume that all Ukrainians citizens were "victims" of state corruption. Many stood to gain from it because it provided them with a certain flexibility (e.g., wealthy parents whose children were not doing well in school could ensure that they graduate anyway). An eleventh grader claimed that "The problem in this country is that everybody steals, from the lowest bum [*bomvzh*] to the president." Nevertheless, a Yushchenko campaign leaflet described the situation in Ukraine thus: "Criminalized clans during the Kuchma government gained control over the economy, bank system, television, Parliament, and courts. . . . This happens at the expense of the impoverishment of the majority of people [*za rakhunok zubozhinnia osnovnoi masy liudey*], who lost faith in the fairness and power of the law." Here, Yushchenko poses the divide between bandits and honest people not only in moral terms but also in economic terms: the bandits are responsible for the impoverishment of honest people. (This is a clear inversion of the noble "social bandit" described by Hobsbawm [1969].) Therefore, Yushchenko's slogan and electoral promise "Bandits will be put in jail!" (*Bandyty syditymut' v tiurmakh!*) resonated powerfully with the protesters. Students on Maidan captured the slogan thus: "*Zek na nary, todi my pidem na pary* [When the convict (in this case, Viktor Yanukovych) is (back) on his prison bed, then we'll go back to class]."

A sixteen-year-old high school student explained how "bandits" stole from the population thus: "As I see it, those who want to come to power think, 'I'll be president for a month,' for example, 'and I need to grab all the money I can, everything that I can from Ukraine.' There are no rules in the economic sphere, so if you want to do something like that, you can do it, there's no law for you." A sign on Maidan read, "*Borshch, Tak! Balanda, Ni*" ([Ukrainian] soup, not [prison] soup). This seemed to be an appeal to the state in which citizens articulate their need for the basics (in this case, food) while also grounding these in the rule of law (i.e., prison food won't do). This is in line with Yushchenko's constant articulation of the necessary link between economic improvement and the restoration of the rule of law. Other protesters framed illegal plunder in moral terms. Nina, a street vendor in her sixties, explained it thus: "Those bandit oligarchs steal money from people, and then people have to live in the garbage [*smitnyk*]. It's not that the Soviet government didn't steal, of course they stole, but still, we had enough to get by." A young mother from a village close to Kyiv told me: "Those bandits take everything for themselves first, and then nothing is left for the people. As usual, it's the poor [*bidni*], the simple people [*prosti*], who end up suffering."

Soviet citizens had used the expression "simple" people to refer to the divide between Communist Party leaders (involved in politics and the particular kind of scheming that this was thought to entail) and ordinary citizens (innocent of political machinations). On the one hand, the word *prosti* connotes exclusion from political power and decision-making, and thus lack of agency. Lack of agency could in turn translate into a lack of responsibility, one that allowed citizens to remain "innocent" or untainted by "dirty politics." On the other hand, in the official Soviet discourse, the "simple people" had been the deserving recipients of entitlements from the state (see Brooks 2003), a form of rule that Verdery (1996) refers to as "socialist paternalism." The term *prosti* possessed flexibility similar to that of the term "child" in that it could evoke notions of exclusion and powerlessness, but also notions of innocence and entitlement to protection. Its use constituted one of the ways in which demonstrators positioned themselves vis-à-vis the authorities during the Orange Revolution.

The term *prosti* also reinforced the moral dichotomy between rich and poor (superimposing it to government/people). This was true despite the fact that the revolution was not essentially a revolution of the dispossessed (many of the protesters on Maidan were part of a rising middle class, Kyiv being the richest city of Ukraine), and that Yushchenko enjoyed the support of several oligarchs. In fact, some of the people I interviewed referred to themselves as *prosti* (simple people), even though, by their own account, they were relatively well off and/or influential. By identifying themselves as *prosti*, they could not only deflect attention from their personal wealth, but also present themselves as untainted by the activities of the "bandit government."

Posing themselves as *prosti* also enabled citizens to continue articulating some of their expectations of the state. According to my informants, the Kuchma government had not only failed to provide for the people but had also directly threatened the few entitlements people had left. The demonstrators perceived the government's inability and unwillingness to provide for their citizens as a great unfairness or injustice (*nespravedlyvist'*). "It's not fair," teenagers would often tell me, "that's why we came." A sixteen-year-old student stated that "A person wants to feel protected by (*zakhyshchena*) and not plundered by (*obikradena*) their state." This young woman posed protection as the opposite of plunder, and imagined the state through the idiom of care. As young people on Maidan denounced the "predatory" practices of their government, they simultaneously articulated a kind of citizenship in which economic protection was at least as important as political rights.

If the bandit became a way to talk about the government, then the slave became a way to talk about the people. A sign on Maidan during the revolution claimed: "We are not slaves! [*My ne raby!*]" What did this mean, I asked my informants, whose slaves? A few of the protesters, and particularly those from Western Ukraine, said, we are not *Russia*'s slaves. To them, the fact that then President Putin had congratulated Yanukovych on his "stolen" victory only showed the extent to which Ukraine was still under the influence of Russia (*pid vplyvom Rosii*). Along those lines, others referred to Shevchenko's poetry (in which the slave is a major theme), declaring, "We are not slaves means that we are not 'Little Russians.'"

While protesters referred to Yanukovych as a "bandit," I had also heard him referred to as a "slave" in the school context. During a ninth-grade Ukrainian language class at the public school, the teacher, a woman in her fifties, had the class read a text entitled "*Rab Mankurt*" (Slave Mankurt, by Chingiz Aitmatov). Students took turns reading, and the teacher paraphrased: "Mankurt didn't know who he is [in terms of identity, of nationality], he didn't feel like a person. When he was asked something, he was silent. He didn't recognize his own mother." When they were done, the teacher asked, "So, you now understand the meaning of Mankurt? A Mankurt doesn't know and doesn't want to know. Are there any Mankurts among us?" And the children protested, "No!" The teacher said, "I did not mean in this class, I mean in this country. We have some, for example our prime minister, who speaks neither Russian nor Ukrainian." The fact that Yanukovych spoke a sometimes clumsy mixture of both languages was not taken as evidence of a hybrid identity, but rather as proof that he was nationally amorphous/unconscious. Not only was he considered a slave in the cultural sense, but he was also portrayed as Russia's slave because of the way he supposedly bowed to President Putin's demands. (His characterization as someone who oppressed others but was in turn oppressed from above points to the realization that one's power is relative and may change according to context.)

A majority of the people I interviewed on Maidan interpreted *My ne raby* as meaning, We are not the *government*'s (*vlada*) slaves. Many respondents spoke of the slave in terms of political apathy. Vadim, a professor of political science in his late fifties, elaborated: "What are slaves? A silent amorphous mass. Slaves carry out the tasks [*vykonuiut' zavdannia*] given to them, otherwise, they know their heads will be cut off. Slaves are mute, but now, now we can already talk, we have freedom [*volia*]." A student of philology at a Kyiv university explained: "As Skovoroda [famous Ukrainian poet and philosopher] said, 'The people is sleeping' [*Narod spyt'*]. But now we have stood up from our knees, and we're saying 'No!' to our criminal government [*zlochynna vlada*]." "The government made us into slaves, and doesn't want to set us free [*vidpuskaty*]," said a high school student. "When you're a slave, you have no rights. We came here to defend our rights." Citizens claimed to have become slaves as the result of the government's intimidation and disregard for the law, but the above statements also emphasized the fact that the people, through protest, was breaking away from this model. In fact, another sign in the tent city read: "Slaves are not allowed in heaven [*Rabiv do raiu ne puskaiot'*]." The claim that slaves are not deserving of heaven moved away from an indictment of the government to a call for collective action.

Many of my respondents' statements presented a combination of political and economic understandings of the slave. Halya, an engineer in her early thirties, explained: "We are not slaves means that we will not allow the *vlada* to manipulate us, to deprive us of our right to vote and our right to be truthfully informed. For years, we worked not for ourselves but for criminals. Now it's time for us to work for our country." Similarly, a sixteen-year-old high school student claimed: "We have been slaves of our corrupt politicians for a long time. *My ne raby* means, We are not slaves of the government. They [the government] can close factories, they can take money from us, bribes. Now, Yanukovych wants to become president [through falsification of election results], and this is the peak of this lie [*brekhnia*], of this unfairness [*nespravedlyvist'*]." Other interpretations of the slave revolved solely around an economic relation to the economically defined bandit. In that sense, slaves referred to people who could be plundered with impunity. "We work like slaves, and for what? For *kopiiky* [kopeks, the smallest denomination of Ukrainian money, in other words, "for peanuts"]!" claimed Maria, a construction worker in her sixties. Petro, a fifteen-year-old high school student, said, "We are not slaves means that we want to be free." Free from what? I asked.

"Free from Kuchma!"

"Oh, so you were Kuchma's slaves?"

"Kuchma stole money and always stole money."

The term "slave" has an interesting genealogy in relation to collective action. I have noticed its use during the 1917 Bolshevik Revolution (on banners, in political slogans) where it referred to a state of slavery (in the sense of economic exploitation, but also perhaps in the social sense, as a lack of respect and equality) that had outlasted the Emancipation of 1861. The term "slaves" is also invoked during the 1991 "Russian Revolution" or response to the coup that aimed at restoring the Soviet Union. In a CNN documentary about the event entitled "The New Russian Revolution" (1991), interviewees state that they "no longer want to live like slaves." Living like slaves seemed to entail both political repression and economic deprivation (the latter exacerbated by Soviet citizens' exposure—through film and television—to so-called "Western living standards"). It is significant that self-labeling as slaves marks both the formation and the dissolution of Soviet power. The term appears once again during the Orange Revolution, this time in response to *post*-Soviet conditions and modes of rule, and especially the new tactics of the "bandit state."

The term slave has obviously undergone significant transformations since 1917. It would be interesting to investigate (and this would require an in-depth analysis beyond the scope of this book) whether people are reacting to, and collectively protesting, what they see as the persistence of *feudal-like* systems of rule in which they are perpetually cast as slaves. In her book *What Was Socialism and What Comes Next?* (1996), Verdery explores the local metaphor of transition as a "return to feudalism." In the Ukrainian context, people often referred to their government as a "clan [*klan*]," or criminal clan (*kryminal'nyi klan*). This perception was not limited to Yushchenko supporters. Nina, the teacher of Ukrainian in the public school, told me shortly before the revolution, "People say that they don't want to be ruled by Yanukovych's 'clan.' You think Yushchenko's people are not a clan? We've always had a clan, and we will always have a clan [*U nas zavzhdy buv klan, i zavzhdy bude*]." Depending on the historical moment, the "clan" could refer to feudal lords, Communist leaders, or post-Soviet (criminal) oligarchies. The idea of the clan suggests a kind of continuity (from pre-Soviet to post-Soviet times) in political rule, continuity against which a definition of justice (*spravedlyvist'*) (differently constituted in different historical periods) may emerge. Of course, people may judge clans against one another, and the Soviet "clan" that seemed (to some) so corrupt and criminal is often judged less harshly in relation to the post-Soviet oligarchy. That is why even people who condemned the Soviet regime in the early 1990s can now invoke some semblance of order (predictability, regulation, decency, etc.) under Soviet rule. This in turn suggests that the *post*-Soviet experience (and especially the experience of the so-called "bandit state") is largely responsible for the kind of overlap and engagement, at the discursive level, of Western and Soviet discourses of rights and justice.

The term slave in its local articulations connotes obedience, compliance, lack of consciousness of oneself as a person or as a Ukrainian. In addition, the slave is "beneath the law," has no rights or entitlements, and is undeserving. The slave is more animal than human in some respect. As students told me, "It is time that we break our chains!" Yushchenko's use of "honest people" suggests less dismal prospects. For one, it gives citizens a moral advantage over the "bandits in power." We must ask, however, whether the term "honest people" really constitutes an alternative to the term *prosti*, which also poses the people as somehow blameless (*and* deserving). The *prosti* were better off than the slaves in that they enjoyed a kind of moral superiority and were entitled to certain resources. But it is the term "person" (*liudyna*) that arises as the real alternative to the slave. As Petro, the fifteen year old quoted above, stated, "*My ne raby* means that we want to change something, to have a better life."[6] The expression "living like a person" allowed my respondents to picture a better life, one in which they would be free from oppression, and especially, from need. Young people's references to a "better life" revealed both a desire to move away from Soviet and post-Soviet standards of living toward those found in Western Europe, *and* a desire for the restoration of some Soviet-style social protections.

From Slaves to Persons

The song "I don't want to [*Ia ne khochu*]," composed by the Ukrainian hip hop group Tartak, became a hit during the revolution and was performed on Maidan. It was very popular among high school students. Its lyrics mused on the kind of country Ukraine could become was every person able to live "like a person." The expression "living like a person [*zhyty iak liudyna* or *zhyty po-liuds'ky*]" was widely used around the time of the revolution. Although not all my informants brought up the concept in exactly those terms, most people articulated a desire for living a "normal life [*normal'ne zhyttia*]," or living like "normal people [*normal'ni liudy*]." A medical student from Kyiv told me: "People want to live like people [*zhyty po-liuds'ky*], not [just] survive." It seemed that for many, living like a person meant having "the basics." "Why did you come to Maidan?" I asked Olya, a retired woman in her late sixties from a small town in Kyiv oblast. "Because we want to live like people [*po-liuds'ky*]. Our level of life is so low. I was a school teacher, and then school principal for twenty-five years. My pension is 60 *hryvnias* [approx. $30] per month, but prices are rising, so I can barely afford a loaf of bread. What kind of country is this in which a person can no longer afford bread?" Marko, a student of foreign languages in his early twenties, said to me, "Living like a person is like living a normal life. To have an apartment. To be secure financially." "There are no jobs," claimed an accountant in her forties. "Even educated people cannot find work. There are a lot of poor people, a lot of rich people, but no middle class. For me, to live like a person is to have a job, a stable job." Katya, a business lawyer in her late twenties, claimed: "In general, [living like a person is] to have job security, an apartment, a car, a cell phone, and a vacation on the seashore every year." Similarly, the high school students to whom I spoke tended to expand the definition of basic needs to include material goods that were thought to be "standard" in Western European countries (including apartment, country house, car, and cell phone).

Since some of my respondents' statements seemed to expand on what we might think of as basic necessities, I needed to find out whether there existed a general consensus on what constitutes a decent life. I asked my respondents: Are there people in Ukraine who "live like people?" and got the following answers. A fourteen-year-old exclaimed: "Well I think Akhmetov lives like a person!" (Rinat Akhmetov is Ukraine's wealthiest oligarch, net worth: US$11.8 billion), or "Yes, of course, there are a lot of rich people," or "Bandits live like people." A carpenter in his forties from Western Ukraine confirmed: "For a lot of people, living like a person means to have a pile of money [*kupa hroshei*], a palace, and a *bumer* [expensive car, prototypically a BMW], like those bandits."

The lavish (and highly visible) lifestyle of the country's oligarchs provided the kind of standard that ordinary citizens could both despise *and* emulate. In fact, despite the Orange Revolution's strong positioning against "bandits" in power, it seems that the latter still provided a way of imagining the person (and thus perhaps also the citizen). Indeed, as a bandit, one could live like a person. Many people associated bandits with a certain kind of freedom: freedom from need.[7] One could argue that it is precisely this freedom from need that allowed them to also enjoy *political* freedoms. In fact, bandits were "rights-bearing people." Importantly, there seemed to be an implicit equation between "living like a person [*zhyty iak liudyna*]" and enjoying human rights, or literally in Ukrainian, "rights of the person [*prava liudyny*]." Thus, a certain kind of livelihood allowed for a certain kind of relationship to rights, and thus made one not only a person but a *citizen*. In the case of the "bandits," their wealth allowed them to live "above the law," and therefore to enjoy even those "rights" connected with whim and desire. Here an important parallel can be drawn with the freedom that students seek (through the bandit repertoire) in the school context (see Chapter 3). There, the "class bandits'" power was based on physical force rather than wealth; yet at the level of society in the post-Soviet context, it is precisely the combination of wealth and the wielding of force that seem to guarantee (a gangster-like form of) "respect" as well as the respect of one's rights. While the equation between being wealthy and having "all possible rights" is attractive to young people, this scenario (as emphasized on Maidan) is one in which individual liberty hinders equality, and the "excessive" rights enjoyed are gained at the expense of other people's rights.

Ukraine's exposure to so-called "Western" living standards had also shaped the idea of living like people. After independence, Ukrainian citizens had begun watching soap operas such as *Dynasty*, had seen Western European department stores and supermarkets on television, had traveled to Western Europe for pleasure or work, and had visited relatives living abroad. This was especially true of the students I worked with in the private school, who had often traveled extensively. Therefore, it was common for Yushchenko supporters, young and old, to say, We want to live "like everyone [*iak vsi*]"; or "like everywhere [*iak skriz'*]." The longing to live like a person could then provide a link to the world, and especially to the imagined West. It also made a claim about the universality of the category of the person, and (at least up until then) Ukraine's exclusion from it.

Scholars of the post-Soviet region have often encountered what Fehérváry calls the "discourse of the normal" (2002: 370), where the term "normal" is "used to refer to the extraordinary, to things that are neither customary nor normative within their local context, but since the fall of state socialism, are expected to become so in the future" (373; see also Rausing 2002). The adjective "normal" also describes a standard of living "imagined to be part of 'average' lifestyles in Western Europe or the United States" (Fehérváry 2002: 370). Thus, the statement "We want to live like everyone" seems to signal a desire to partake in the "decent living" that is thought to be characteristic of the West. According to Rausing, in post-Soviet Estonia, the "normal" is framed as the "unfamiliar," and the "not normal" is the familiar (Rausing 2004: 37), that is, the Soviet experience (Fehérváry notes something similar in the Hungarian context). In Ukraine, however, the normal *could* be the familiar. In fact, for some, living like people could be traced back to the Soviet period. For example, a Yanukovych supporter stated: "Before this 'independent Ukraine,' we lived like normal people." A woman in her sixties, a Yushchenko supporter, reminisced about the Soviet Union: "Of course, there were problems, we had to watch what we said, but essentially, we lived like people. There was no variety in products, but we had enough to survive. Now, with all those bandits, you never know what can happen." The expression *zhyty iak liudyna* was already in use during the Soviet period, where it could mean, for example, having an apartment of one's own (i.e., separate from one's parents) to raise one's family. Thus, living like a person could be grounded in Western (Western European especially), post-Soviet, or Soviet models.

A few respondents also associated "living like a person" with living in security or safety (*zhyty u bezpetsi*), for example being safe from bandits, or anyone who might cheat them. Some of my informants from Western Ukraine expressed, in addition to the economic dimension, a political one. A bank employee in her twenties from L'viv said that for her, living like a person meant not being afraid to speak out in general. A young university student from Ternopil' explained that living like a person meant living a decent life (in the material sense), but that it also had to do with certain freedoms. "It's freedom [*svoboda*] to express what I want, freedom to do what I *want* and not what I'm *told* to do. I have my own opinion and I want it heard. To live like a person means to be treated with respect [*z povahoiu*]." Thus, while living like a person could mean living decently (however defined), it could also have connotations of liberty and absence of oppression, a meaning that spoke to students' articulations of freedom and dignity in the school context. (Yet as seen above, it appears that human dignity could not be completely disentangled from the freedom [*volia*] of the bandit to satisfy desire.)

It is significant that *some* of the things that defined living like a person (e.g., a reasonable and stable price for bread, job security, and a yearly vacation on the seashore) were present during the Soviet period in the form of entitlements, or things that "deserving citizens" were granted from above. (Entitlements defined Soviet citizenship to a large degree: a Soviet citizen's political fall from grace was signified by the immediate removal of entitlements, including job and dwelling [Wanner 2005].) According to Verdery, socialism "encouraged subjects to see themselves as entitled to things" (1996: 166). The Communist Party was charged with collecting the total social product and redistributing it in accordance with people's needs. The benevolent Party acted "like a father who gives handouts to the children as he sees fit" (1996: 24). This "turned economic relationships into *moral* relationships" (Brooks 2003: 49) that involved relations of debt and gratitude. Brooks (2003) argues that the "economy of the gift" was a central feature of the Soviet state, where the state was portrayed as a selfless benefactor, and the citizenry as deserving recipients. Citizens' needs were defined by the state and thus were constituted as rights (Verdery 1996: 166). Citizens also came to think of certain consumer goods as their right because mass media "touted the material standards of living enjoyed in their countries as among the best in the world and as rising all the time" (Patico 2005: 483). In her book *How We Survived Communism and Even Laughed* (1993), Drakulic argues that the state's monopoly over the definition of needs also implied its ability to proclaim anything (e.g., toilet paper) a "luxury." The "right" to consumer goods was in fact continually frustrated by shortages (Patico 2005: 484). As Verdery argues, however, the socialist system made people into a type of "rights-bearing subjects," a category that could be transposed to the post-socialist context to make *new* claims (the right to private property, etc.) (1996: 166).

Were some of Yushchenko's supporters (re)constituting themselves as rights-bearing citizens under new circumstances? Obviously, we cannot argue that Ukrainian citizens understand Soviet entitlements in the same way as they did during the Soviet period. Post-Soviet governance, including the use of political tactics that threatened the goods and services that citizens had taken for granted under Soviet rule, has altered the meaning of entitlements, as has marketization and the resulting polarization of wealth. In the summer of 2003, I was walking with Ivan, an informant of mine and a professor of philosophy in his sixties, in a Kyiv neighborhood formerly known as "Stalinka." There, we came across graffiti on a cement block supporting a billboard with an advertisement for Panasonic televisions. The graffiti read: "*Khochemo zhyty!* [We want to live!]" I asked him what this meant, and he explained that with the introduction of capitalism after the collapse, people had understood what was meant by *Khto koho zist'*, or "Who eats whom," a Soviet-era portrayal of the class struggle. Now, people could barely make a living, he said. Ivan was cynical about Communist rule. He described the Bolsheviks as reasoning that "if the bourgeoisie oppresses the workers, there will be no communism, but if the workers oppress the bourgeoisie, then it will be a communist paradise." Despite his negative views, he added: "You know, before, the Communists took into account people's minimum needs.

Figure 8. "We want to *live!*" has been written on the base of a billboard. Photo by the author, 2003.

Now, the leadership thinks that people don't need anything [*A teper vlada vvazhaie shcho liudiam nichoho ne treba*]." Ivan was reproducing the idea that persons have certain minimum needs that must be met (by the state). The idea of basic needs had emerged anew with the experience of a leadership that did not seem to "care" about people's basic needs. Contact with "Western living standards" had also brought an expansion of the category of basic needs. During the Orange Revolution, demonstrators framed (economic) rights both in terms of material *needs* and in terms of *desires* based on "Western" or post-Soviet images of conspicuous consumption. Clearly, we need not pose these as antagonistic, for as Patico argues, "impulses toward both social justice and consumerist plenty are not entirely contradictory to one another" (2008: 208; see also Patico 2005). On the one hand the blurriness between rights and desires accounts for the difficulty in pinpointing what constitutes "basic" needs, or a "decent" standard of living. In other words, it makes it difficult to identify with certainty the kind of rights that might make one into a "person" and thus also a citizen. On the other hand, the expression "living like a person" also bridges the gap between generations because it can be filled with a range of different expectations.

The question is, who did protesters think was responsible for making them into full-fledged "persons" or citizens? How were these perceived rights articulated as claims, both by adults and young people, during the Orange Revolution?

Calling upon the State

Before, during, and after the Orange Revolution, one could often hear people say, "Yulia [Tymoshenko] will increase teachers' salaries!" or "Yushchenko will fix everything!" While we might expect these kinds of claims to be limited to people who had spent most of their lives under Soviet rule, young people had similar expectations of their leadership. Shortly after Yushchenko's inauguration, I had a discussion with eleventh-grade students in the public school where I conducted research. I asked them, "What do you expect Yushchenko to do, what do you want him to do exactly?"

> *Lesya:* To change everything, and especially, to give back the money that the previous government took from us, they stole a lot—
> *Danylo:* from our pockets.
> *Lesya:* Through illegal privatization!
> *Danylo:* Not only.
> *Lesya:* On the border, when they took other "taxes" [bribes] from us.
> *Taras:* Our government should do what people want done. They should help people, make their lives better, more comfortable, help them to reach a higher standard of living.

Students expected Yushchenko to recuperate the money stolen by the previous government. He was to do this, for example, through the reprivatization of former national assets and the prosecution of former members of the government. This money would then be put to work for the improvement of people's lives, whether through job creation or the restoration of social programs. In general, the students with whom I interacted considered the government to be responsible for improving the life of its citizens.

Diuk (2004) notes a similar phenomenon among Russia youth born after 1986. When asked, in the fall of 2002, "What should be the relation between the government and its people?" as much as 64.3 percent of young people in an eighteen-to-thirty-five-year-old cohort agreed with the statement "The government should care for all of its people providing for all their needs" (Diuk 2004: 61). Noting that the Russian state has not engaged in any major media campaigns in an effort to promote itself as a provider of care, Diuk surmises that "younger Russians have acquired this belief from their elders, who heard the rhetoric of state paternalism every day under Soviet rule. In at least this one respect, then, Russian youth seem to be close to the assumptions and expectations of their parents' generation" (2004: 61). While there may exist what Hann calls "strong threads of continuity" with the Soviet era (2002: 5), the question is how these threads become entangled with a Western orientation in a way that produces something new and relevant to young people's lives, a topic that will be addressed at the end of the chapter.

Only a few students in the six classes with which I discussed this topic articulated a different perspective, arguing that *people* were responsible for their own economic well-being. One student captured this sentiment when she said that economic growth and people's well-being (*blaho*) did not depend on the government, but rather on "how hard the Ukrainian people will work on the state's [*derzhava,* meaning country] and on its own welfare. The best way for us to solve our problems is to become more independent from the government." In this, young people seemed to reproduce the ideals of "individualism, initiative, and independence that are increasingly valued . . . in contemporary Ukraine" (Phillips 2011: 197).

President Yushchenko's press conference on the occasion of the first hundred days of the new government revealed a widespread "top-down" vision of change. The press conference (more like a live conversation) aired live on several television channels (5 Kanal [Fifth Channel], CTB, Novyi Kanal, ICTV) in April 2005, and lasted more than two hours. People from anywhere in Ukraine could ask the president questions by calling, emailing, writing, or speaking live from one of four city squares in L'viv, Kyiv, Donetsk, and Simferopol. The president answered the questions one by one. The simple fact of giving people the opportunity to address their president directly provided an opportunity to restore the link between people and state, and especially to reframe the relation between the president and his citizens as one between equals. One was struck, however, by the way in which both Yushchenko supporters and Yanukovych supporters addressed their new president, and the manner in which they articulated their needs to him. Some people read their questions (in Russian or Ukrainian) from a sheet of paper, so that Yushchenko felt compelled to say that he wishes people would not read their questions, so that they could have a live conversation (*shchob v zhyvomu u nas bulo spilkuvannia*).

At one point, the member of a city council asked a question to the president, but the journalist who hosted the press conference said that from now on, "we would like to get questions from simple citizens [*prosti hromadiany*]," meaning those not in power. She had already couched the conference as an opportunity for the simple people (*prosti liudy*) to be heard. This reproduced the very divide between people and government that the press conference sought to bridge. Clearly, the use of such categories as *prosti* illustrates the extent to which the press conference itself artificially constrained the sorts of views (of change, of the relation between state and citizens) that could be exposed or voiced. Defining "the people" as *prosti* at the outset might have had the effect of allowing for the expression of a certain set of concerns (including the issue of entitlements) above others. Thus, the kinds of discourses put forth during this press conference differed in some respects from the discourses I accessed during the revolution. What I wish to illustrate here, however, is the way in which some citizens articulated the state in relation to livelihood. The examples below suggest that many perceived the state (or even Yushchenko himself: the distinction between state and leader is at times blurry) as responsible for providing them with jobs, salaries, and social benefits that would "make their lives better."

While people asked questions about such diverse topics as Crimean autonomy, NATO membership, the prosecution of members of the former government, and the defense of the Ukrainian language and culture, the majority of the questions dealt with economic protection and social welfare (healthcare; veterans' pensions; assistance to mothers, orphans, and the disabled, etc.). This was not in itself surprising. In his campaign leaflets (one of which I observed circulating among students in the public school), Yushchenko had made ten major promises to his people. At the top of the list were: "Create five million new jobs," "Prioritize the financing of social programs," "Increase the budget and decrease taxes," "Make pensions and salaries higher, and prices and taxes lower," "Make the minimal pension higher than the living minimum," and "Insure accessible, quality healthcare" (other promises dealt with the restoration of moral and family values, respect for veterans, and the development of villages).

The following questions by citizens are representative of the tone of the press conference. A woman in her sixties from Donetsk read on camera: "Viktor Andrievych, you promised during the elections campaign to create five million jobs. . . . So far, it's been only promises, you didn't do anything to make people's lives better. Our lives are becoming worse, our factories are closing. Tell us please, What are we to feed our children, your promises?" A young mother from L'viv asked why she could not benefit from financial assistance for her child, who was born right before the law on assistance to mothers was implemented. She said that her friend had stood on Maidan (during the revolution) while eight months' pregnant, and had rejoiced in knowing that she would get financial help once she gave birth, but that she too would be excluded now. A miner from Donetsk in his fifties ended his question to the president by saying: "How will you improve the life of simple miners [*prosti shakhtari*]?" A young medical student emailed the president to explain the sacrifices one had to make to become a doctor (eleven years of study), only to earn 350 *hryvnias* per month. He asked the president, "How can one live on that money, and what should I do?"

While Yushchenko affirmed several times that the new government would do everything possible to improve people's lives, on occasion, he also said something to the effect that the particular question raised had nothing to do with the government or the president (i.e., the government could not solve all of people's problems). This points to a slight gap between some citizens' expectations of the state, and Yushchenko's understanding of what the state, with its few resources (he alluded to the fact that citizens should be willing to pay their taxes), could take on. Keeping in mind the particular staging of the press conference, what came across was that most people who asked questions about economic improvement looked to the state, personified in Yushchenko, as the provider of a "better life."[8] In other words, citizens sought not only "liberty rights," but also "claims rights" (Shnapper 1997). While liberty rights guarantee "the rights of citizens against the power of the state by ensuring their freedom to think, speak, meet, work, or trade" (1997: 202), claims rights imply receiving services from the state, including "the right to a job, material well-being, education, [and] time off" (1997: 202).

Did collective civic action (action against and *independent* of the state) arise in order to restore a certain degree of *dependency* (especially economic) on the state? This would seem to negate the very notion of the country's mass protests as a "revolution," that is unless we conceive of the revolution in terms of putting an end to the government's "carnivalesque" excess and "bringing back the state"[9] (the latter understood here as a law-abiding, accountable government that "cares" about citizens).

As the press conference makes clear, however, the better life "from above" was only half of the transaction. What the people gave for this better life was their effort and labor (mining, studying medicine, or bearing children). When asked what they considered to be their responsibilities as citizens, most adult protesters told me "voting" (an activity imbued with new meaning in the context of the revolution) and "working."[10] Young people mostly said, "Being here/protesting," but some also said "studying." My point here is that the idea of "care" issuing from above is understood as half of the flow that constitutes the *reciprocal* relation of citizenship. People's labor constituted the other half. As Brooks (2003) argues, the Soviet "economy of the gift" was also a "moral economy" that rested on citizens' image of themselves as *deserving* recipients (of welfare or care in the form of basic services and resources). In some sense, the imagined reciprocal relationship was also one of economic and moral dependency. Therefore, rather than looking at the articulation of democracy simply in economic terms, we should perhaps emphasize the centrality of a "*moral* economy" as an element borrowed from Soviet experience and reconfigured in the local encounter with capitalism.

A More Just Capitalism?

The chapter began with high school students' statements about the meaning of living in a European state. Their imaginaries of citizenship seemed to be, for the most part, firmly anchored in Soviet-inspired idioms of care and welfare, and this, despite the fact that these young people had no first-hand experience of the Soviet system. We cannot speak here of nostalgia or of a desire to go back to the Soviet way of life, for young people's idea of a "better life" is tied to Western European rather than Soviet living standards. Yet there appears to be a longing for a form of government that could combine elements of both the Western European and Soviet models of the "welfare state." In the discourses of the Orange Revolution, the local category of "order" was flexible enough to allow for an engagement between Soviet and

Western modernities, and through it, young people could begin articulating
new imaginaries of rights and social justice that were neither Soviet nor
Western, and thus comprised a new political vision for the future.

It is significant that a protest movement that appeared at first glance to
be an unambiguous "return to Europe" also contained salvaged elements of
Soviet modernity. This allows us to question the idea of "European normality" as a neoliberal project imposed upon and transformative of local populations, and to focus rather on the process by which local populations
appropriate and transform "normality." As Kürti and Skalník (2009) argue,
there has been a tendency in the scholarship on post-socialist states to focus
on the deleterious effects of capitalism and view local populations as "victims" of transition. The discourses on Maidan seem to reveal, instead,
people's—and especially young people's—agency in transforming the meaning and experience of capitalist transformation. In his work on human
rights in Bolivia, Goodale (2007) speaks of social resistance as being "articulated within a rights framework at the same time it formally opposes a
western or neoliberal 'oppression' of the Bolivian people" (134), a situation
in which one part of neoliberalism (the rights discourse) is used to contest
another (e.g., the right of companies or other actors to pursue economic self-
interest) (134). The young people cited in this study did not overtly resist the
capitalist model. In fact, demonstrators did not blame capitalism per se (this
is in contrast to other post-Soviet countries where indictments of capitalism
itself are common), but rather the carnivalesque form it had acquired at the
hands of the ruling elite. But while young people refrained from condemn-
ing capitalism, they subtly (and perhaps unconsciously) transformed and
displaced it by infusing it with elements that were meaningful to them.

Chapter 6

From Revolution to Conversation?

What we need in the future [in our school and in our country] is a conversation, not a revolution.
                    (Nadia, eleventh grade, April 2005)

After the revolution, the terms of engagement and negotiation between students and school authorities underwent significant change. The school as an institution had not witnessed the radical transformations experienced in other areas of society, and young people now seemed even more aware of its shortcomings in the area of democratic practice. Crucially, the school still lacked a space for face-to-face "conversation" between students and school authorities. The pedagogies of nonviolent street protests had altered students' quest for (civic or other) freedoms, so that the new strategies they used in schools blurred the boundary between democracy and force, or conversation and confrontation.

Overthrow

Students, and especially the younger ones, were fond of bringing the streets into the school, chanting political slogans in unison. Exasperated teachers constantly reprimanded them: "*Vy ne pryyikhaly na mitynh! Vy na urotsi!* [You are in class, not at a political rally!]." A tenth grader recounted how during the revolution, "we were told in school that we shouldn't go to Maidan. The principal said, 'You don't have your own opinion. You're too young.' And you know, you become rude when they tell you what to do." In another school, the principal attempted to forbid students from singing the revolution theme song, *"Razom nas bahato"* ("Together we are many," a thinly veiled reference to the fact that students outnumbered their teachers), but the kids continued singing, undeterred.

During the period of the mass protests, students in both the public and private schools began plotting the overthrow of their own "unfair [*nespravedlyvi*]" leaders: their school principals. The tenth graders in the public school shared their plan with me. They hoped to record in some way evidence of what they considered their principal's abuses of power (including what they described as threats and the verbal humiliation of students), and bring this evidence to the district to have the principal removed and replaced. They did not go through with their plan, however, because they feared that it might not work (the district authorities would not listen to "children"), and that if the principal found out, her revenge would be terrible. In the private school, eleventh graders plotted similar action. A student was designated to record on his cell phone camera the way the principal taught his class and verbally humiliated students. However, the students did not go through with it because as it turned out, "50 percent [of the students] did not know whether or not they were right [in doing this]," and therefore could not take decisive action. This indecision had to do in part with the sense that despite his unfairness, the principal was able to "keep things together" and to maintain order in the school. There was always considerable ambivalence about this among students and teachers. On the one hand, they felt that they needed a strong leader to maintain order, but on the other hand, they could barely tolerate the unjust practices of such a leader. Students borrowed the overthrow as a form of dissent from the revolutionary mode of action. It was not meant to be a violent overthrow in either context, yet the perceived need for an overthrow points to the absence of conditions for dialogue or conversation, conditions that persisted in the school even after the revolution.

Defacement

The tradition in the private school was to have a portrait of the president of Ukraine in each classroom. The configuration was that of president-flag-trident (*tryzub*, the Ukrainian coat of arms). Until the 2004 elections, a picture of President Kuchma had adorned every classroom. With Yushchenko's victory, however, teachers had to change the portrait, and some teachers (especially the pro-Yanukovych ones) lingered longer than others. The interesting fact is that all the new portraits of Yushchenko available for display were of him prior to his alleged poisoning by a high dose of dioxin during the campaign (rumored to be the work of Kuchma forces), that is, looking young and handsome. In fact, after the revolution had left Yushchenko in power, images of him appeared everywhere. One image in particular was of postcard size and portrayed him against a pure white background. With its slightly blurry edges, it looked like a holy picture. Although some images depicted the new president after his poisoning (e.g., during his inauguration), the pictures intended for display in classrooms or offices were all "before" portraits. Teachers could get these "before" portraits at any newspaper stand in the city. There was no tradition of putting up a picture of the president in the public school's classrooms, but students there claimed that in other schools, teachers who disliked Yushchenko had selected "after" pictures.

One incident took place in the private school. Svetlana was the one who related it to me, and only she, the school nurse, and the students involved knew of its occurrence. Three students in a tenth-grade class had been anti-Yushchenko since the beginning of the campaign, presumably because their parents were likely to lose some of their status under his presidency. One day, they went into their mathematics teacher's classroom, and opened the armoire in which he kept school supplies and some personal belongings (all teachers have one, and students usually have no access to it). They found and took the frame with a picture of Kuchma that had been left there until the teacher had a moment to replace it with the new president's portrait. They then replaced Kuchma's picture with a picture of Yushchenko they had especially sought out and printed from the internet, one in which he looks terribly disfigured (after the poisoning). After putting this picture in the frame, they hung it in the designated space on the wall above the blackboard. They did not want anyone to know that they had done this, but a fellow student who was aware of the plan told on them. Svetlana was warned, and immediately warned the school nurse, who was also her friend of many years. They rushed to the classroom and Svetlana climbed onto a chair to remove the picture immediately, before the mathematics teacher got back to his class (at his age, they thought, he might go into cardiac arrest seeing what had been done).

Svetlana confronted the students involved and told them that there were laws against tampering with the image of the president (I have never been able to find these laws). She met with each student individually and threatened them with legal action. One of them, a female student, kept quiet and seemed unafraid. Svetlana told her that having well-connected parents would be of no help since her offense was so serious. The teacher also brought up the fact that if the rest of the students (*kollektiv* was the word used), pro-Yushchenko in majority, learned about the incident, they would "hang" the perpetrators.

The night of the incident, the phone kept ringing at home, as Svetlana attempted to negotiate some kind of solution or punishment. She told me, still fired up: "Those enemies of the people [*vorohy narodu*, a Soviet formula coined by Stalin] took it from the Internet! They found an *ugly* [Rus. *urodlivyi*] picture, you can't imagine. They don't sell pictures like that; it doesn't exist otherwise. There is an article (of law) [*stattia*], and I told the students they could go to prison. No one is above prison, even if their father knows someone at the top." In the end, the students went unpunished and no legal action was taken.

The teacher's strong reaction to the incident seems to signify something about the sacredness of authority that in some sense "resides" in the portrait. Defacement is not a practice that started after the revolution. The huge campaign billboards portraying Yanukovych's face were subjected to graffiti and profanity of all kinds. These alterations were meant to show what his detractors considered his "real" face, be it that of a convict (*zek*), that of Stalin (the leader or *Vozhd*), or that of Bulgakov's "Sharikov" (a man implanted with the heart of a dog, a metaphor for the engineering of the "Soviet Man").[1] Vandalism reached such a point that in some places, a police officer could be seen standing guard under Yanukovych billboards, presumably to protect the candidate's image against potential defacement. This suggests that the image of the candidate was thought to bear an iconic relation to the actual candidate. As in sympathetic magic, it became possible to harm the person by harming his image, thus the need for "bodyguards." Because of the constant threat of defacement, the authorities eventually had to "disappear" Yanukovych's face. As Kyivites went to work one morning and saw regular advertisement instead of the face, some could not help but laugh: this had been a small victory. Yanukovych's image was soon replaced with life-sized pictures of his most popular supporters (television anchors, the former president Leonid Kravchuk, etc.). Yet campaign leaflets continued to be distributed that showed this same face, in smaller proportions.

A couple of weeks after Yanukovych's face had been officially disappeared in Kyiv, Yushchenko had been literally defaced. One night, Svetlana had come back home late from work and simply declared: "[They] poisoned him [*Ioho otruily*]." She had no doubt that the Kuchma government was responsible for this. For Yushchenko supporters, this constituted evidence that the Kuchma government would stop at nothing to ensure Yanukovych's victory. Echoing the government channel's reports that Yushchenko had suddenly and unexpectedly fallen ill, Yanukovych supporters at the private school had suggested instead that Yushchenko had contracted syphilis, or that his "alcoholism" had simply caught up with him. "Too much homemade vodka" was a version I heard at the market.

Speaking on Maidan during the Orange Revolution, Yushchenko declared, raising his hand to his face: "This face is the face of Ukraine," going on to talk about how the government had plundered and destroyed Ukraine. Through this statement, Yushchenko, the "people's president" (*narodnyi prezydent*), could claim to have on his body, as citizens did on theirs (recall the election observer's reference to his black eye as the "seal of the state" in Chapter 4), the traces of the state. Thus the candidate's *face* had become the terrain on which people and government met. It seems that in the absence of the conditions for a *conversation* (or "face to face") between citizens and government, the two had spoken to one another *through* the face, and particularly, through the *defacement* of both Yanukovych (his image), and Yushchenko (his actual face). But what lay behind defacement? Defacement involved a willful transformation. But was defacement simple unmasking? Was it an exercise in "making legible" in some way by bringing the "insides outside" (Taussig 1999)?

The transcripts of a private phone conversation between unknown interlocutors in Kyiv and Moscow following Yushchenko's poisoning is revealing: [Kiev]: "The point was to make [Yushchenko's] face ugly, to disfigure the Messiah, and to brand him with the mark of the beast" (quoted in Wilson 2005: 101). The expectation seems to have been that the "Messiah" (the secret police's code name for Yushchenko, an ironic acknowledgment of his charisma and the quasi-religious fervor he inspired in some people) could be transformed from "superhuman" to "less than human." Some Yanukovych supporters claimed that the poisoning had revealed Yushchenko's *true* (ugly) face. In contrast, when speaking with Yushchenko supporters, one got the sense that underneath the disfigured Yushchenko lay the real, or true Yushchenko (the one preserved in memory as the "before" picture). Taussig claims that the face is at the crossroads of mask and window to the soul (1999: 3). Here, the logic at work on both sides of the political divide was that "Our candidate's face is a window to his soul; your candidate's face is a mask."

What constituted one's true face was framed in a particular way in a political atmosphere where everyone is accused of being a "political chameleon [*prystosuvanets*]" who switches alliances at will, caring only about his or her own personal interests. As Taussig demonstrates in his book *Defacement: Public Secrecy and the Labor of the Negative* (1999), defacement is not a simple exercise of revealing truth. Defacement further empowers the secret, the "public secret" that can be defined as "that which is generally known, but cannot be articulated" (Taussig 1999: 5). In this case, it may be that the secret that everyone shares (from politicians to "ordinary citizens" across the political divide) is, ultimately, that "Things are not as they seem." There is no depth to the surface of the face, no "real face" behind the mask, but merely a proliferation of masks. The category of the *prystosuvanets,* or political chameleon who switches political alliances and political programs at will, essentializes the idea of a multitude of equally deceitful faces.[2]

To get back to the incident in school, what might we say about students' "second defacement"? Pro-Yushchenko students were not particularly well disposed toward defeated Yanukovych supporters. They often taunted and humiliated them, just as they felt they had been humiliated when a Yanukovych victory was apparently secured. In some sense, the pro-democracy candidate's victory had led to his domination (through image), and not (or not yet) to the conditions of possibility for a conversation among people on different sides of the political divide. With conversation still rare in the school context, defacement provided an effective form of political dissent. Both sides were still talking to one another "through" the face rather than face to face. The fact that the "perpetrators" wished to remained unseen and unknown emphasized this. The teacher's use of "enemies of the people" to describe the students is also significant, as the term "people" in this context no longer refers to the proletariat, but to a victorious majority of Yushchenko supporters. Because the perpetrators had an alternate loyalty, they were the enemies of the majority. For this, the majority could potentially "hang" them. Is democracy in this case arising as the dictatorship of the majority?

Perhaps most striking is the teacher's response to the defacement of the president's image. Invoking "the law," she threatened students with imprisonment. It is probable that she was thinking of Soviet laws that criminalized defamation (especially that of leaders and powerful individuals). The "Law against Defamation" of the 2004 Civil Code of Ukraine stated that "negative information disseminated about an individual is considered false" (Article

277). This allowed politicians and other powerful individuals to define criticism or any inconvenient statements about them as defamation, and to sue or jail the accused (usually journalists). The law was amended in December 2005, a year after the Orange Revolution, to be more compatible with free speech. The new "Law on Amendments to the Civil Code as to the Right to Information" states that "negative information disseminated about a person is false unless the person who disseminated it can prove the contrary." The point is that for years after the collapse of the Soviet Union, one could be jailed for portraying authority in a negative light, and Svetlana's invocation of the law was in line with this. The students' actions do not seem to fall neatly under the category of defamation, however, because the latter is usually expressed orally or in written form. The constitution of Ukraine considers it the duty of all citizens to respect state symbols, identified as the coat of arms, the national anthem, and the flag. Under the criminal code of Ukraine, punishment for public mockery of these symbols may include six months of imprisonment or a fine. Here again, there is no mention of the image of the president constituting a state symbol, or no provisions for the punishment of defacement. In any case, the students did not "alter" the picture of the president in any way. The picture depicted the president as he appeared after the poisoning: terribly disfigured. While Svetlana invoked "the law," perhaps what lay beneath her aversion for the students' actions was an unwritten law, a kind of taboo against the defacement of one's leader. It was not simply that "the representation becomes the represented" (Taussig 1999: 4), which would suggest that by defacing the picture, students were harming Yushchenko himself. Svetlana may have reacted against what she considered to be the *desecration* of the image. In his discussion of totemism, Durkheim argues that the prohibitions around the representation are "more numerous, stricter, and more severely enforced than those pertaining the totem itself" (1965: 155). This leads Durkheim to conclude that "the images of totemic beings are more sacred than the beings themselves" (1965: 156). If the representation or image is more sacred than what it represents, it would follow that the defacement of the image would appear a worse crime than the defacement of the actual person. After his poisoning, Yushchenko had claimed that his face was "the face of Ukraine." His face now stood in a metonymic relation to society, and thus became, more than a human face, society's totem. In this particular context, society refers to the people who are at the mercy of the government in power. Thus Yushchenko's defacement was

more than his *own* disfigurement. Crucially, it possessed that "strange surplus of negative energy" that arises from the desecration of a nation's flag,
currency, or monuments (Taussig 1999: 2).

Svetlana's outrage may have had something to do with what Soviet historians have termed the "Cult of Personality," in which the portrait played
such a central role. The cult of personality had developed under Lenin, but
was consolidated under Stalin. Many scholars have pointed to a parallel between worship of the Soviet leader's image and icon and tsar worship among
the peasantry. In 1936, a diarist described Bolshevik revolutionary holidays
thus: "the portraits of party leaders are now displayed the same way icons
used to be: a round portrait framed and attached to a pole . . . just like what
people used to do before on church holidays" (in Fitzpatrick 1999: 30). In his
book *Art Under Stalin* (1991), Bown describes how after World War II, "Artists no longer portrayed the man [Stalin], as it were, but the idea of the man;
as flesh and blood he might have ceased to exist; he had become a bundle of
concepts, the embodiment of all virtue, a divinity" (178). The All-Union
Agricultural Exhibition of 1939 included a larger-than-life sculpture of Stalin by the artist Mercurov. Bown interprets the search for a bomb inside the
sculpture of Stalin as "an indication of the almost supernatural significance
that was now attributable to images of the leader: as if a terrorist, intent on
doing maximum damage to the Soviet state, might therefore choose to blow
up not a railway bridge or pipeline, but a statue of Stalin" (1991: 83). In the
Eastern Orthodox tradition, the destruction or alteration of an icon (e.g., of
Jesus or the Virgin Mary) is perceived as an attack on the figure it represents. Here, in contrast, the destruction of Stalin's image would amount to
the destruction of the *Soviet state* itself. A similar logic was perhaps at work
with the picture of Yanukovych during the Ukrainian elections. If Yanukovych's face was the face of "the state" (meaning here, of established authority), then it became more susceptible to attack, and thus had to be guarded
with special care. Its disappearance could be interpreted as the government's sudden "retreat."

Yurchak (2006) provides us with an alternate approach to defacement
when he claims that Lenin was not just one of many Soviet symbols, but
"a central organizing principle of authoritative discourse, its master signifier
and external canon through which all other symbols and concepts were le-
gitimized" (2006: 88). We are told of a young girl, Masha, who draws a picture of Lenin (one of which she is very proud) in her Pioneer notebook, only
to be reprimanded by her teacher. The teacher tells Masha that if she cannot

draw faces, she should not attempt to draw Lenin (i.e., one cannot "experiment" with Lenin's face) (Yurchak 2006: 89). One could argue that the child's drawing of Lenin constitutes a kind of defacement by virtue of the fact that it is a deviation from the official portraits of Lenin that only specially qualified Soviet artists could paint. These portraits were based on the "original," a cast of Lenin's head or a death mask (Yurchak 2006: 89). Masha's teacher was afraid that her pupil's drawing would point to her own "ideological carelessness" (Yurchak 2006: 89). Regardless of the "perpetrator's" intentions, it is perhaps "repetition with a difference" that constitutes defacement. Masha's well-intentioned drawing of Lenin, or the Ukrainian students' ill-intentioned portrayal of Yushchenko, are both instances of defacement. While Lenin, as the "central organizing principle of Soviet authoritative discourse," cannot be compared to Yushchenko, it seems that defacement in both cases arises *as the appropriation of that which may not be individually appropriated.* The students are making the portrait *theirs* when it is not theirs to be altered. Perhaps portraits of Soviet leaders, like other collectively owned goods, belonged "to everyone" and therefore to "no one" in particular. The students knew that their somewhat spectacular defacement of Yushchenko would produce a surplus of negative energy (Taussig 1999). Nevertheless, the incident could also be regarded as just another manifestation of "cynicism" (see Chapter 2). In fact, cynicism may be thought of as defacement not because it exposes a secret, but because it repeats "with a difference." For many teachers, cynicism repeats reality while also defiling it in some way.

Barricade

In both the public and private schools, I observed on numerous occasions a daily ritual through which students negotiated their "captivity" (see Chapter 3). Shortly after the revolution, I was sitting next to the doors in the main hall waiting to interview a student and witnessed for the nth time the ritual of rushing toward the school doors during the break to go out. The guard had locked the door and this time was standing outside. Grade eleven students were desperate to get out, and kept knocking and banging on the door, pushing it violently. A male student decided to put a chair in front of the door and sit on it so that the guard could not get back in. He said to the others, "If he doesn't let us out, we won't let him in." Another student took another

chair, and soon there were three students sitting in front of the door, surrounded by another ten or so. Then a girl suggested bringing *palatky* (tents)
the next day, to which another girl replied, "yeah, let's make an Orange
Revolution," and then the first one said, "or a green one, or a violet [gay] one,
anything." Other students came down to get out, and one of them remarked,
"Oh, there's a barricade." Then one of the guys walked up to the "patriotic
corner" of the front hall and took the Ukrainian flag displayed there to the
students' improvised "camp." The guard yelled from the other side of the
door, wanting to get back in, and students yelled back to him meanly, staying
firmly in their chairs. Finally, the bell rang and the kids slowly dispersed,
allowing the guard back in.

As this example makes clear, after the revolution, students no longer
drew solely on the bandit repertoire to negotiate their passage to the outside.
Force is still present, of course, in the form of shouting and banging on the
door. It is also present, to a certain extent, in the strategy central to this episode: the barricade. The barricade as a technique is traditionally associated
with warfare and perhaps siege, as in the French or Bolshevik Revolutions.
The barricade is interesting because it is both a boundary and an invitation to
storm (but not usually an invitation to conversation). In this case, we have
the establishment of a *boundary* (chairs against the door), where, effectively,
the representative of authority (the guard) and the students were back to
back rather than face to face.

Students also mimicked nonviolent techniques observed on Maidan,
however. What could a partial reliance on democratic strategies add to students' action? By borrowing from the revolution's repertoire, students re-
framed a demand that school authorities (principal, teachers, and security
guard) considered "excessive" as a *legitimate* demand. In other words, the
revolutionary form affixed a seal of legitimacy to what would otherwise
appear to school authorities as mere "disorder." In fact, through this form,
students could reconfigure themselves as agents for change, or revolutionaries within their own institution.

Students now understood something of the power of collective action,
itself grounded in the will of the majority: "*Razom nas bahato* [Together we
are many]." They couched their demands within the framework of democracy, that is, presenting themselves not only as a popular (in this case, student)
majority, but also drawing on national symbols (i.e., the Ukrainian flag) to
add weight to their demands. Teachers claimed that the purpose of the patriotic display at the entrance of the school (it included a large flag, the words

Figure 9. "Freedom will not be defeated," reads the Orange Revolution sticker on this street sign in Kyiv. Photo by the author, 2004.

of the national anthem, and the Ukrainian trident) was to instill in students respect for the Ukrainian nation and state. This put them in a relation of subservience, further emphasized by the prohibition on touching the flag. By removing the flag from its usual context and appropriating it for their impromptu "revolution," however, students de facto redefined the "patriot." No longer obedient or respectful of authority, the patriot, anchored in national symbols, could potentially become a force that authorities had to recognize and with which they had to contend. Crucially, students constituted themselves as a potentially equal *interlocutor.* The fact that they rallied around the Ukrainian flag gave their action a certain legitimacy (it was not, after all, a pirate flag), and thus they could no longer be as easily dismissed as "outlaws" or "bandits." While the barricade central to the students' performance seemed anything but an invitation to discussion, certain elements of it seemed to establish some of the conditions necessary for a conversation with authority.

The revolution indeed provided students with new ways to express their longing for freedom (however defined) in the context of specific institutional constraints. But students did not merely repeat disciplines and strategies observed in the revolutionary context. Rather, they domesticated these so that they would become relevant to power struggles specific to the school. This appropriation of the revolution was reminiscent of Peter Weiss's play *The Persecution and Assassination of Jean-Paul Marat as Performed by the Inmates of the Asylum of Charenton Under the Direction of the Marquis de Sade* (1966). In the play, we see how the specificities of the inmates' plight come through in their *reenactment* of the French Revolution. "Who keeps us prisoners / Who locks us in," chant the patients, "We're all normal and we want our freedom / Freedom Freedom Freedom" (1966: 12). One thing is common to both school and asylum: the revolution has not fundamentally changed the conditions of the "confinement." The institutions themselves remain "special" spaces, and thus the inmates' or students' demands, inspired by revolutionary action, take on a certain urgency: "We want our rights and we don't care *how* / We want our Revolution NOW," chant the Charenton inmates (1966: 11).

The specificity of the school as an institution means that one cannot pose it simply as a microcosm of society. Both the demonstrators on Maidan and the high school students shared the impulse to destabilize their so-called unfair leadership (*nespravedlyve kerivnytstvo*). Nevertheless, there were crucial differences in the kinds of repertoires and self-representation deployed to achieve this goal. Revolutionary discourses reproduced by the self-proclaimed "pro-democracy" candidate and his supporters posed banditry as ideologically *incompatible* with human rights. There was no "conversation" to be had between these. In schools, in contrast (and the above incident in which students used both force and democratic strategies for getting out of the school illustrates this well), the democratic repertoire often *merged* with the bandit repertoire. There, students often claimed rights by invoking the figure of the bandit, and used the bandit repertoire to mobilize against the unfair practices of the authorities.

Students told me repeatedly that they had learned something new, that "Together we can achieve *whatever* we want." The key here is perhaps the "whatever." What is it teenagers want, and how did Maidan teach them to fight for it? It sometimes seemed that students had understood the revolution as successful mass disobedience, and that this could be transposed to the school context not only to defend actual rights, but also to obtain whatever they felt entitled to. That is to say, there was a thin line between what Brooks (2005) refers to as *svoboda*, associated with civic freedoms, and *volia*, another kind of freedom associated with will and desire. Young people indeed seemed to be defending something along the continuum of "the bandit-like freedom of wanton desire [and] the liberal freedom to realize oneself in an orderly world" (Brooks 2005: 16). The example of exiting the school points to this subtlety: Is it students' *right* to get out of the school during breaks, or is it rather a privilege? Where would one draw the line?

The Orange Revolution constituted the promise of "freedom within the law [*svoboda*]" rather than "freedom outside the law [*volia*]." Arbitrary rules, whether those of the so-called bandit government (the informal rules of *poniattia*), or those of schools' principals, have become visible as "unfairness." While students do not abandon the repertoire of the bandit entirely (the school as an institution has not become democratic overnight), they begin to portray themselves as persons with civic rights (rights *within* the law). They imagine a new set of school rules within which they could enjoy certain rights and freedoms.

As illustrated in Chapter 2, there was a tendency in the school context to perceive *svoboda* as something that would automatically degenerate into *volia* (e.g., democracy could only become "excessive" democracy). And indeed, in the school setting, where students constantly tested limits, *volia* could still constitute an expression of freedom. Students claimed that they were sometimes overwhelmed by their own "disorder." I had asked a group of ninth graders if there had been anything good about the Soviet Union. One of them, a well-known troublemaker, replied that yes, there was discipline. And what about now? "Now we have a new president [Viktor Yushchenko], but the country's still a *durdom* [nut house]!" Other students longed for order as well, claiming that lessons were sometimes so chaotic that they ended up wasting their time entirely, unable to hear what the teacher was saying. Others claimed: "You come to school, and you don't know where you are, in a school or in a saloon." A student once pointed to me, ashamed: "You see that big hole in the wall behind the teacher's desk? We punched that in one day while fooling around during the break."

I became painfully aware of the way freedom could manifest itself during an excursion with a class of eleventh graders from the private school. To celebrate the end of the school year, they had asked me and their teacher of mathematics to accompany them to Western Ukraine. The week-long trip ended with the teacher and I woken up in the middle of the night by some activity in the hallway. Following a drunken binge, some students had succeeded in flooding their hotel bathroom, causing commotion and damage of the kind the hotel staff claimed to have never seen. When, close to a breakdown, the teacher began reprimanding them, they simply said, "You don't understand us [*Vy nas ne rozumiiete*]." When I later queried the students about this, they claimed that this was their only week away from parents and school, and that they had needed to feel free (*vidchuvaty sebe vil'nymy*).

In order to understand concepts of freedom circulating in this particular class, upon return from the excursion I asked the teacher of Ukrainian language to have students write essays on "What is freedom for me [*Shcho dlia mene svoboda*]." Not all the students who wrote about freedom associated it with civic freedom. Many wrote of freedom as the possibility of realizing one's desires or wishes (*bazhannia*). However, one student stated that "complete freedom [*povna svoboda*]" cannot be realized. "Freedom [*Svoboda*] is like Einstein's theory of relativity," he wrote. Many students defined freedom in relation to its limits, that is, responsibility, moral norms, and order (*poriadok*). For example, one student mentioned the upholding of the constitution as a mechanism that could counter "limitless freedom [*bezmezhna svoboda*] and license [*vsedozvolenist'*]." Others defined their personal freedom as something already within the limits of the law: "Freedom for me is when I'm free to do whatever does not contradict existing laws," wrote Tanya, a student famous for her temper tantrums. Another student, wealthy and well connected, stated, "For me, freedom is to live within the law [*za pravylamy*], when everyone has equal means (livelihood) and everyone is equal under the law."[3] The majority of the students made a distinction between the kind of freedom they wish for today and in the future. The freedom sought in the present had to do with "independence from parents," especially financial; "the possibility of independently choosing one's career, without pressure from parents," "freedom to spend time the way I want to," and "freedom to make my own decisions." Future freedom, associated with adult rights and responsibilities, was more closely connected with citizenship and with living "in a free country in which my rights and freedoms are protected." What emerges from the texts is that freedom may be associated with desires and wishes, or with rights and civic freedoms.

The themes of rights, desire, and excess also arose in a conversation with a tenth grader in the public school. Reflecting on what she perceived as students' excessive ways of defending their freedom, she said: "There should be a boundary between students' *rights* and their *freedom*." What she was in fact pointing to is the lack of distinction between *svoboda* and *volia*, and students' willingness to defend anything along this continuum through excess. She added, "Pupils' sense of democracy [within the school] is different from democracy in our country. Democracy for us students is, 'We can do whatever we want.' In the country, it doesn't work that way. Democracy in our country is based on laws and on doing things for other people to make their lives better." On the one hand, this student reproduced the civics teacher's concept of *povna demokratiia* (complete/excessive democracy), or democracy as a "free for all" (see Chapter 2) in explaining students' expressions of democracy. On the other hand, she also showed awareness of a *different* kind of democracy rooted in mutual respect, care, responsibilities, and the law. In this, she reproduced the definitions of democracy put forth by protesters on Maidan.

Capitalism as Carnival, Capitalism as Fairy Tale

The week following the end of the revolution (in early December 2004), when students returned to class, I asked some teachers of Ukrainian at the private school to distribute an in-class questionnaire to eleventh graders about their experience of the revolution. Had they been on Independence Square? If so, how had it felt? Did they agree with Yulia Tymoshenko that Ukraine had "become a nation" during the revolution? How did they now view the relation between people and state? and so on. Not all students had been present on Maidan. Some of the students whose parents supported other candidates, or were apolitical, had abstained. Several students, regardless of political affiliation, had thought it safer to watch the events on television. Those students who had gone had been there with their parents; more rarely with friends. Most students offered some thoughts about the revolution or recounted experiences on Maidan. Other students refused to answer, however, or put random Yes No Yes No answers next to the questions. Several others wrote that "children" should not be involved in politics and should concentrate on things appropriate for their age, for example, should "study, study, study, as Lenin said." Yet others declared that this kind of questionnaire was an instance of political pressure put on students in the school context. Apparently, at least one of the teachers (a Yushchenko supporter) had presented this assignment to her class as a way to earn extra points for the course. "If you write well and good things, it will help you with your grade in the class," she had claimed. Therefore, it was necessary to choose a different strategy. For the public school, I chose lyrics from a song that had been very popular with youth during the revolution (*Ia ne khochu*, or "I Don't Want

to"; see Chapter 2), and asked students to elaborate on them. Group interviews were also conducted with students in grades 10 and 11 in both schools.

Many different expressions were put forth to describe the revolution,
including "festival," "carnival," and "theatrical celebration." Yet the most
compelling metaphor arose while in conversation with a group of eleventh-
grade students in the private school. Remembering her experience on Maidan,
one student simply said that it was "like a fairy tale." The metaphor of the
fairy tale can be applied to different dimensions of the revolution. A friend
of mine who had spent every day on Maidan agreed that the *structure* of the
fairy tale resembled that of the revolution in many ways. For one, fairy tales
present a clear picture of the difference between good and evil. Fairy tales
also have a plot and a direction: they are comprised of a quest, some trials
and tribulations, and then the restoring of balance which leads to a (usually)
happy ending. They are often stories of empowerment. Based on student accounts of the event, it seems that the fairy tale, limited in space (Independence
Square) and in time (seventeen days), referred to a space of enchantment in
which what Kideckel (1995) calls the "actually existing turbulence" of everyday life had been temporarily suspended. It appears that the "fairy tale,"
more than a description of revolution-era sociality, came to stand for a new
(more just) kind of capitalism. Exhausted by the lawlessness, violence, and
excess that they had dubbed "the carnival," demonstrators longed for a different sort of capitalism.

Based on the material collected, it appears that dimensions of citizenship (the relation among citizens, the relation of citizens to the "state," and
the relation of citizens to themselves) had undergone sudden and dramatic
transformation. Students described the relation among citizens with particular fondness. "It was so cold on Maidan, but there was such warmth!"
stated Natasha, a tenth grader. Students described Maidan as the site of
the "highest moral values," "solidarity of the people," and "mutual aid." "One
could feel a powerful flow of warmth and kindness," stated one student. She
continued: "On Maidan I saw a lot of people from all corners of Ukraine,
people of all professions, social rank and age groups—students and businessmen, teachers and soldiers, athletes and artists. . . . All stood together,
chanting, 'Together we are many and we will never be defeated!' discussing
and joking, [and] in their eyes burned the same fire—orange." "I cannot convey with words what I saw in the eyes of the protesters, one has to experience
it," claimed another student. A university student and friend of mine had
marveled at the number of friends and acquaintances she had met on Maidan

(the crowd there had at some point reached one million). "How do you think this happened?" I asked. "Because you know, people were actually *looking* at one another, looking into each other's eyes, for a change." This sudden "face to face" was itself an invitation to conversation, even with strangers. Several students pointed out how bumping into other people had resulted not in the usual aggressive behavior, but in new, sometimes lasting, friendships. Conversation even became possible across the political divide. Yushchenko supporters offered food and blankets to Yanukovych supporters who had traveled all the way from Eastern Ukraine, and arguments between them, though sometimes animated, did not result in violence.

It became obvious that the relation between people and state was being reconfigured when people interviewed on *Maidan* began addressing their leaders (Kuchma and his people) as "*ty*" (or the informal "you"), hailing them and instructing them on the course of action to take. This was in sharp contrast with the previous use of "they" or "them" to refer to the government. A student also told me how she had felt listening to politicians addressing the crowd: "It was the only time when important politicians like Yushchenko and Tymoshenko spoke to people like to people. And you feel like you are the same as them, and you don't feel that they are different, that they are better or smarter than you." This was in contrast to those "bandits [who] think they're higher than you [*vyshchi za tebe*]." At that moment, it became possible to imagine that the gap between people and government had been bridged. Another student wrote: "We were afraid for all the people on Maidan, because we are a big family, I think, and we were afraid of blood on Maidan, because we came with peace in our heart, like Yushchenko. He showed in a peaceful way how to change something, and how to make things better in our country without the use of weapons. As in the song *Razom nas bahato* [Together We Are Many], he showed the power of our country, the power of our people, and the power of our *nation,* that we are all Ukrainians."

The relation of demonstrators to themselves also changed. Students in the private school pointed out in their accounts that among the protesters in the orange camp, "not one swear word was heard, there was not one drunk, not one violator of the civic order [*porushnykiv hromadians'koho poriadku*]." While this picture of complete civility is perhaps not entirely accurate, it suggests a desire among the demonstrators to transcend the image of "disorder" commonly associated with the "postcolony" or states deemed "in transition."[4] People proudly told me, a few days into the revolution, You know that the crime rate in Kyiv has dropped by half? One of the students in the public school told me how she had lost her cell phone on Maidan and called her own number from her friend's phone. She was so pleasantly surprised when the person who had found her phone answered to let her know that she could come pick it up under the central clock (a traditional downtown meeting place)! Of course, as everywhere, there were people trying to use the event to their own advantage. While walking with a friend (a university student) around Maidan, we encountered a man selling a cell phone. My friend is by nature reserved, but she immediately approached him: "Why are you selling this phone? Is this a phone you just found and now want to make money on? Shame on you!" Through small incidents like these, and through *self-policing*, a kind of moral, self-ruling community was being reproduced. We might interpret these practices of self-regulation as evidence that people were "buying into" the neoliberal model. Yet as Matza (2009) has argued about Russia, "projects that may appear 'neoliberalizing' also articulate with other political rationalities to produce unpredictable results" (493). As seen in Chapter 5, self-regulation coexisted with longing for state protection and care.

Although by all accounts very little had changed in the power relations specific to the school context, students could now imagine a context in which more teachers would be "fair [*spravedlyvi*]," and principals would be younger and more attuned to students' needs. Power, in its essence, was being rethought. "We need a father," said Serhiy, an eleventh grader in the private school, "but one who will help us, not beat us." His fellow student Nadia, commenting on relations with authority in the school and the country, said to me (with great insight, I think): "What we need in the future [in the school and in the country] is a conversation, not a revolution."

Conclusion

The tendency in much recent writing on post-Soviet states has been to view "transition" as the transformation, through exposure to new "Western" models, of post-socialist subjectivities, collectivities, and socialities. This book challenges such a partial view by focusing on the ways in which post-Soviet citizenries themselves actively transform, negotiate, and localize the very concepts aimed at shaping them. Change in the region can thus be viewed in terms of a constant engagement or conversation. This model restores a particular concept of local agency: not so much the agency of outright "resistance" as the agency that arises from reproducing imported political practices while also localizing and appropriating them. The notion of engagement elaborated here has further potential for understanding cultural encounters and social change, including the transformations associated with globalization.

The possibilities and complexities of change as engagement become apparent when examined through the prism of the school. The educational context becomes a space where both officially sanctioned and unofficial engagements with Western models come to meet through practices such as "cynicism." In Ukrainian schools, the repertoires of the "patriot" and the "bandit" as different forms of engagement are constantly weighed against one another and at times become intertwined. While the figure of the "bandit" or violent entrepreneur emerges out of the engagement with *capitalism*, in the school as a specific institution, students appropriate the figure of the bandit to engage with *democracy*. Young people's negotiation of the tension between the kinds of freedom associated with marketization and those associated with democratization points to citizenship as an exercise in "self making and being made by power relations" (Ong 1996: 737). Thus we may speak not only of the effects of schooling on students, but also of students' impact on the educational process, as the first generation of post-Soviet children engages creatively with different models.

Human rights as the "archetypal language of democratic transition" (Wilson 2001: 1) can be filled with different meanings. The human rights literature has at times reproduced the assumption that the terms "human" and "rights" are everywhere understood in a similar way. Recent anthropological work on the "vernacularization" of human rights has challenged this view (Goodale and Merry 2007). Students of rights must not only contend with variations (e.g., cross-cultural, but also along class, gender, and generational lines) in the definition of "human," but also trace the various conceptualizations of "rights" that may be present within a single cultural context. In addition, Goldstein (2007) observes that "as with all cultural phenomena, the meanings of human rights shift and change over time, as local actors redefine them in response to current material conditions and sociopolitical configurations" (52). My study demonstrates the extent to which the everyday meanings of rights tend to be unstable, flexible, and dependent on the power dynamics within which they emerge. In fact, in the Ukrainian context, human rights as a "floating signifier that represents a new form of human dignity and moral worth" (Goodale 2007: 160) may be variously construed as needs, entitlements, duties, freedoms, privileges, or desires.

As "incomplete" (or incompletely socialized) citizens, young people are in a particularly good position to recast official idioms for social action (Herzfeld 2005), and thus have more leeway in subverting and/or expanding the definition of rights. As a result, some of their imaginaries of rights may be grounded in a concern for equality and social justice, while others are grounded in whim, will, and desire. While we might be tempted to associate young people's articulation of rights beyond the purview of the law (i.e., seemingly excessive or unjustified rights) with children's supposed "natural" unruliness or rebelliousness, this study has shown the importance of examining the conditions of possibility for this kind of behavior. Jenks enjoins us to look at children's transgressions as "critiques of the current order rather than as disruptions of a properly normative life" (2005: 150). This perspective allows for an analysis of the way young people navigate different configurations of power, whether the hierarchies of school, state, or global dynamics.

In their articulation of "outlaw" freedom, young people draw on the performances of the post-Soviet "violent entrepreneurs" (this kind of appropriation points to the importance of going beyond the official discourses of rights wielded by states, supranational entities, or NGOs, to explore unofficial sites of pedagogy). While violent entrepreneurs had come to position themselves at the margins of the law in order to survive emergent capitalism, students appropriate bandit behavior and demeanor to gain the upper hand (sometimes in a forceful fashion) in the power struggle with school authorities. Like young people elsewhere, students must negotiate the tension between the growing focus on children as rights-bearing individuals, and what Ariès points to as the "quarantine" of childhood. In Ukrainian schools, the tendency (found in Soviet pedagogies) to relegate young people to the realm of "childhood" is often replicated, though based on a different logic, in new national pedagogies. Under these circumstances, young people's quest for rights and dignity comes to be enacted via the bandit who demands "respect." This kind of performance speaks to young people's increasing exposure to "technologies of the self" (independence, initiative, risk-taking) deemed necessary to survival in a market economy (e.g., Matza 2009, Phillips 2011). Yet by modeling the most extreme of "market subjectivities" (i.e., the bandit who wields violence and whose personal freedom and wealth are gained at the expense of others), young people simultaneously reproduce and subvert pedagogies associated with neoliberal self-making.

Students' claims and performances of rights "outside the law" are also partially rooted in long-standing cultural discourses (still prevalent in Ukraine and Russia) that distinguish between civic freedom (*svoboda*), and the freedom based on will and desire (*volia*). In the context of engagement with the West, this discourse posits that the Western-style civic freedoms granted to the people are likely to degenerate into license and chaos. This does not mean that children's oscillation between civic freedom and freedom "outside the law" should be read as proof that Ukrainians (or, more generally, the "East Slavic") people are in fact prone to disorder. Rather, young people's self-representation as "unruly children" allows them the flexibility to both explore a range of possible subject positions vis-à-vis school authorities, *and* to keep "Western" norms and standards at bay, if they so desire.[1] Indeed, the image of one's people as "inherently disorderly" allows space for imagining a kind of freedom that operates not only outside of regulation, but also outside of self-regulation as the essence of neoliberal governmentality.[2] This points to the importance of examining the connection between a region's position in the global hierarchy and its inhabitants' articulations of rights (especially when the region under study tends to be stereotyped by Western actors as "prone to disorder" because it is, e.g., "postcolonial," or as in the case of Eastern Europe, because it has become emblematic of the civilizational boundary between "Europe" and the "unruly beyond").

The association of rights with excess is context-specific, however. As young people circulate between different social spheres (e.g., from school to streets), the nature of their engagement with rights changes. In their involvement with "democratic revolution," a form that is now spreading to Africa and the Middle East, young people are being "hailed" by certain Western/global articulations of democracy and more generally, of the "normal." Yet the effects of this exposure are not predictable, as every instance of peaceful protest has its own pedagogies and locally relevant forms of order. In Ukraine, students combined selected elements of Soviet modernity and Western/global concepts of rights so as to forge new imaginaries of human rights and social justice. The post-Soviet generation's incorporation of Soviet elements not only complicates the picture of change as "failed reproduction"; it also suggests that Western standards may be appropriated and infused with elements relevant to young people's vision of a just future. What emerges from the different takes on rights described in this book is that young people value both freedom and justice, but that the balance between them changes according to the context in which rights are being claimed. Participation in mass political mobilization gave young people the opportunity to express dissent directly, and not, as in schools, "behind the back" of power (e.g., defacement), or through deceit (e.g., the bandit posing as patriot). It is essential to examine how the power relations inherent in a particular context influence the kinds of articulations of rights put forth by young people.

The "state" in post-Soviet Ukraine comes across as highly *diffuse* (e.g., inhabiting the realm of chance) and at the same time as highly *personalized* (e.g., essentialized in the leader's image). Yet in both instances, it manifests itself to citizens as "two-faced" (i.e., the bandit/state, or the mask/real face of political leaders). The local concept of "bandit state" emerges as the expression of a form of authority rooted equally in paternalism and violence (and where surveillance and protection have become blurred), and this entanglement comes through in the students' image of "the father who beats us." Thus citizens may construe the state as the usurper of rights and freedoms, or personify it as the agent that bestows entitlements. This tension becomes apparent in electoral contests in Ukraine, and recent political developments illustrate the ambiguity felt toward the state. In parliamentary elections deemed free and fair in March 2006, Viktor Yanukovych's Party of Regions (the party that Yushchenko supporters associated with "criminals") came out victorious. "What happened," I asked a friend of mine from Kyiv. "How could Yanukovych be back in power so soon after the Orange Revolution?" "Because people want democracy, but they also want a strong leader who will care for them. They want both [*i te i te khochut'*]." Is it really the case that Ukrainian citizens wished for seemingly contradictory things, or is it rather that the kind of democracy for which many (though not all) people longed needed to be compatible with a strong benevolent state? In February 2010, the people of Ukraine elected Viktor Yanukovych as their president. In a runoff election, he collected 48.83 percent of the votes, while Yulia Tymoshenko, one of the key figures of the Orange Revolution, obtained 45.59 percent of the votes. The incumbent, Viktor Yushchenko, dubbed "least popular president in the world," got a measly 5.45 percent of the popular vote in the first round, slightly more than the category "Against all [*proty vsikh*]" chosen by 4.36 percent of citizens in the runoff election.

This was the very first presidential election in which the first post-Soviet generation, now legal adults and full-fledged citizens, could vote, and thus it is difficult to assess their impact on the final results. Yet it is doubtful that this new generation would settle for democracy without social justice, or higher living standards without political liberties. This study has shown how young people crafted a synthetic discourse that combined concerns for rights, freedom, and social justice to respond to the local engagements with capitalism, and my expectation is that they will forge new political imaginaries in which these elements continue to coexist, though not necessarily in a predictable fashion. While some Western journalists have described Yanukovych's recent victory as the triumph of a pro-Moscow, Soviet-style authoritarian leader, my findings suggest that there can be no real return to Soviet-style politics in Ukraine. The first post-Soviet generation's engagement with rights in their textbooks, in the media, and on the streets cannot be easily undone, and their exuberant quest for civic rights in school, even when couched in the language of "bandits," reveals their awareness of the possibility of "freedom within the law." Thus as these young people emerge as new political players in the next few years, their political orientation will likely be neither nostalgic nor blindly West-centric.

Notes

Chapter 1. Young Citizens and the Meanings of Rights in a Globalizing World

1. All names have been changed to protect my informants' privacy.

2. Markowitz (2000) notes a similar use of the term "children [*deti*]" in Russian schools in the mid-1990s.

3. Recent studies conducted on the subject of adolescent rebellion have questioned the universality of this phenomenon, both within particular social contexts and across cultures. Some have suggested that youth rebellion is a powerful discourse that has contributed to the marginalization of adolescents (e.g., Graham 2004).

4. Several scholars have argued that the boundary between "state" and "society" is a construction. This is part of a larger critique of the concept of "civil society" (e.g., Hann and Dunn 1996, Gupta 2006, Hemment 2007, Phillips 2008, Creed 2011).

5. Or what John and Jean Comaroff (2006) have described as the criminal, "uncivil society" that tends to emerge under conditions of state withdrawal (274).

6. Another response relevant to this study and to citizenship in general is citizens' attempts at making themselves similarly "illegible," a strategy that may be used in dealings with the state and other forms of authority.

7. The concept of "zone" and "exception" may also be useful in conceptualizing young people's *perceived* relationship, as "minors," to the law and to citizenship rights.

Chapter 2. Order, Excess, and the Construction of the Patriot

1. It seems that the nationality had to be compatible with denationalization of the kind necessary to what became known under Brezhnev as *sblizheniie* and *sliianie*, processes central to the formation of a "Soviet people." *Sblizhenie* meant "coming closer together," and was used to describe "the concept of nationalities living closer together, losing some of their distinctiveness and sense of separateness," while *sliianie* went one step further, relating to the "flowing together" and fusion of nationalities (Henze 1985: 6).

2. One should probably be wary of the new political projects associated with "recovering" identities, be they projects around membership in the EU or membership in the CES.

3. A look at the difference in identification between the Soviet census of 1989 and the 2001 Ukrainian census reveals the fluidity and context-dependent character of self-identification. For example, the percentage of citizens who claimed "Russianness" went from almost 22 percent in 1989 to 17 percent in 2001.

4. That is, a "deliberate" famine to the extent that the little grain produced was expropriated from rural communities and their inhabitants prevented from leaving to search for food.

5. The extent to which the concept of genetic code represents a move away from nationalism is debatable; however, in the Ukrainian context, the concept is associated with passivity (it is something one simply "has" and cannot change) rather than with assertive or chauvinistic nationalism.

6. There remains a tension in the neoliberal state, however, whereby "on the one hand, the state maintains 'law and order,' while on the other it produces subjects who are autonomous and self-regulating" (Speed 2007: 175).

7. The making of students into decent persons seemed all the more critical in a context marked by capitalist transformations and what many teachers saw as the resulting deterioration of morals.

8. This type of portrayal was common in the Soviet Union as well (see, e.g., *Diary of a Russian Schoolteacher*, 1960).

9. As Burawoy and Verdery (1999) have argued, much of what may appear at first glance as Soviet "inertia" may in fact arise as a conscious response to *post*-Soviet challenges.

10. In her ethnography of post-Soviet Russian schools, Patico (2008) notes that in her informants' discourses, "the continent of Africa held special power as a condensed representation of lack of status, power, and sophistication" (2008: 137).

11. For example, Argenti (2007) has talked about the treatment of social subordinates as children in Cameroon, and Bayart (1979) has used the term "social cadets" to speak of the infantilization of subordinates.

12. In this case, however, one could argue that it may contribute to a sense of *supranational* intimacy and cohesion, at least when "our people" stands for Ukrainians, Russians, and Belarusians. I say "*may* contribute" because some Ukrainians, like the Estonians described by Rausing, regard Russians as "inherently excessive and disorderly" while viewing themselves as characterized by "restraint and order" (Rausing 2004: 36).

Chapter 3. Seeking Rights, Performing the Outlaw

1. The word *brigada* comes from the Soviet labor camp setting, where it referred literally to a "work brigade." The brigade was comprised of several prisoners organized according to an informal hierarchy, with a "leader," his sidekicks, and a number of subordinates.

2. Perhaps the bandit also provided post-Soviet citizens with a way of "being somebody" in a post–Cold War context in which identification with the Soviet super-power is no longer possible, and where national identity does not necessarily con-stitute a source of self-assertiveness.

3. In her analysis of popular responses to marketization in Russia, Patico notes that "'culturedness' evokes Soviet norms of propriety and has been used to critique post-Soviet class developments and crass nouveau riche materialism" (2005: 480).

4. In his study of gangs and gangster behavior in inner cities, Garot (2007), draw-ing on Goffman's (1959, 1976) work on impression management, notes that "identity is increasingly recognized not as an obdurate quality but as a resource whose relevance is strategically and conceptually determined" (2007: 50), so that "at times, a young per-son is definitely a gang member, and at other times, the same young person definitely is not" (2007: 51).

5. Students seemed particularly taken with the depictions of everyday racism in rap lyrics.

The combination of African American gangster slang and Russian resulted, for example, in some eleventh graders hailing each other thus: "Niga, idi siuda! [Come here, "niggah"!]" (with the latter used as a term of address between equals, and seem-ingly without racist connotations in this particular context).

6. I could not help but be reminded of the informal leaders' attitudes toward work in the gulag setting. The institution of the Soviet labor camp was premised on the pos-sibility of rehabilitation (of criminals and political prisoners) through work. Yet, out of principle, the informal leaders of the prison setting usually performed no work in the camp (Finkelstein 2001: 3), leaving it to the other members of the *brigada* (work brigade) to meet work targets. In fact, among the prisoner elite or so-called "thieves-in-law" (*vory v zakone*), work had to be avoided at all costs: "Since the true thief can live only on what has been stolen," writes Volkov, "any physical labor would undermine his honor or status" (2002: 56).

Chapter 4. The "Bandit State"

1. Ukrainian folklore does not portray fate as entirely dissociated from human agency, however. For example, certain Ukrainian myths and popular sayings, includ-ing some used in classrooms, clearly convey the message that "one makes one's own fate." This local version of fate is perhaps partly responsible for Ukrainian citizens' uprising against their government in the 2004 Orange Revolution.

2. One could suppose that this "illegibility" gave state authorities a certain kind of flexibility, so that were the men to engage in some form of violence, the authorities would be in a position to stage a dissection: "These men were not ours, they were just thugs."

3. A former gulag inmate, Lev Razgon, describes the behavior of the prisoner "elite" toward other prisoners: "They did not work [in the labor camp] but were allocated a

full ration; they levied a money tribute from all the 'peasants,' those who did work; they took half of the food parcels and purchases from the camp commissary; and they brazenly cleaned out the new transports, taking all the best clothes from the newcomers. They were, in a word, racketeers, gangsters, and members of a small mafia. All the ordinary criminal inmates of the camp—and they made up the majority—hated them intensely" (quoted in Applebaum 2003: 283). That is not to say that informal hierarchies and rules are unique to the gulag setting. Sets of informal rules, sometimes referred to as the "convict code," exist in prisons in the United States, where, for example, inmates may be expected to pay "rent" to their informal leader.

4. The schools in which I conducted research often marked "Victory Day," a celebration of the Soviet victory over the Nazis, with a visit from a veteran of the "Great Patriotic War," and students sometimes cried listening to their war stories.

5. In July 2005, a few months after Viktor Yushchenko had been sworn in as president of Ukraine, he decided to break with tradition by traveling to a neighboring city in an unmarked sedan, without a presidential escort. After his car was stopped by DAI officers every thirty minutes or so over the course of his trip, he decided to liquidate the Inspectorate (Korshak 2005).

6. This kind of discretionary power in applying the law is of course not unique to Ukraine. It exists, to a greater or lesser extent, in every society ruled by law.

Chapter 5. Citizenship Between Western and Soviet Modernities

1. This use of carnival to describe the government is consistent with Mbembe's (2001) argument that the *popular* spectacles and grotesque, excessive forms associated with carnival can also be appropriated by the ruling elite. My informant's comment seems to evoke not only excess but also lawlessness. As Bakhtin argues, "During carnival time life is subject only to its laws . . . the laws of its own freedom" (1984: 7).

2. Note that the concern with order was not reserved for the "orange" politicians. Many Ukrainian politicians used it to different ends. For example, in 2006, newly appointed Prime Minister Viktor Yanukovych said of his party that "We are ready to take power and restore order in the country" (ABC News Australia, March 25, 2006).

3. Here as elsewhere, all my respondents' names have been changed.

4. The homeless seemed to be, for many, a source of anxiety or fear. In fact, during my fieldwork, I heard a parent tell her young daughter: "If you don't eat your vegetables, the *bomvzh* will come upstairs and get you," suggesting that the homeless person had been substituted for the boogie man.

5. Not all respondents evoked the Soviet Union in positive terms, however. Some of my informants stressed the continuity between Kuchma's rule and Soviet rule, telling me, for example, "You think bandits in the government are new for us? No, first we had Lenin, and then, we got an even scarier [*strashnishe*] bandit, Stalin." Thus, some

posed, implicitly or explicitly, the revolution as a move away from Soviet (or reconstituted Soviet) rule. Yet I noticed in several people the *coexistence* of nostalgia for certain aspects of Soviet life and the straightforward rejection of other aspects (on the production of nostalgia in the post-Soviet space, see Boym 2001).

6. Interestingly, demonstrators posed "bandits" in government and oligarchs as the agents of plunder. No one among my informants directly referred to "capitalism" or "marketization" as forces that could produce (economic) "slaves." This is in contrast to the indictment of capitalism in other settings, e.g., Kazakhstan (see Nazpary 2002).

7. In contrast, honest, moral citizens remained poor precisely because of their honesty.

8. One question (the one by the member of the city council) dealt with regulation and taxation for small businesses. In this case, the expectation was the government (the executive) would regulate business so that entrepreneurs could support themselves and their families through their own economic activity.

9. Before the Orange Revolution, it was common to hear citizens claim that "There is no government [*Nema vlady*]," or "There is no caretaker/owner [*Nema hospodaria*]." (This is what Aretxaga [2003], in another context, has referred to as discourses of "state deficit.") It is therefore unsurprising that actions aimed at restoring the state would appear "revolutionary."

10. A few respondents also mentioned paying taxes, while still fewer suggested that they should take an active role in the development of civil society through participation in NGOs.

Chapter 6. From Revolution to Conversation?

1. Similarly, Yushchenko's detractors portrayed him, e.g., as a sellout to the United States, thus the nickname "Bushchenko."

2. The Ukrainian political ballot itself seems to acknowledge this disenchantment by offering the voter a chance to vote "against all" (*proty vsikh*). The existence of this additional category (one that follows the names of candidates on the ballot) allows a citizen to make her vote count (the percentage of those voting "against all" is at times significant) while also allowing her to endorse a principle that rejects the artifice at the root of politics. The powerful refusal in *proty vsikh* points to the perpetual illegibility of the state itself, regardless of who is in charge, and is perhaps, in its own strangely *official* way, the ultimate form of defacement.

3. It is significant that even the concept of freedom may be imbued with a concern with economic well-being and equality.

4. See Comaroff and Comaroff, eds., *Law and Disorder in the Postcolony* (2006).

Conclusion

1. This is especially so in the era of EU integration and the attempt at harmonizing standards (from democratic standards to hygienic standards).

2. On the subject of self-regulation as a form of bondage, see Talal Asad, "Conscripts of Western Civilization" (1992).

References

Abrams, Philip. 2006 (1977). Notes on the Difficulty of Studying the State. In *The Anthropology of the State: A Reader*. Aradhana Sharma and Akhil Gupta, eds. Oxford: Blackwell.

Agamben, Giorgio. 2000. *Means Without End: Notes on Politics*. Minneapolis: University of Minnesota Press.

———. 1998. *Homo Sacer: Sovereign Power and Bare Life*. Stanford: Stanford University Press.

Allina-Pisano, Jessica. 2010. Social Contracts and Authoritarian Projects in Post-Soviet Space: The Use of Administrative Resource. *Communist and Post-Communist Studies* 43: 373–382.

Alonso, Ana Maria. 2005. Sovereignty, the Spatial Politics of Security, and Gender: Looking North and South from the US-Mexico Border. In *State Formation: Anthropological Perspectives*. Christian Krohn-Hansen and Knut G. Nustad, eds. London: Pluto Press.

———. 1994. The Politics of Space, Time and Substance: State Formation, Nationalism, and Ethnicity. *Annual Review of Anthropology* 23: 379–405.

Althusser, Louis. 1971. Ideology and Ideological State Apparatuses. In *Lenin and Philosophy and Other Essays*. New York: Monthly Review Press.

Anderson, Benedict. 1991. *Imagined Communities: Reflections on the Origin and Spread of Nationalism*. London: Verso.

Apple, Michael W. 1979. *Ideology and Curriculum*. Boston: Routledge and Kegan Paul.

Applebaum, Anne. 2003. *Gulag: A History*. New York: Anchor Books.

Arel, Dominique. 2005. The "Orange Revolution": Analysis and Implications of the 2004 Presidential Election in Ukraine. Third Annual Stasiuk-Cambridge Lecture on Contemporary Ukraine, Cambridge University, February 25.

Arendt, Hannah.1963. *On Revolution*. Harmondsworth: Pelican.

Aretxaga, Begoña. 2003. Maddening States. *Annual Review of Anthropology* 32: 393–410.

Ariès, Philippe. 1962. *Centuries of Childhood: A Social History of Family Life*. New York: Knopf.

Argenti, Nicolas. 2007. *The Intestines of the State: Youth, Violence, and Belated Histories in the Cameroon Grassfields*. Chicago: University of Chicago Press.

Asad, Talal. 1992. Conscripts of Western Civilization. In *Civilization in Crisis: Anthropological Perspectives*, vol. 1 of *Dialectical Anthropology: Essays in Honor of Stanley Diamond*. Christine Ward Gailey, ed. Gainesville: University of Florida Press.

Austin, John. 1999. *How to Do Things with Words*. Oxford: Clarendon Press.

Bakhtin, Mikhail. 1996. *The Dialogic Imagination: Four Essays*. Michael Holquist, ed. Austin: University of Texas Press.

———. 1984. *Rabelais and His World*. Bloomington: Indiana University Press.

Bakka, T. V. 2005. *Liudyna i svit: zrazky vidpovidey do ekzamenatsiynykh biletiv, 11klas* [Study Guide]. Kyiv: Nachal'nyi Tsentr Shkola.

———. 2004. *Liudyna i suspil'stvo: zrazky vidpovidey do ekzamenatsiynykh biletiv, 11klas* [Study Guide]. Kyiv: Nachal'nyi Tsentr Shkola.

Banks, Marcus. 1996. *Ethnicity: Anthropological Constructions*. London: Routledge.

Bayart, Jean-François. 1979. *L'Etat au Cameroun*. Paris: Presses de la Fondation Nationale des Sciences Politiques.

Bayart, Jean-François, Stephen Ellis, and Béatrice Hibou. 1999. *The Criminalization of the State in Africa*. Oxford and Bloomington: James Currey and Indiana University Press.

Baybara, T. M., and N. M. Bibik. 2004. *Ia i Ukraina. Pidruchnyk dlia 4 klasu*. Kyiv: Forum.

Benei, Véronique. 2008. *Schooling Passions: Nation, History, and Language in Contemporary Western India*. Stanford, Calif.: Stanford University Press.

Benjamin, Walter. 1986. Critique of Violence. In *Reflections: Essays, Aphorisms, Autobiographical Writing*. Peter Demetz, ed. New York: Schocken Books.

———. 1969. *Illuminations: Essays and Reflections*. Hannah Arendt, ed. New York: Schocken Books.

Berdhal, Daphne. 1999. *Where the World Ended: Re-unification and Identity in the German Borderland*. Berkeley: University of California Press.

Berlin, Isaiah. 1978. *Russian Thinkers*. New York: Penguin.

Bhabha, Homi. 1990. *Nation and Narration*. London: Routledge.

Bilaniuk, Laada. 2005. *Contested Tongues: Language Politics and Cultural Correction in Ukraine*. Ithaca, N.Y.: Cornell University Press.

Birch, Anthony Harold. 1993. *The Concepts and Theories of Modern Democracy*. London: Routledge.

Bloch, Alexia. 2004. *Red Ties and Residential Schools: Indigenous Siberians in a Post-Soviet State*. Philadelphia: University of Pennsylvania Press.

Blok, Anton. 1974. The *Mafia of a Sicilian Village, 1860–1960: A Study of Violent Peasant Entrepreneurs*. Prospect Heights, Ill.: Waveland Press.

Blum, Douglas W. 2007. *National Identity and Globalization: Youth, State, and Society in Post-Soviet Eurasia*. Cambridge: Cambridge University Press.

Borneman, John. 1992. *Belonging in the Two Berlins: Kin, State, Nation*. Cambridge: Cambridge University Press.

Bourdieu, Pierre. 1990. *In Other Words: Essays Toward a Reflexive Sociology.* Stanford, Calif.: Stanford University Press.

Bourdieu, Pierre, and Jean-Claude Passeron. 1977. *Reproduction: In Education, Society, and Culture.* Beverly Hills, Calif.: Sage.

Bowles, Samuel, and Herbert Gintis. 1976. *Schooling in Capitalist America: Educational Reform and the Contradictions of Economic Life.* New York: Basic Books.

Bown, Matthew Cullerne. 1991. *Art Under Stalin.* New York: Holmes and Meier.

Boym, Svetlana. 2001. *The Future of Nostalgia.* New York: Basic Books.

Brandtstadter, Susanne. 2007. Transitional Spaces: Postsocialism as a Cultural Process: Introduction. *Critique of Anthropology* 27 (2): 131–145.

Brocklehurst, Helen. 2006. *Who's Afraid of Children? Children, Conflict, and International Relations.* London: Ashgate Publishing.

Bronfenbrenner, Urie. 1970. *Two Worlds of Childhood: U.S. and U.S.S.R.* New York: Russell Sage Foundation.

Brooks, Jeffrey. 2005. How Tolstoevskii Pleased Readers and Rewrote a Russian Myth. *Slavic Review* 64 (3) (Fall): 538–559.

———. 2003. Stalin's Politics of Obligation. In *Totalitarian Movements and Political Religions,* special issue on Stalinism. London: Routledge, 47–68.

———. 2003. *Thank You Comrade Stalin! Soviet Public Culture from Revolution to Cold War.* Princeton, N.J.: Princeton University Press.

Brysk, Alison, ed. 2002. *Globalization and Human Rights.* Berkeley: University of California Press.

Buchowski, Michał. 2001. *Rethinking Transformation: An Anthropological Perspective on Post-Socialism.* Poznan: Humaniora.

Buck-Morss, Susan. 2002. *Dreamworld and Catastrophe: The Passing of Mass Utopia in East and West.* Cambridge, Mass.: MIT Press.

Burawoy, Michael, and Katherine Verdery. 1999. *Uncertain Transition: Ethnographies of Change in the Postsocialist World.* Lanham, Md.: Rowman and Littlefield.

Caldwell, Melissa L. 2011. *Dacha Idylls: Living Organically in Russia's Countryside.* Berkeley: University of California Press.

———. 2008. Domesticating the French Fry: McDonald's and Consumerism in Moscow. In *The Anthropology of Globalization: A Reader,* 2nd ed. Inda Jonathan Xavier and Renato Rosaldo, eds. Oxford: Blackwell Publishing.

———. 2004. *Not by Bread Alone: Social Support in the New Russia.* Berkeley: University of California Press.

Catt, Helena. 1999. *Democracy in Practice.* London: Routledge.

Cheney, Kristen E. 2007. *Pillars of the Nation: Child Citizens and Ugandan National Development.* Chicago: University of Chicago Press.

Clastres, Pierre. 1974. *La société contre l'état.* Paris: Les Editions de Minuit.

Comaroff, Jean, and John L. Comaroff, eds. 2006. *Law and Disorder in the Postcolony.* Chicago: University of Chicago Press.

Coronil, Fernando. 1988. *The Magical State: History and Illusion in the Appearance of Democracy*. Notre Dame, Ind.: Helen Kellogg Institute Studies.

Corrigan, Philip Richard, and Derek Sayer. 1985. *The Great Arch: English State Formation as Cultural Revolution*. Oxford: Blackwell.

Cowan, Jane K., Marie-Benedicte Dembour, and Richard A. Wilson, eds. 2001. *Culture and Rights: Anthropological Perspectives*. Cambridge University Press.

Creed, Gerald W. 2011. *Masquerade and Postsocialism: Ritual and Cultural Dispossession in Bulgaria*. Bloomington: Indiana University Press.

Darden, Keith. 2001. Blackmail as a Tool of State Domination: Ukraine Under Kuchma. *East European Constitutional Review* 10, nos. 2–3 (Spring–Summer): 67–71.

Das, Veena. 2004. The Signature of the State: The Paradox of Illegibility. In *Anthropology in the Margins of the State*. Veena Das and Deborah Poole, eds. Santa Fe: School of American Research Press.

———. 1995. *Critical Events: An Anthropological Perspective on Contemporary India*. Oxford: Oxford University Press.

Das, Veena, and Deborah Poole. 2004. State and Its Margins: Comparative Ethnographies. In *Anthropology in the Margins of the State*. Santa Fe: School of American Research Press.

Deleuze, Gilles, and Claire Parnet. 1987. *Dialogues*. London: Athlone Press.

Derrida, Jacques. 1990. Force of Law: The Metaphysical Foundations of Authority. *Cardoza Law Review* 11: 919–1045.

Diuk, Nadia. 2006. The Triumph of Civil Society. In *Revolution in Orange: The Origins of Ukraine's Democratic Breakthrough*. Anders Aslund and Michael McFaul, eds. Washington, D.C.: Carnegie Endowment for International Peace.

———. 2004. The Next Generation. *Journal of Democracy* 15, no. 3 (July): 59–66.

Donnelly, Jack. 1982. Human Rights and Human Dignity: An Analytic Critique of Non-Western Conceptions of Human Rights. *American Political Science Review* 76, (2): 303–316.

Drakulic, Slavenka. 1993. *How We Survived Communism and Even Laughed*. New York: Harper Perennial.

Dunn, Elizabeth C. 2005. Standards and Person-Making in East Central Europe. In *Global Assemblages: Technology, Politics and Ethics as Anthropological Problems*. Stephen J. Collier and Aihwa Ong, eds. Oxford: Blackwell.

———. 2004. *Privatizing Poland: Baby Food, Big Business, and the Remaking of Labor*. Ithaca, N.Y.: Cornell University Press.

Durham, Deborah. 2000. Youth and the Social Imagination in Africa: Introduction to parts 1 and 2. *Anthropological Quarterly* 73 (3): 113–120.

Durkheim, Emile. 1965. *The Elementary Forms of the Religious Life*. New York: Free Press.

———. 1956. *Education and Sociology*. Glencoe, Ill.: Free Press.

Ennew, Judith, and Brian Milne. 1990. *The Next Generation: The Lives of Third World Children*. Philadelphia: New Society.

Farmer, Paul. 2004. On Suffering and Structural Violence. In *Violence in War and Peace*. Nancy Scheper-Hughes, ed. Oxford: Blackwell.

Fehérváry, Krisztina. 2002. American Kitchens, Luxury Bathrooms, and the Search for a "Normal" Life in Postsocialist Hungary. *Ethnos* 67 (3): 369–400.

Ferguson, James, and Akhil Gupta. 2005. Spatializing States: Toward an Ethnography of Neoliberal Governmentality. In *Anthropologies of Modernity: Foucault, Governmentality, and Life Politics*. Oxford: Blackwell.

Finkelstein, Leonid. 2001. The Russian Lexicon. *Prism* 7, no. 3 (March 30).

Fitzpatrick, Sheila. 1999. *Everyday Stalinism: Ordinary Life in Extraordinary Times: Soviet Russia in the 1930s*. New York: Oxford University Press.

Foley, Douglas E. 1990. *Learning Capitalist Culture: Deep in the Heart of Tejas*. Philadelphia: University of Pennsylvania Press.

Foucault, Michel. 1991. Governmentality. In *The Foucault Effect: Studies in Governmentality*. Graham Burchell, Colin Gordon, and Peter Miller, eds. London: Harvester Wheatsheaf.

———. 1978. *The History of Sexuality, An Introduction*, Vol. 1. New York: Vintage Books.

Fournier, Anna. 2010. Ukraine's Orange Revolution: Beyond Soviet Political Culture? In *Orange Revolution and Aftermath: Mobilization, Apathy, and the State in Ukraine*. Paul D'Anieri, ed. Washington D.C. and Baltimore: Woodrow Wilson Press and Johns Hopkins University Press.

———. 2007. Patriotism, Order, and Articulations of the Nation in Kyiv High Schools Before and After the Orange Revolution. *Journal of Communist Studies and Transition Politics* 23, no. 1 (March): 101–117.

Fowkes, Ben. 1997. *The Disintegration of the Soviet Union: A Study in the Rise and Triumph of Nationalism*. London: Macmillan Press.

Franklin, Bob, ed. 1986. *The Rights of Children*. Oxford: Basil Blackwell.

Friedman, Jonathan. 1990. Being in the World: Globalization and Localization. *Theory, Culture and Society* 7: 311–328.

Gal, Susan, and Gail Kligman. 2000. *The Politics of Gender After Socialism: A Comparative-Historical Essay*. Princeton, N.J.: Princeton University Press.

Garot, Robert. 2007. "Where You From!": Gang Identity as Performance. *Journal of Contemporary Ethnography*, 36 (1) (February 2007): 50–84.

Gellner, Ernest. 1983. *Nations and Nationalism*. Ithaca, N.Y.: Cornell University Press.

Golden, Deborah. 2001. Storytelling the Future: Israelis, Immigrants and the Imagining of Community. *Anthropological Quarterly* 75 no. 1 (Winter): 7–35.

Goldstein, Daniel M. 2007. Human Rights as Culprit, Human Rights as Victim: Rights and Security in the State of Exception. In *The Practice of Human Rights: Tracking Law Between the Global and the Local*. Mark Goodale and Sally Engle Merry, eds. Cambridge: Cambridge University Press.

Goodale, Mark. 2007. The Power of Right(s): Tracking Empires of Law and New Modes of Social Resistance in Bolivia (and elsewhere). In *The Practice of Human*

Rights: Tracking Law Between the Global and the Local. Mark Goodale and Sally Engle Merry, eds. Cambridge: Cambridge University Press.

———. 2007. Locating Rights, Envisioning Law Between the Global and the Local. In *The Practice of Human Rights: Tracking Law Between the Global and the Local.* Mark Goodale and Sally Engle Merry, eds. Cambridge: Cambridge University Press.

Goodale, Mark, and Sally Engle Merry, eds. 2007. *The Practice of Human Rights: Tracking Law Between the Global and the Local.* Cambridge: Cambridge University Press.

Graham, Philip Jeremy. 2004. *The End of Adolescence.* Oxford: Oxford University Press.

Gramsci, Antonio. 1971. *Selections from the Prison Notebooks of Antonio Gramsci.* New York: International Publishers.

Green, Linda. 1992. *Fear As a Way of Life: Mayan Widows in Rural Guatemala.* New York: Columbia University Press.

Gregory, Steven, and Daniel Timerman. 1986. Rituals of the Modern State: The Case of Torture in Argentina. *Dialectical Anthropology* 11, (1): 63–72.

Grisso, Thomas. 1981. *Juveniles' Waiver of Rights: Legal and Psychological Competence.* New York: Plenum Press.

Gupta, Akhil. 2006. Blurred Boundaries: The Discourse of Corruption, the Culture of Politics, and the Imagined State. In *The Anthropology of the State: A Reader.* Aradhana Sharma and Akhil Gupta, eds. Oxford: Blackwell.

Hall, Kathleen D. 2002. *Lives in Translation: Sikh Youth as British Citizens.* Philadelphia: University of Pennsylvania Press.

Hann, Chris. 2002. Farewell to the Socialist "Other." In *Postsocialism: Ideals, Ideologies and Practices in Eurasia.* C. M. Hann, ed. London: Routledge.

———. 2001. Comments. *Current Anthropology* 24, no. 1 (February): 133–134.

Hann, Chris, and Elizabeth Dunn, eds. 1996. *Civil Society: Challenging Western Models.* London: Routledge.

Hardman, Charlotte. 1973. Can There Be an Anthropology of Children? *Journal of the Anthropological Society of Oxford* 4 (1): 85–99.

Hare, Paul, Mohammed Ishaq, and Saul Estrin. 1998. Ukraine: The Legacies of Central Planning and the Transition to a Market Economy. In *Ukraine: State and Nation-Building.* Taras Kuzio, ed. New York: Routledge.

Harris, John. 1996. Liberating Children. In *The Liberation Debate: Rights at Issue.* Michael P. T. Leahy and Dan Cohn-Sherbok, eds. London: Routledge.

Harris, Judith Rich. 1998. *The Nurture Assumption: Why Children Turn Out the Way They Do.* New York: Free Press.

Hawkesworth, Mary. 1980. Ideological Immunity: The Soviet Response to Human Rights Criticism. *Universal Human Rights* 2 (1): 67–84.

Hemment, Julie. 2007. *Empowering Women in Russia: Activism, Aid, and NGOs.* Bloomington: Indiana University Press.

Henze, Paul B. 1985. The Spectre and Implications of Internal Nationalist Dissent: Historical and Functional Comparisons. In *Soviet Nationalities in Strategic Perspective*. Enders S. Wimbush, ed. London: Croom Helm.

Herzfeld, Michael. 2005. *Cultural Intimacy: Social Poetics in the Nation-State*, 2nd ed. New York: Routledge.

———. 2001. *Anthropology: Theoretical Practice in Culture and Society*. Malden, Mass.: Blackwell.

———. 1982. *Ours Once More: Folklore, Ideology and the Making of Modern Greece*. Austin: University of Texas Press.

Hirshfeld, Lawrence A. 2002. Why Don't Anthropologists Like Children? *American Anthropologist* 104 (2): 611–627.

Ho, Karen. 2008. Situating Global Capitalisms: A View from Wall Street Investment Banks. In *The Anthropology of Globalization: A Reader*. 2nd ed. Jonathan Xavier Inda and Renato Rosaldo, eds. Oxford: Blackwell.

Hobsbawm, Eric J. 1969. *Bandits*. New York: Delacorte Press.

Hoffman, David L., and Yanni Kotsonis. 2000. *Russian Modernity: Politics, Knowledge, Practices*. Houndmills: Macmillan Press.

Holston, James. 2008. *Insurgent Citizenship: Disjunctions of Democracy and Modernity in Brazil*. Princeton, N.J.: Princeton University Press.

Holston, James, and Teresa P. R. Caldeira. 1998. Democracy, Law, and Violence: Disjunctions of Brazilian Citizenship. In *Fault Lines of Democracy in Post-Transition Latin America*. Felipe Agüero and Jeffrey Stark, eds. Miami: University of Miami North-South Center Press.

Holt, John. 1974. *Escape From Childhood*. New York: E.P. Dutton.

Honderich, Ted, ed. 1995. *The Oxford Companion to Philosophy*. Oxford: Oxford University Press.

Humphrey, Caroline. 2002. *The Unmaking of Soviet Life: Everyday Economies After Socialism*. Ithaca, N.Y.: Cornell University Press.

Hurtig, Janise. 2008. *Coming of Age in Times of Crisis: Youth, Schooling and Patriarchy in a Venezuelan Town*. Houndmills: Palgrave Macmillan.

Ichilov, Orit, ed. 1998. *Citizenship and Citizenship Education in a Changing World*. London: Woburn Press.

Inda, Jonathan Xavier, and Renato Rosaldo, eds. 2008. *The Anthropology of Globalization: A Reader* 2nd ed. Oxford: Blackwell Publishing.

Ivannikova, L., ed. 1995. *Blahoslovy, Maty. Uroky ukrains'koho narodoznavstva v shkoli (5–8 klasy)*. Kyiv: Osvita.

Jacoby, Susan. 1974. *Inside Soviet Schools*. Toronto: Doubleday Canada.

Jenks, Chris. 2005. *Childhood*. 2nd ed. London: Routledge.

Joseph, Suad. 2005. Teaching Rights and Responsibilities: Paradoxes of Globalization and Children's Citizenship in Lebanon. *Journal of Social History* 38 (4): 1007–1026.

Kaplan, Samuel. 2006. *The Pedagogical State: Education and the Politics of National Culture in post-1980 Turkey*. Stanford, Calif.: Stanford University Press.

Kasianov, G. V. 1998. Ukrains'kyi natsionalizm. Problema naukovoho pereomyslennia. *Ukrains'kyi istorychnyi zhurnal*, no. 2: 39–53.

Kharkhordin, Oleg. 1999. *The Collective and the Individual in Russia: A Study of Practices*. Berkeley: University of California Press.

Khazanov, Anatoly. 1995. *After the USSR: Ethnicity, Nationalism, and Politics in the Commonwealth of Independent States*. Madison: University of Wisconsin Press.

Kideckel, David, ed. 1995. *East European Communities: The Struggle for Balance in Turbulent Times*. Boulder: Westview Press.

Kornai, Janos. 1980. *Economics of Shortage*. Amsterdam: North Holland Publishers.

Korshak, Stefan. 2005. A Bribe Too Far! Ukraine Scraps All Traffic Cops. July 26, 2005. www.motoring.co.za

Kremen', Vasyl'. 2003. *Osvita i nauka Ukrainy: shliakhy modernizatsii*. Kyiv: Hramota.

Kundera, Milan. 1978. *Le livre du rire et de l'oubli*. Paris: Editions Gallimard.

Kürti, Laszlo, and Peter Skalník, eds. 2009. *Postsocialist Europe: Anthropological Perspectives from Home*. New York: Berghahn Books.

Kuzio, Taras. 2006. Everyday Ukrainians and the Orange Revolution. In *Revolution in Orange: The Origins of Ukraine's Democratic Breakthrough*. Anders Aslund and Michael McFaul, eds. Washington, D.C.: Carnegie Endowment for International Peace.

———. 2002. Ukrainian-Russian Historical Commission Raises Storm. *RFE/RL*, Poland, Belarus, Ukraine Report, 4 (26), 2 July 2002.

———. 1998. *Ukraine: State and Nation-Building*. New York: Routledge.

Lancy, David F. 2008. *The Anthropology of Childhood: Cherubs, Chattels, Changelings*. Cambridge: Cambridge University Press.

Lansdown, G. 1994. Children's Rights. In *Children's Childhood: Observed and Experienced*. B. Mayall, ed. Washington, D.C.: Falmer Press.

Latour, Bruno. 1987. *Science in Action: How to Follow Scientists and Engineers Through Society*. Cambridge: Harvard University Press.

Lazar, Sian. 2010. Schooling and Critical Citizenship: Pedagogies of Political Agency in El Alto, Bolivia. *Anthropology & Education Quarterly* 41 (2): 181–205.

Levinson, Bradley A. U. 2005. Citizenship, Identity, Democracy: Engaging the Political in the Anthropology of Education. *Anthropology and Education Quarterly* 36 (4): 329–340.

Levinson, Bradley A., and Dorothy Holland. 1996. *The Cultural Production of the Educated Person: Critical Ethnographies of Schooling and Local Practice*. Albany: State University of New York Press.

Livschiz, Ann. 2006. Children's Lives After Zoia's Death: Order, Emotions and Heroism in Children's Lives and Literature in the Post-War Soviet Union. In *Late Stalinist Russia: Society Between Reconstruction and Reinvention*. Juliane Furst, ed. London: Routledge.

Luykx, Aurolyn. 1999. *The Citizen Factory: Schooling and Cultural Production in Bolivia*. Albany: State University of New York Press.

Markowitz, Fran. 2000. *Coming of Age in Post-Soviet Russia*. Urbana: University of Illinois Press.

Marshall, J. D. 1984. John Wilson on the Necessity of Punishment. *Journal of Philosophy of Education* 18 (1): 97–104.

Marshall, Kathleen. 1997. *Children's Rights in the Balance: The Participation-Protection Debate*. Edinburgh: Stationery Office Books.

Marshall, T. H. 1950. *Citizenship and Social Class*. Cambridge: Cambridge University Press.

Matza, Tomas. 2009. Moscow's Echo: Technologies of the Self, Publics, and Politics on the Russian Talk Show. *Cultural Anthropology* 24 (3): 489–522.

Mazawi, Ander Elias. 1998. Contested Regimes, Civic Dissent, and the Political Socialization of Children and Adolescents: The Case of the Palestinian Uprising. In Orit Ichilov, ed. *Citizenship and Citizenship Education in a Changing World*. London: Woburn Press.

Mbembe, Achille. 2001. *On the Postcolony*. Berkeley: University of California Press.

Melton, G. B., and Limber, S. P. 1992. What Children's Rights Mean to Children: Children's Own Views. In *The Ideologies of Children's Rights*. M. D. A. Freeman and P. Veerman, eds. Netherlands: Kluwer Academic Publishers.

Merry, Sally Engle. 2007. Introduction. In *The Practice of Human Rights: Tracking Law Between the Global and the Local*. Mark Goodale and Sally Engle Merry, eds. Cambridge: Cambridge University Press.

———. 2005. Transnational Human Rights and Local Activism: Mapping the Middle. *American Anthropologist* 108, issue 1, 38–51.

———. 2001. Changing Rights, Changing Culture. In *Culture and Rights: Anthropological Perspectives*. Jane K. Cowan, Marie-Benedicte Dembour, and Richard A. Wilson, eds. Cambridge: Cambridge University Press.

Montgomery, Heather. 2009. *An Introduction to Childhood: Anthropological Perspectives on Children's Lives*. Oxford: Wiley-Blackwell.

Montgomery, Heather, and Martin Woodhead. 2002. *Understanding Childhood: An Interdisciplinary Approach*. Chichester: John Wiley and Sons/Open University.

Moos, Elizabeth. 1967. *Soviet Education: Achievements and Goals*. New York: National Council of American-Soviet Friendship.

Morrow, Virginia. 1999. "We Are People Too": Children's and Young People's Perspectives on Children's Rights and Decision-Making in England. *International Journal of Children's Rights* 7: 149–170.

Nagengast, Carole. 1994. Violence, Terror, and the Crisis of the State. *Annual Review of Anthropology* 23: 109–136.

Nagengast, Carole, Michal Buchowski, and Edouard Conte, eds. 2001. *Poland Beyond Communism: Transition in Critical Perspective*. Fribourg, Switzerland: University Press.

Nazpary, Joma. 2002. *Post-Soviet Chaos: Violence and Dispossession in Kazakhstan*. London: Pluto Press.

Nelson, Diane M. 2004. Anthropologist Discovers Legendary Two-Faced Indian! Margins, the State, and Duplicity in Postwar Guatemala. In *Anthropology in the Margins of the State*. Veena Das and Deborah Poole, eds. Santa Fe: School of American Research Press.

Ong, Aihwa. 1999. *Flexible Citizenship: The Cultural Logics of Transnationality*. Durham: Duke University Press.

———. 1996. Cultural Citizenship as Subject-Making: Immigrants Negotiate Racial and Cultural Boundaries in the United States. *Current Anthropology* 37 (5): 737–762.

Ortner, Sherry B. 1989. *High Religion: A Cultural and Political History of Sherpa Buddhism*. Princeton, N.J.: Princeton University Press.

Paley, Julia. 2002. Toward an Anthropology of Democracy. *Annual Review of Anthropology* 31: 469–496.

Patico, Jennifer. 2008. *Consumption and Social Change in a Post-Soviet Middle Class*. Washington, D.C., and Stanford, Calif.: Woodrow Wilson Center Press and Stanford University Press.

———. 2005. To Be Happy in a Mercedes: Tropes of Value and Ambivalent Visions of Marketization. *American Ethnologist* 32 (3): 479–496.

Perice, Glen. 1997. Rumors and Politics in Haiti. *Anthropological Quarterly* 70 no. 1 (January): 1–10.

Petryna, Adriana. 2005. Science and Citizenship Under Postsocialism. In *Anthropologies of Modernity: Foucault, Governmentality, and Life Politics*. Oxford: Blackwell.

———. 2002. *Life Exposed: Biological Citizens After Chernobyl*. Princeton, N.J.: Princeton University Press.

Phillips, Sarah D. 2011. *Disability and Mobile Citizenship in Postsocialist Ukraine*. Bloomington: Indiana University Press.

———. 2008. Women's Social Activism in the New Ukraine: Development and the Politics of Differentiation. Bloomington: Indiana University Press.

Pilkington, Hilary. 2002. Introduction. In *Looking West? Cultural Globalization and Russian Youth Cultures*. Hilary Pilkington, Elena Omel'chenko, Moya Flynn, Ul'iana Bliudina, and Elena Starkova, eds. University Park: Pennsylvania State University Press.

———. 1994. *Russia's Youth and Its Culture: A Nation's Constructors and Constructed*. London: Routledge.

Platz, Stephanie. 2000. The Shape of National Time: Daily Life, History, and Identity During Armenia's Transition to Independence, 1991–1994. In *Altering States: Ethnographies of Transition in Eastern Europe and the Former Soviet Union*. Ann Arbor: University of Michigan Press.

Polyzio, Eleoussa, Michael Fullan, and John P. Anchan. 2000. *Change Forces in Post-Communist Eastern Europe: Education in Transition*. London: Routledge Falmer.

Pometun, O., et al. 2002. *My – Hromadiany Ukrainy 9 (10)*. Kyiv: NBF Ukrains'ki tekhnolohii.

Poole, Deborah. 2004. Between Threat and Guarantee: Justice and Community in the Margins of the Peruvian State. In *Anthropology in the Margins of the State*. Veena Das and Deborah Poole, eds. Santa Fe: School of American Research Press.

———. 1994. Introduction: Anthropological Perspectives on Violence and Culture—A View from the Peruvian High Provinces. In *Unruly Order: Violence, Power, and Cultural Identity in the High Provinces of Southern Peru*. Boulder, Colo.: Westview Press.

Poulantzas, Nicos. 1974. *Fascism and Dictatorship: The Third International and the Problem of Fascism*. London: NLB.

Povinelli, Elizabeth. 2002. *The Cunning of Recognition: Indigenous Alterities and the Making of Australian Multiculturalism*. Durham, N.C.: Duke University Press.

Radcliffe-Brown, A.R. 1940. Preface. In *African Political Systems*. M. Fortes and E.E. Evans-Pritchard, eds. London: Oxford University Press.

Rausing, Sigrid. 2004. *History, Memory, and Identity in Post-Soviet Estonia: The End of a Collective Farm*. Oxford: Oxford University Press.

———. 2002. Reconstructing the "Normal": Identity and the Consumption of Western Goods in Estonia. In *Markets and Moralities: Ethnographies of Postsocialism*. Ruth Ellen Mandel and Caroline Humphrey, eds. Oxford: Berg.

Reed-Danahay, Deborah. 1996. *Education and Identity in Rural France: The Politics of Schooling*. Cambridge: Cambridge University Press.

Reynolds, Pamela. 1995. Youth and the Politics of Culture in South Africa. In *Children and the Politics of Culture*. Sharon Stephens, ed. Princeton, N.J.: Princeton University Press.

Ries, Nancy. 2002. Honest Bandits and Warped People: Russian Narratives About Money, Corruption and Moral Decay. In *Ethnography in Unstable Places: Everyday Lives in Contexts of Dramatic Political Change*. Carol J. Greenhouse, Elizabeth Mertz, and Kay B. Warren, eds. Durham, N.C.: Duke University Press.

Rigi, Jakob. 2007. The War in Chechnya: The Chaotic Mode of Domination, Violence and Bare Life in the Post-Soviet Context. *Critique of Anthropology* 27 (1): 37–62.

Rival, Laura. 1996. Formal Schooling and the Production of Modern Citizens in the Ecuadorian Amazon. In *The Cultural Production of the Educated Person: Critical Ethnographies of Schooling and Local Practice*. Bradley A. Levinson, Douglas E. Foley, and Dorothy C. Holland, eds. Albany: State University of New York Press.

Robertson, Roland. 1992. *Globalization: Social Theory and Global Culture*. London: Sage.

Rodgers, Peter W. 2008. *Nation, Region and History in Post-Communist Transitions: Identity Politics in Ukraine, 1991–2006*. Stuttgart: Ibidem-Verlag.

Roitman, Janet. 2005. *Fiscal Disobedience: An Anthropology of Economic Regulation in Central Africa*. Princeton, N.J.: Princeton University Press.

Rose, Nikolas. 1989. *Governing the Soul*. London: Routledge.

Ryabchuk, Mykola. 2004. From "Dysfunctional" to "Blackmail" State: Paradoxes of the Post- Soviet Transition. Paper presented at the 38th Shevchenko Annual Lecture, University of Alberta, March 12, 2004.

Sahlins, Marshall David. 1981. *Historical Metaphors and Mythical Realities: Structure in the Early History of the Sandwich Islands Kingdom*. Ann Arbor: University of Michigan Press.

Sanford, Victoria. 2004. Contesting Displacement in Colombia: Citizenship and State Sovereignty at the Margins. In *Anthropology in the Margins of the State*. Veena Das and Deborah Poole, eds. Santa Fe: School of American Research Press.

Sarat, Austin, and Thomas R. Kearns. 1997. Editorial Introduction. In *Identities, Politics, and Rights*. Austin Sarat and Thomas R. Kearns, eds. Ann Arbor: University of Michigan Press.

Scheper-Hughes, Nancy, and Carolyn Sargent. 1998. Introduction: The Cultural Politics of Childhood. In *Small Wars: The Cultural Politics of Childhood*. Nancy Scheper-Hughes and Carolyn Sargent, eds. Berkeley: University of California Press.

Sharma, Aradhana, and Akhil Gupta. 2006. Introduction: Rethinking Theories of the State in an Age of Globalization. In *The Anthropology of the State: A Reader*. Aradhana Sharma and Akhil Gupta, eds. Oxford: Blackwell.

Shaw, Thomas A. 1996. Taiwanese Schools Against Themselves: School Culture Versus the Subjectivity of Youth. In *The Cultural Production of the Educated Person: Critical Ethnographies of Schooling and Local Practice*. Bradley A. Levinson, Douglas E. Foley, and Dorothy C. Holland, eds. Albany: State University of New York Press.

Shnapper, Dominique. 1997. The European Debate on Citizenship. *Daedalus* 126 (3): 199–223.

Slezkine, Yuri. 2000. The USSR as a Communal Apartment, or How a Socialist State Promoted Ethnic Particularism. In *Stalinism: New Directions*. Sheila Fitzpatrick, ed. London: Routledge.

Speed, Shannon. 2007. Exercising Rights and Reconfiguring Resistance in the Zapatista Juntas de Buen Gobierno. In *The Practice of Human Rights: Tracking Law Between the Global and the Local*. Mark Goodale and Sally Engle Merry, eds. Cambridge: Cambridge University Press.

Sushko, Oleksandr, and Olena Prystayko. 2006. Western Influence. In *Revolution in Orange: The Origins of Ukraine's Democratic Breakthrough*. Anders Aslund and Michael McFaul, eds. Washington, D.C.: Carnegie Endowment for International Peace.

Taussig, Michael. 1999. *Defacement: Public Secrecy and the Labor of the Negative*. Stanford, Calif.: Stanford University Press.

———. 1992. *The Nervous System*. New York: Routledge.

Taylor, Diana. 1997. *Disappearing Acts: Spectacles of Gender and Nationalism in Argentina's "Dirty War."* Durham, N.C.: Duke University Press.

Taylor, Nicola J., and Smith, Anne B. 2009. Preface. In *Children as Citizens? International Voices.* Nicola J. Taylor and Anne B. Smith, eds. Dunedin: University of Otago Press.

Tilly, Charles. 1985. War Making and State Making as Organized Crime. In *Bringing the State Back In.* Peter B. Evans, Dietrich Rueschemeyer, and Theda Skocpol, eds. Cambridge: Cambridge University Press.

Todorova, Maria. 1997. *Imagining the Balkans.* New York: Oxford University Press.

Topalova, Viktoriya. 2006. In Search of Heroes: Cultural Politics and Political Mobilization of Youths in Contemporary Russia and Ukraine. *Demokratizatsiya* 14 (1): 23–41.

Trouillot, Michel-Rolph. 2001. The Anthropology of the State in the Age of Globalization: Close Encounters of the Deceptive Kind. *Current Anthropology* 24, no. 1 (February): 125–138.

Turner, Victor. 1967. *The Forest of Symbols: Aspects of Ndembu Ritual.* Ithaca, N.Y.: Cornell University Press.

Tykhosha, V.I., L. I. Ursulenko, A.I. Movchun. 2004. *Ukrains'ka Mova: zbirnyk tekstiv dlia perekaziv iz tvorchymy zavdanniamy, 11 klas.* Kyiv: Kimo.

Usenko, I. B., et al. 2003. *Osnovy Pravoznavstva. Pidruchnyk dlia 9 klasu.* Kyiv: Perun.

Varese, Federico. 2001. *The Russian Mafia: Private Protection in a New Market Economy.* Oxford: Oxford University Press.

Veloso, Leticia. 2008. Universal Citizens, Unequal Childhoods: Children's Perspectives on Rights and Citizenship in Brazil. *Latin American Perspectives* 35 (4): 45–60.

Verdery, Katherine. 2002. Whither Postsocialism? In *Postsocialism: Ideals, Ideologies and Practices in Eurasia.* Chris Hann, ed. London: Routledge.

———. 1996. *What Was Socialism, and What Comes Next?* Princeton, N.J.: Princeton University Press.

———. 1994. From Parent-State to Family Patriarchs: Gender and Nation in Contemporary Eastern Europe. *East European Politics and Societies* 8 (2): 225–255.

Vigdorova, F. 1960. *Diary of a Russian Schoolteacher.* Westport, Conn.: Greenwood Press.

Volkov, Vadim. 2002. *Violent Entrepreneurs: The Use of Force in the Making of Russian Capitalism.* Ithaca, N.Y.: Cornell University Press.

Volkov, Vladimir. 2003. Russian Elections: Putin Consolidates Regime of "Managed Democracy." *World Socialist Website,* 18 December, 2003. http://www.wsws.org.

Wanner, Catherine. 2005. Money, Morality and New Forms of Exchange in Postsocialist Ukraine. *Ethnos* 70, no. 4 (December): 515–537.

———. 1999. Crafting Identity, Marking Time: An Anthropological Perspective on Historical Commemoration and Nation-Building in Ukraine. *Harvard Ukrainian Studies* 23, nos. 3/4 (December):105–131.

———. 1998. *Burden of Dreams: History and Identity in Post-Soviet Ukraine.* University Park: Pennsylvania State University Press.

Weiss, Peter. 1966. *The Persecution and Assassination of Jean-Paul Marat as Performed by the Inmates of the Asylum of Charenton Under the Direction of the Marquis de Sade*. New York: Atheneum.

Willis, Paul. 1977. *Learning to Labor: How Working Class Kids Get Working Class Jobs*. New York: Columbia University Press.

Wilson, Andrew. 2005. *Virtual Politics: Faking Democracy in the Post-Soviet World*. New Haven, Conn.: Yale University Press.

———. 2000. *The Ukrainians: Unexpected Nation*. New Haven: Yale University Press.

Wilson, Richard. 2001. *The Politics of Truth and Reconciliation in South Africa*. Cambridge: Cambridge University Press.

———. 1997. *Human Rights, Culture and Context: Anthropological Perspectives*. London: Pluto Press.

Woodhead, Martin, and Heather Montgomery. 2002. *Understanding Childhood: An Interdisciplinary Approach*. New York: Wiley.

Yurchak, Alexei. 2006. *Everything Was Forever, Until It Was No More: The Last Soviet Generation*. Princeton, N.J.: Princeton University Press.

———. 2002. Entrepreneurial Governmentality in Postsocialist Russia. In *The New Entrepreneurs of Europe and Asia*. Victoria E. Bonnell and Thomas B. Gold, eds. Armonk, N.Y.: M. E. Sharpe.

Index

Abramian, Levon, 68
Abrams, Philip, 13
adminresurs, 129–30
adolescents, 4, 137
Africa, 182
African Charter on the Rights and Welfare
 of the Child, 81
Agamben, Giorgio, 18, 76, 122
Aitmatov, Chingiz, 146
Akhmetov, Rinat, 101, 150
Allina-Pisano, Jessica, 130
All-Union Agricultural Exhibition of 1939,
 168
Alonso, Ana Maria, 32
Anderson, Benedict, 32
Andropov, Yuri, 29
Andryivskiy Uzviz (street), 35
anthropologists, 8, 19, 22
Applebaum, Anne, 117
Arendt, Hannah, 18
Armenia, 28
Art Under Stalin (Bown), 168

Bakhtin, Mikhail, 142
bandit capitalism, 101–2, 136
bandit repertoire, 84–92, 100–102;
 class bandits and, 116, 151; and democratic repertoire, 172; effect of Orange
 Revolution on, 170; and New Rich, 87–88;
 patriot repertoire vs., 90–92, 179; and
 prison slang, 85; and repertoire of state,
 112–14
bandits, 143–45; as heroes, 85–87; honest
 people vs., 143; and "living like a person,"
 150; and maintenance of order, 104–5;
 in media, 84–88; as metaphor for state,
 114–15; and narratives of capitalism,
 101–2; old leaders as, 177; as political

force, 101; and prison culture, 119–20;
 randomness of, 106; as scapegoats, 106;
 Soviet "thieves" vs. post-Soviet, 86–87,
 144–45; as symbols of chaos, 111–13
bandit state (*bandyts'ka vlada*), 14, 16–19,
 113, 182; citizens' view of, 120; concept of,
 104; Orange Revolution and image of,
 136, 137; students' view of, 115–17
barricade, 169–71
basic needs, 150, 154
Bayart, Jean-François, 14
Belarus, 37, 63
Belinsky, Vissarion, 67
belligerent nationalism, 39
Benei, Veronique, 37, 45
Benjamin, Walter, 18
Berdahl, Daphne, 17
Beslan hostage crisis, 27
Bilaniuk, Laada, 37
bila vorona (white crow), 42, 81, 90
Birch, Anthony, 84
blat, 3
Bloch, Alexia, 50
Blok, Anton, 104
Bolivia, 21, 45, 160
Bolshevik Revolution, 147–48, 170
Bolsheviks, 31, 119, 153–54, 168
The Book of Laughter and Forgetting
 (Kundera), 112–13
Bourdieu, Pierre, 46
bourgeois nationalism, 30–32
Bown, Matthew, 168
Brandtstadter, Susanne, 22
Brigada, 85–87
Brocklehurst, Helen, 9
Brooks, Jeffrey, 153, 172
Buck-Morss, Susan, 22–23
Bulgakov, Mikhail, 164

Acknowledgments

First and foremost, I would like to thank my hosts, friends and informants in Kyiv for allowing me to share in their lives, and for tirelessly answering my questions and discussing various issues, even as the political climate in Ukraine became more volatile. I was humbled by the everyday acts of courage I witnessed during difficult times, and by the tolerance and mutual respect shown by citizens on different sides of the political divide during the Orange Revolution.

I wish to thank the Ministry of Education and Science of Ukraine for granting me permission to carry out research in schools. My gratitude also goes to school administrators for agreeing to have me in their schools, and to teachers for allowing me into their classrooms. I only hope that my analysis of power relations in the school has not overshadowed most teachers' exceptional dedication to their students. Perhaps my biggest debt is to the young people who so graciously shared their perspectives on life in Ukraine and hopes for the future. I am grateful for their trust and friendship, and also for their creative approaches to navigating radical social change. Their insights have been crucial to my understanding of the way larger social and moral struggles come to be played out in the school context and beyond.

This project could not have been brought to fruition without the generous support of various organizations and individuals. I wish to thank the Shevchenko Scientific Society in the USA (Yuri Kuziw Fund) for supporting field research in Ukraine. I am grateful for the support provided by the Canadian Institute of Ukrainian Studies (Helen Darcovich Memorial Doctoral Fellowship) for data analysis. I also wish to thank Inga Shmorhun and the late Alek Iwashchenko for their contribution and faith in me. Additional financial support in connection with the project was provided by the Social Sciences and Humanities Research Council of Canada (SSHRC), the Fonds pour la Formation de Chercheurs et l'Aide à la Recherche (FCAR), the Harvard

Ukrainian Research Institute, the Department of Anthropology, Johns Hopkins University, and the Office of the Dean, Zanvyl Krieger School of Arts and Sciences, Johns Hopkins University.

At Johns Hopkins, I am much indebted to Niloofar Haeri, whose dedication, intelligence, and wisdom have been critical to this project. Deborah Poole's enthusiasm, commitment, and fine-tuned feedback on my work have been truly inspiring. Jeffrey Brooks read countless drafts of this book with good humor and a critical eye, and I am grateful for his creative approach to scholarship and for his unwavering support and friendship. My gratitude also goes to Sidney Mintz for the stimulating discussions that challenged my assumptions at every stage of this research and helped me refine my work. Many thanks to Steven David for believing in my work and for his support of teaching and research on Europe's new democracies at Johns Hopkins.

My sincere appreciation goes to Michael Herzfeld for so graciously and generously sharing his time and expertise, and for his invaluable insights into my work over the years. Alexander Motyl offered much needed encouragement and help along the way. My gratitude also goes to the Ukrainian communities of Baltimore and Washington, D.C., for their openness and genuine interest in my work.

I would like to thank the Department of Anthropology, the Dean's Office, Faculty of Arts, and my colleagues at the University of Manitoba for their support during the last phases of this project. Portions of my research were presented at various conferences, seminars, and lectures, and I am grateful for the valuable feedback I received from colleagues there.

At the University of Pennsylvania Press, I wish to thank Peter Agree for his strong support and dedication to this project. I am also grateful to Julia Rose Roberts, Noreen O'Connor-Abel, and the staff at the Press for their contributions to the project. The thoughtful comments provided by anonymous reviewers have greatly benefited my work.

I bear sole responsibility for the content of this book. The views and ideas expressed in this work are my own and not those of any of the individuals, organizations, and institutions that supported my research in its different stages.

Selected material in Chapters 2 and 6 appeared previously in the *Journal of Communist Studies and Transition Politics*, 23, no. 1, as "Patriotism, Order, and Articulations of the Nation in Kyiv High Schools Before and

After the Orange Revolution" (Taylor and Francis, 2007, http://www.tandf online.com). A portion of Chapter 5 also appeared in the edited volume *Orange Revolution and Aftermath: Mobilization, Apathy, and the State in Ukraine*, published by the Woodrow Wilson Center Press and the Johns Hopkins University Press. I would like to thank the publishers for granting permission to include the materials here.